I
Want
To
Quit
Winners

by Harold S. Smith, Sr.

with John Wesley Noble

♠ ♦ ♣ ♥

Prentice-Hall, Inc., Englewood Cliffs, N. J.

I
Want
To
Quit
Winners

To the one woman who so perfectly demonstrated her love of God through her fellow man that it lives on these forty years since she went to her rest and has inspired me to strive just a little harder for the spiritual values she cherished.

DELIA DANYOW

of Vergennes, Vermont

My Great Grandmother

September 8, 1961

GRANT SAWYER
GOVERNOR

Mr. Harold S. Smith, Sr.
Harolds Club
Reno, Nevada

Dear Harold:

     I just finished reading "I Want to Quit
Winners." It is absolutely one of the most fascinating
expositions I have ever read.

     I do not know whether I feel this way be-
cause I know, or know of, most of the people and the
situations narrated by you or whether it is just a darned
interesting account of a man's life.

     Seemingly, without trying to do so, you have
pretty well told the story of Nevada gambling and placed
it in its proper perspective in the past and present.

     If everyone reacts to your book as I did,
you will surely have a best seller.

     Kindest personal regards.

                Cordially,

                Grant Sawyer
                Governor

GS-ec

My Openers

I never lay my money on the line until I understand clearly the game I'm going to play. Readers, I believe, should receive the same consideration when they open a book. Before you gamble your time on a long book like this one, about gambling, my life, my club, gamblers and so forth, you want to see my openers. Let me draw you a picture.

This is a book about gambling and you. You're in it even if you've never thrown dice, bet on a horse or drawn a hand of cards. You're in the game of life with all its odds, aren't you? Well so am I, my friend, and there's a real game.

As they say out here in western Nevada, twenty-five years encompasses a heap of living. It has for me certainly, through good cycles and disastrous ones, millions of dollars won and millions gone, hopes raised and dashed, and heartaches money won't cure. I'm going to tell you about them in painful detail. I'm going to let you peek inside this gambler's heart.

Far too much has been written already on gaming itself. Most of it, like the thievery stores real gamblers avoid, is completely dishonest. At least it isn't the whole story. I believe it is time for some considered findings. Some facts.

Gambling, by its name, means playing games of chance wherein the risks can never be eliminated. There is no system—and I believe I have seen them all—which can make gambling a sure thing. That is a hard, cold fact. Yet I see good people dropping millions of dollars in needed money every year. That is unfortunate. It is definitely silly.

They are adults. They think they know what they are doing. Some do; most don't. How could they? They don't have funds, time or the temperament to make a close study of games of chance. I have had, believe me, over the past twenty-five years. I know too well. A millionaire could retire on what my education has cost.

But that's partly because I'm me, Harold S. Smith, Sr., professional gambler, doting father and grandfather, and founder of the biggest gambling house in the world (bigger than Monte Carlo ever was), Harolds Club of Reno. Did I fail to point out

I am also a sentimentalist? In part, then, this must be the narrative of a human being.

To be a good gambler, a man must be able to see to the marrow of your bones. He must size you up the way a good waitress does, or a smart bellboy, a bartender, or a prostitute. I intend to show you the marrow of many a bone, some still living, some no longer with us. Along the way, we may have to dodge a bullet or two.

Someone has said every psychiatrist should spend his first year of practice in Harolds Club. I'll buy that. The gaming tables reveal a great deal about people, both the best and the worst. You do not have to be a genius to observe them.

I believe there are findings here for the consideration of clergymen, with whom I try to maintain the best of relations, as well as for the otherwise astute businessman who gambles, and for women—wives, sweethearts, career ladies—especially those who should tend to their knitting and leave gambling to experts. May I also suggest that there is a message for young people? Those teenagers particularly who believe bitterly, as I once did, that life's odds are stacked. I warn you, however, I propose to speak bluntly. I didn't finish high school, myself.

But, if you please, I am not stupid. I know some readers will want from me only a how-to book on gaming. How to cut your losses; how to recognize hunches; how to break the casino. I'm with you. Why play if you can't win? And quit winners? I hate to leave my own money on the table. So I'll include herein my primer on gambling. I'll show you how you can play, and have fun, at these games.

I plan to take you behind the tables of Nevada's legal gaming houses, from upstart Jackpot to flamboyant Las Vegas, and see how you look to real operators. We'll meet big gamboliers from Ray Ryan to Nick the Greek and see how they play their games. And I'm going to deal you in on some of the biggest games ever played.

I will demonstrate extrasensory perception to you and attempt to describe the vital difference between hunches and wishful thinking. I will give you the precise mathematical percentages for and against you in any game from "friendly" poker to cent-a-point bridge, gin rummy and 21, how I bet the horses, why there are big winners and big losers. I will give you my findings on lucky streaks. You will even see how the mechanical slot machines can go crazy at times and befuddle us club operators. This will not be a dull book.

On the desk in my office at Harolds Club I keep a fifteen inch ruler. I tell people it represents me, Harold S. Smith, Sr., the man, the gambler. "Most of the time," I tell them, "you see one or two inches of the rule. Sometimes even three or four inches. Rarely more. Don't jump to conclusions unless you can see at least six inches clearly." You, the reader of this book, are going to see more of that ruler than anyone—private secretary, family, friends—ever has.

These are my openers, then. If you like the shape of the game, ante up and read on.

One caution. I'm very human, as you will see. In no way do I wish to appear braggadocio or know-it-all. Mistakes make even the bravest gambler humble. I will tell you of mine frankly. Maybe they will help to change the odds of your game, whatever it be, cards, dice, business, marriage, or just plain living.

Yours seriously,

Harold S. Smith Sr.

And here I must acknowledge the help I have had in writing this book. It came from John Wesley Noble, a professional writer and a man who has lived a little, drunk a little and been tripped up, as have I, by human nature. I poured out everything, the good, the bad, my hopes and fears. John listened thoughtfully, considered carefully and directed my thoughts to paper. Only he, I and Mercedes Hoover, my secretary, saw the growing manuscript in the craftsman's hands. He was guiding me to put my story down in my own way and it was uncanny. Today ours is one of those rare all-the-way partnerships that will outlive ordinary author-subject relationships. Mention must be made too of the fact that it was Hilary Sax, then on the faculty of the University of Nevada, who first pursuaded me to gather material for this book.

Contents

1

♣ ♣ ♣ ♣

As I See Me

NOT LONG AGO, after bedding down with a virus and certain vexing family problems for several days, I stepped out to the sidewalk in front of Harolds Club for a breath of fresh air. It was late afternoon and the Sierra snows to the west were pale pink in the fading sunlight as I stood a moment watching rosy neon blossom from the gambling clubs along North Virginia Street. It was precisely at that moment I felt the hunch.

It came on in a surge, like a gust of wind off the desert or a sudden chiming of bells, electric, keening, impelling. I suddenly felt strong, bold, confident. I wanted to gamble. For big money.

A true hunch hits like that. It flames into your consciousness like the crimson flare you come upon suddenly at a highway accident. Through the thickest fog of illness, preoccupation or dulling medication, it blazes. Your senses are alerted. The next conscious move is yours.

Unlike highway flares though, a hunch fades swiftly. The deed must be done fast. Going for big money, moreover, is not child's play. It's for blood, thick blood, your own or the other man's.

13

When the hunch hits, there's no time for planning or debate, though you may come home later carrying your head in your hands. All this I knew.

I strode across the street and into the Horseshoe Club of my friend Bernie Einstoss. The dice table nearest the door, I noticed, was empty save for two dealers idly clinking silver dollars. This I like; other players might obstruct perceptions. Keyed to the hunch, I agreed quickly to terms. The limit of my losing, if it went that way, would be $25,000. I gave the house my marker, or IOU, and took $10,000 in chips. I laid $400 on the Line and took the dice. Never have dice felt so right to me. In forty minutes I won $29,500.

Thanking the dealers with a $500 "toke," or tip, I left to have dinner with my son, Harold Jr., at the new Elks Club south of town. Junior is a tall, dark, good-looking lad of twenty-nine who has grown up with gaming and likes to believe he's a fair gambler. He isn't bad, either, for his tender years; before the state law that operators may not gamble in their own clubs, he won $100,000 at one setting of dice in our place. And, hunches to the contrary, he was to be lucky this night. We played bridge with two brother Elks at a penny a point and side bets. Junior won $1,000 from me and went off contentedly to keep a date with Kay Starr, the lovely night club singer.

I still felt good as I parked my car in the club garage. Losing a thousand isn't too bad if it's all in the family; my bread seemed still to be falling jam-up. So, rather than return to my sick bed, I dropped in at the Horseshoe for a cup of coffee. I was sitting with my friends Jack and Esther Filtzer, talking of business, the weather, everything but gambling, when the flash came again.

"Just a year ago today," I heard myself blurt, "we were in this booth—these identical places—when I capriciously marked that big Keno ticket!" Capriciously, I said, because Keno is like the age-old Chinese lottery; your chances of marking the right eight spots on a ten-spot ticket might occur once in 200 years. "I'm going to play a ticket!" I announced, and did. Five minutes later it paid $5,000. Then, fantastically, it repeated for $600 more.

I knew then I had a very lucky streak going. Not, I hasten to assure you, because of the amounts won, but because I was receiving those sharp, clear hunches and recognizing them instantly. I went to a 21 table and bet $300. Consider now, if you please, exactly what happened there. The dealer dealt me two face cards, a pat hand; he had to hit his own 13 and broke. Next he gave me a ten and two and I hit with a nine for a perfect 21. He had twenty and lost. On my next hand, I turned up ace-queen; blackjack. No question but this was it. Immediately I bet heavily and fast to catch the tide while it was running. I won $32,000 more.

At 9 PM, five hours after coming out for air, I was headed back winners by $67,500, less the thousand Junior took at bridge. Five hours on other occasions have cost me $40,000. I fairly floated across the street to my own club. Just inside the door I saw a man hit a $1,000 jackpot on the dollar slot machine. He whooped like a tomahawked Comanche. I knew how he felt. Precisely. I was feeling the same way. There, however, the similarity ends. My round blue eyes may have twinkled as I got on the public address system to order drinks for the house, but I didn't whoop. I couldn't. I am a professional.

Seeing me for the first time, you might not believe it. I don't fit the popular conception of a gambler. Not in any way. Tourists stopping at Harolds Club after seeing our red billboards on highways and byways across the continent constantly are amazed by this. Obviously they expect something else; probably a darkly sinister and suave man with lizard eyes, manicured nails and loud-checked suit. Someone points me out, perhaps when I'm cowboying around the club like a weekend square, and they just can't believe I'm the Harold of this big operation.

I'm a gambler—make no mistake about that. I have romanced Lady Luck in every possible way, from marriage to money. I love my fellow man but I have a pure passion for taking the money of other operators when I visit their clubs or when they come into mine. I will bet my money with you in any amount you name and I keep a million dollars cash on the premises to pay off if I lose. Once I even had the club on the line for a single throw of the dice. We'll come to that later.

♥

Some people, in fact, say I am an improbable man in an improbable business and an impossible state. To them, the Reno stopover on the sagebrush side of the Sierra, between the Great Salt Lake and San Francisco, is of itself never-never land. Possibly. It is true, in Nevada, that gaming for money is as legitimate a business as a soda fountain or department store and you find slot machines everywhere but in the post office and undertaking parlors. For that matter, prostitution still is legal under local option in some of our towns, though no longer in Reno. In Nevada, you can play chuck-a-luck before breakfast, if you choose, or buy a drink at any hour of any day or night, election day excepted. There's still a lot of the wide-open pioneer West out here and we like it that way. But make no mistake. We're not so provincially wild and woolly we don't know pepper from salt. I was born elsewhere and I wouldn't trade one clump of Nevada's sagebrush for all of Central Park. I have been there too.

So this is my playground, and while I may look to you like a Rotarian from Sioux Fall S.D., I am the proprietor of the biggest gambling club there is. I am, to be sure, a pretty average looking guy at 5 feet 10 and 170 pounds, and I do wear dark, horn-rimmed glasses. My big blue eyes haven't been so good since a childhood bout with measles. Nevertheless, they have witnessed un-average sights and, I like to believe, fill with childlike wonder at a lovely sunset just as quickly as delight at a royal flush on the card table.

I cannot explain my healthy, ruddy complexion—it seems to defy the weird hours and indoor life—except to say that I come of solid, long-jawed Vermont stock and I have trained myself to sleep fast. The tall, ramrod-straight gent behind me with the gaudy Harolds Club cravat and July 4th suspenders is my Daddy. He's seventy-three and can play vicious bridge all night, his hands being good. That's his only vice, though; he doesn't smoke, doesn't drink and doesn't waste his substance at the gaming tables. Him, I cannot explain. I can, however, explain my nose, which appears to have been broken in combat and is probably my only sinister feature. We Smiths all have hawk-like beaks and mine has been pummeled a few times in the back alley here, and before that in the boxing ring. I can't endow its rubbery curves with glamour. The truth is I had an obstructed septum when I was sixteen and Daddy hired specialists to knock about with hammers, chisels and pliers, removing cartilege so I would breathe more easily. It cost $300 when that was a lot of money to us and I have to laugh now. Considering the occupational hazards I live with, it seems I'm breathing harder most of the time.

I live with chicanery, as you might have guessed, not to mention a large and strong-willed family. This may be cause enough for the recent infiltration of gray in the dark, wavy hair I inherit from my French-Canadian mother. There's noticeable bulge to my hips, too, but don't ascribe it to middle-aged obesity, please. If you look closely, you will notice I wear a heavy leather belt with a solid silver buckle. Over my right hip it supports a tremendous bunch of keys—maybe five pounds in all—which open a number of important locks hereabouts, as well as some interesting doors elsewhere. In due time we'll pass through them. The point is I must, at all times, have this impedimenta. When a tailor starts measuring me for a close fit, I have a little talk with him.

For instance, I need three wallets. One is for necessary documents, including my official gambling licenses. One is the decoy for stray pickpockets who invariably gravitate to me. The third is for currency I may wish to use myself. I also carry twenty or more cartwheel silver dollars which I, as head of fabulous Harolds Club, am expected to distribute as though we manufactured them here. Sometimes, for excellent reasons, I have a loaded pistol in my trousers pocket.

The result is I cannot be a clothes horse. I dress as neatly as I can in good tweeds, woolens, silks or synthetics; in conservative blues, grays, browns or white, as the desert seasons demand. I also maintain a wardrobe of formal evening wear. Not, as you might expect, for wear in our plush baccarat room or for emcee-ing the floor show in our seventh floor Fun Room, which I often like to do. They're for my real love, my serious work, presenting great artists and great music for my appreciative fellow Nevadans in a scholarly hall far removed from the rattling dice.

My wardrobe of western clothes, including satin-lined western-cut tuxedos, would dazzle a movie cowboy. The theme and spirit of Harolds Club, authentic Old West, explains them. Some of the best fun I've had in old Reno has been on horseback with my hell-for-leather friends, and after a while I'll trot out my fine palomino, Yankee Doodle, and we'll canter through some of those episodes. At times I simply feel like dolling up and cowboying around the club. You might even have caught me in one of those moods or in my Gay 90's bit, red-striped blazer, cane and straw skimmer, a hangover from one of the shows we stage here. Did I overlook my New York Yankees uniform? It's a real one I collected after Ol' Casey had romped to another world's championship and I personally led a band down Virginia Street to celebrate.

Is any of this so improbable? I'm a professional gambler but I like to have fun, too. Maybe at times I do behave like a big kid where you expect a coldly calculating, gimlet-eyed man. Well, I'll let you look a little farther along my personal ruler now. I am somewhat of a quick-silver character comprising many contradictions. I can be flamboyant, true, where most gamblers are self-effacing. I am loquacious in an industry where the tight lip is standard equipment; my neighbor, Bill Harrah, for example, deliberately sets times when he won't utter a word. That's just for practice, and he runs two fine clubs, one here in Reno and one up at Lake Tahoe. I am outgoing, outgiving and trusting in a business where human greed can curdle the milk of human kindness in an instant. I am a brooder and a laugher. When I laugh, I guffaw so loud you hear me from the first floor escalator to the revolving searchlights above the big red sign on our roof. When I brood, as I do too often, it's in genuine sorrow for myself and my fellow man. At least once in the past I fell into such a blue funk I had to enlist psychiatric help to get out.

Please, though, don't shed any tears. That would be quite unnecessary. I have learned the tools of my trade and I never forget how they're used, come funks or frustrations. My brother Raymond, my Daddy, my first wife and I built this $500 hole-in-the-wall into a $25,000,000 enterprise and we didn't do it by being silly. Emotion, sentiment, may cause me to root louder than anyone in the stadium for the San Francisco Forty-Niners to beat the Green Bay Packers, say, in a playoff for the National

Football League title. But my money will be riding on the Packers if cold, hard logic says they're the money team on that particular day. You learn a lot in my business about the laws of probability and you obey those laws regardless of personal feelings. Otherwise, you could be out in the street without a business. I learned that a long, long time ago.

◆

But we're speaking of improbables. Maybe I seem improbable because I've sought psychiatric help when I know so much about human nature, my own and yours. I do know a lot about it. I can look to the marrow of my fellow man, as I said. Take that little lady in bobby socks and jeans. Her hair's in pin curlers and she has a dollar's worth of coins clutched in her hand; a young housewife relaxing a few minutes from housework and kiddies. Obviously her husband doesn't earn much—she's sticking with that nickel machine—and a $7.50 jackpot would be a big thrill for her. I hope she hits it. She has a wholesome, happy look about her. Not so the well-dressed blonde angrily tugging the handle of the dollar machine. She's battling frustrations she brought in with her.

Every person who comes into my club interests me. I look at them not casually, but intently. Take the middle-aged gentleman who just sat down at the 21 table. He is new to me; I want to remember him. He's a potential customer and I must know him. I must catalogue him. The way he dresses is significant. Are his shoes neatly polished? Do his socks match his ensemble with taste and judgment? He wears glasses; what type are they? How is his hair cut? By a good barber? Is he, in truth, a genteel man? What sort of jewelry does he affect? Inexpensive? Expensive but gaudy? Or just expensive? I move closer to hear how he speaks to other players at the table, and to the dealer. How does he handle his money? As if it were hot potatoes or something he's accustomed to? Are his nails manicured? How does he bet? Casually? Recklessly? Cautiously? Does he sit his stool confidently? Or is he not quite sure of himself? I won't ask him one question. His manner and appearance tell me everything I need to know.

These are things I, as a businessman, must know about this customer. How much money could he win from me, should he get lucky? Do I have a chance of winning from him? How much credit could we extend him? For what amount could we safely cash his checks? I must notice the way he drinks and if drinks befuddle his judgment. Drunken losers are not good business. Is he argumentative? Apparently not. If he disputes a point, then, he might be mistaken but it would be with justification. He will understand our explanation. This is a real gentleman, in fact. The sort I speak of as a lovely man. We want no chiselers or kibitzers to annoy him.

He's getting up from the 21 table. Perhaps he would like to see our floor show. We have signs telling the customers it's there for their pleasure, but people on vacation don't read signs. This reminds me to get on the PA system and announce the show again. Is he only a 21 player or does he like other games? One man likes only 21, another only dice, still another roulette. This man's next move will be most interesting to me. He's stopping at the dice table. He's laying a big bet. Here is a real player. I am going to like him a lot.

But just a moment here. Who's that other face at the table? I feel my skin crawl. There's a subtle difference about him. I can't say just what, but he's phoney. I can smell it. There's something about his countenance I didn't see in my first man's, or in anyone else at this table. Here is the face of a cheat—crossroaders, we call them in the trade—and I shall give him close attention.

Sharpies turn up in our clubs constantly and they have cuter tricks than loaded dice or simple nicks on cards. We had an example only recently, cards marked with an infra-red dye which can be seen through only a certain type contact lens. It was a caper which could have cost us hundreds of thousands of dollars. But I've come a long, long way since I met my first crossroader. While I wear bifocals, I am not blind. From the first day I heard of contact lenses, I've been waiting. When some of our girl dealers tried them out, in fact, I spent hours gazing into their eyes. Not to flirt, I assure you, but to imprint on my mind how the human eye looks in contact lenses. We caught the infra-red bit before the culprit even had a stake.

Big money, of course, breeds dishonesty. A famous Nevada club actually was built to separate one millionaire from his bankroll. It took only normal perception to smell the fish in an establishment springing up suddenly at the end of nowhere, convenient to only a few hundred passing players, but square on this lamb's road to town. He didn't recognize it because he was a true eccentric from the unkempt hair on his head to the scuffed tennis shoes on his feet. The operators, in their greed, overlooked this nicety. They failed to describe Mr. Lamb's eccentricities to one dealer who just happened to be the sole employee on duty the afternoon the victim walked in. The sleepy dealer saw what he thought was a penniless bum and ordered him out. Offended, the millionaire never stepped foot in there again and the club that was built just for him got not Dollar One of his play.

For such operators I have real scorn. They deliberately created a "flat store," as we call dishonest gambling houses, for the purpose of robbing a customer. I am against that. The inherent odds going for any gambling house are ample, even with the state's take of 5% on our gross. When I risk my own money, I want an honest chance. But I will not attempt to persuade you that I am honest. You must judge for yourself. This is one of my idiosyncrasies, of which at present writing I have a bundle. For example, while I have a good private secretary, I write my most important letters myself on a hunt and peck typewriter. I never sign them "Sincerely"; that is redundant. Why else would I take the time to write? I sign myself "Seriously". By the same token, I never profess to honesty. Either it shows or it doesn't.

♠

Since we're going to be together a while, you might as well know more of my idiosyncrasies. I detest cocktail parties, bosh and unsolicited advice. I will not criticize your grammar, not even to myself, though I may pick lint off your suit if it catches my eye. I love children and good conversation, won't work near a window and despise pencil mustaches. I grit my teeth at showoffs who clank stacks of silver dollars and believe a man should witness at least one legal execution in his life—I've seen two—so he won't be provoked to rash acts. Another of my idiosyncrasies, perhaps improbable in a casino operator, is that I love to see people win. A big winner is, of course, the greatest walking advertisement a club can buy and will, almost inevitably, be back to lose. That is a consideration. Beyond that, though, winners are having fun and fun eliminates many problems of a gambling club. I may, sarcastically, say "Good night, Santa Claus" to a dealer who's lost a chunk of our money but I wouldn't replace her in mid-deal, as some clubs do, and I won't remove a slot machine if it begins to dump unscheduled jackpots. Why? I'm a player myself. I know how it feels to stand ten feet tall when you're winning. When I lose, I am just as sick inside as any laboring man who unwisely drops his paycheck. I have, on occasion, ordered his money refunded, though mine never is.

Other quirks which would make me improbable? Well, I laid off a girl for a week recently, without pay, for chewing gum on the job. Gum chewers aggravate me and may annoy customers. I am a perfectionist and most exacting. As a result, some employees love me and some detest me. I'm not without my feelings either, as witness another girl who irked me. I had lost $50,000 at her 21 table before the tide turned and I recouped with a last hand worth $2600. In gratitude, I handed her a $500 toke and told her to buy a Dior gown. Now I often select my wife's concert gowns and I believe every woman should have at least one dress or piece of jewelry she can't really afford. That was what I had in mind for this young lady. She, however, was a divorcee with two children and other obligations and saw it differently. She didn't buy the Dior and I, with my idiosyncrasies, was annoyed.

Maybe you're getting the impression that money means little to me. That would not be correct. I like money and need it to pay the bills. Waste is utterly abhorrent to me, and I constantly am picking up pennies from the club floor and saving them. When I found one day that I couldn't locate a chukkar partridge I had shot, I gave up bird hunting. It was wasteful not to retrieve my game. But I do spend money. When I take guests to Las Vegas for a weekend, you can believe we have a ball and it doesn't come cheap. I am restless and impetuous as a jack rabbit and we jump around a lot. I may get into a private 21 game with Milton Berle, a deep conversation with Ted Lewis, or take the side bets Dean Martin misses. It isn't all thoughtless gallivanting. I'm judging entertainers I may hire for my Fun Room and studying the garish Vegas casinos to keep my own club in competition. They know me for a big player so I must show my money to demonstrate all is still well with Harolds Club. I never walk into a casino without making a courtesy bet of several hundred dollars though I'm only on my way to the men's room and have no intention of bucking the games. I'm somewhat of a dissembler, you see, at the same time I appear to be wide open. For example, my real treasure at the moment is a Lincoln Continental automobile with a telephone to keep me in touch. Do I keep that lovely car gleaming? Not on your life. A little Nevada dust on the car prevents the neighbors from thinking I'm so prosperous I don't need their patronage.

Coming home on the plane from Vegas, people may see me drag out a bulky wallet and study a typewritten page. A financial statement? No; personal business. Events of the past few years have taught me there are things in this life beside money. I am now searching out eternal truths. When I find something I like, I copy it off and read it over and over. It may be Descartes, the Bible, Elbert Hubbard or Adam Smith (1723-1790) who said something I need to remember. "Prejudice," he said, "was not reasoned into a man; therefore you cannot reason it out." A gambler has as much chance of escaping prejudice as a camel has of passing through the eye of a needle.

Lacking formal education, my thirst for knowledge seems suddenly unquenchable. But, as the Good Book says, nothing in this life shall be easy for man. In 1949, I had a severe attack of iritis, which recurs periodically with pain that would make the electric chair seem like an overstuffed sofa. The only relief is a hypodermic of adrenalin jabbed directly into my eyeball. You should try that sometime if you want a thrill. I can't read all I would like to, then, but I do tempt the fates at least once a year to pore over favorite books like *The Robe*, my *Bible, The Greatest Story Ever Told, Anthony Adverse*. There's a story that tells what a man with conflicts in himself is like! The old bard Shakespeare, who knew people as I would like to, is my favorite. To save my eyes, I have him on records and sit by the hour listening to the insights to be found in Hamlet, Julius Caesar and Macbeth.

In a gambling club? Well, I have a lovely home near the out-skirts of Reno, but I can't always go home. So I have two hideaways at the club. One is behind the double-thick, double-locked doors of my office where you could reach me only if my secretary put the call through. A second phone, for emergencies, connects me directly with the security catwalks which keep an eye on every gaming table in the house. There in my office, in shirt-sleeves and green eyeshade, I probably look as a gambler should as I bend over hated paperwork on my cluttered desk. The hi-fi is playing softly—always with good music that soothes a soul—Aida, Tosca, Meditation from Thais. The knotty pine walls around the gun cabinets which contain my prized shotguns and rifles are almost solid with photos of the great and small who honor me with love and friendship. There I work, listening to the beautiful music, planning my concerts or changes in the club, attending the welfare of 1150 loyal employees, glancing up occasionally to the countenance of good friends like Lily Pons, several wonderful priests, Elizabeth Schwartzkopf, my present wife Lois, my children and grandchildren, Daddy, some solid kinsfolk in Vermont who may never step foot in a gambling club, and my sainted great grandmother who tried to show me years ago what religion is and what it requires.

My absolute sanctum is on still another floor. There I go to brood or meditate, to rejoice or reflect. I keep a little typewritten note on that door which says no one is to knock without bidding and no one, if invited in, is to bring questions or advice. Here again is the difference between me and my Daddy. The sign on his office says bluntly: "PUSH THE DOOR KNOB TO BEAT HELL." Here I have surrounded myself with photos of those I love. Square in the center of them is the crucifix to which my eye turns more and more these days.

Looking back over fifty-one years, I see I have come a far piece from the Jewish neighborhood in Cleveland where I learned so many vital rules of living. I have run wheel and nail games in amusement parks, been a soldier (if I hadn't gone off to become Private First Class Smith in World War II, I'd be just another gambler today and there wouldn't be justification for this book), been an outdoorsman, a millionaire, even a movie actor. Yes, I was drafted to play my pet peeve of all, the gambling game

kibitzer, in the picture *Five Against The House* with Kim Novak
and Guy Madison, which was filmed here in Harolds Club. I gave
a great performance too, though it won me no Academy Award.
Once I thought I had reached the pinnacle of life's happiness—
and was delighted to leave the hundred-dollar chips to change
diapers on my two baby daughters— only to see the marriage
dissolve in divorce, lose a share of my club in the process, and
wallow for a while in booze. I remarried and adopted two more
wonderful children, had a nervous breakdown and gave my
solemn oath not to drink again until 1966. Now I am trying to
do constructive things, to justify the fantastic good fortunes I
have enjoyed.

At the moment I am on the closest of terms with my state's
officialdom. Not long ago, in fact, I bought $55,000 worth of
western hats from Rex Bell, the former cowboy movie star
and lieutenant-governor of Nevada, who has a haberdashery shop
across the street from Harolds Club. One of those hats proved the
finest gift I could have given a rich gentleman from Switzerland,
a dignitary of the recent Winter Olympic Games at nearby Squaw
Valley. We became good friends. But the fact remains I am a
professional gambler, not always sociably acceptable, and there's
a protocol in all relationships. There's a protocol in a whore-
house, too, if you want the blunt truth.

I am, therefore, many things in the minds of my fellow man.
A skilled trapshooter who shot alongside me in several important
meets has said I am absolutely unpredictable. Another man,
watching me lead the band up Virginia Street, says I'm just a show-
off. Two men who know me very well—Dr. Roy H. Parkinson
and M.A. (John) Diskin—one a distinguished doctor and one
a distinguished lawyer—have done me the honor of putting my
photo in their offices with their families. Both know me quite
well, one having stuck a needle in my eyeball, the other having
had me on a witness stand and set me straight when I differed with
him. "You are one of the greatest of human beings," Jan Peerce
wrote to me not so long ago. "To know you and be with you are
highlights of my life." Another voice, not so melodious, growled
at me in the club a few minutes ago: "You've taken every cent
of my money, you dirty, heartless son of a bitch."

So be it. Each man is entitled to his opinion. You play them
as they lay.

2

♦ ♦ ♦ ♦

This Is My Game

NEWSPAPERS FROM COAST to coast carried a story one day that famous Harolds Club was being sold. We did indeed have an offer well up in the millions, which, as businessmen, we had to consider, and somehow the word leaked. Immediately we were besieged by wire, telephone and mail, plus cablegrams from abroad asking if it were true. All this interest in a gambling house way off in Nevada? I was surprised.

The thing that really startled me, though, was the deluge of protests from customers near and far. It was as though we were letting the old homestead go to the first bidder. They pleaded with us not to sell and we didn't.

The incident wouldn't have amazed me so much if this were a fine old hotel or restaurant with which people associate loving memories. Harolds Club is a gambling house. We earn our money by trying to win yours. I wondered at the time if some of these people didn't feel such a personal interest because we're holding money they hope to win back.

I knew this wasn't the case, of course. Somewhere in the furor

27

of publicity there was an interesting statement. It said that the Smith family and Harolds Club, more than any other institution, has, over a quarter of a century, set the standard that has made recreational gambling possible in the Silver State. I would like to believe this is true. Gaming today is Nevada's largest industry— the gross handle for 1960 was $200,127,146, on which casinos paid a State tax alone of $9,857,534. Gambling house payrolls are paying off mortgages on big churches and pretty little homes. It isn't all sinister.

The people it attracts are from all walks of life, including even clergymen whom I have recognized more than once in spite of their disguise. What the Smith family has tried to do is provide those who like to gamble with a place where the dice are truly cubed and the cards are dealt squarely; an environment in which they don't need to fear they will be clipped. The avalanche of protest seemed to indicate we may have been successful. Anyway, I took it as a tribute.

Harolds Club is different, no doubt about it, and the sale talk made me think of things I've come to take for granted. I've visited gambling casinos from Havana, Cuba, to Kentucky, from Miami, Fla., to Dayton, O., and from Tiajuana, Mexico, to San Francisco, where gaming is not legal. As I write this, in fact, San Francisco is again a "closed town." If the Grand Jury ever wonders how successful its policemen are at their job, I suggest it come to Reno for a weekend and see the crowds of San Franciscans flocking here. Any time the city by the Golden Gate clamps down, my business booms. Maybe that's an indication of the relief an "open" state like Nevada affords with legal gaming. Living with it, we know how to control it. Unquestionably we save our neighboring states many law-enforcement headaches.

In this picture, as I have said, Harolds Clubs is the biggest of all. It has mushroomed from the one-room shop we opened February 23, 1936—my twenty-sixth birthday—into a seven-story structure occupying two-thirds of a city block, with offices and other facilities spilling over into a second building across Douglas Alley. With our 1150 employees constantly hiking back and forth on errands and coffee breaks, plus patrons coming to cuss or compliment us, this, I have been told, is the most-traveled alley in the world. We have more gaming tables under one roof than any club; hence more attendants. Well over 1,000,000 people wander through our premises each year; an electric-eye device at just one of our seven outside entrances—none of which is ever locked—counted 15,600 customers in a twenty-four hour period. Some are kibitzers, to be sure, coming to get warm or to cool off. Most, however, are people carrying money to be spent here, and I can hear my merchant readers murmuring an envious "Geewhiz!"

Let me draw the picture a little clearer. If you stand on the west side of Virginia Street, your back to the Prima Donna, Nugget and Horseshoe Clubs, you would be looking at the huge red face of our institution, on which a three-story-high mural in color and lights shows a bigger-than-life wagon train camp. Crouched next to us is the Nevada Club then Harrah's. Behind us in Lincoln Alley is the Bank-Golden Club. All are so close you can wander back and forth without escaping the air conditioning. All have bright signs beckoning you to convenient doors. All want your play. This is the competition keen, alert, never sleeping.

Step through any of the doors, preferably ours, and you see an industry like no other in the world. There are no shelves stacked with merchandise, but rather stacks of gleaming silver dollars as though we were selling money. We are waiting with our money for you to bring yours. Between us, most of the time, there's more cash under this roof than there is in the First National Bank of Nevada at the end of the block. We handle more cash in a year than they do. It is a fact that you can make a purchase at any store in Nevada and pay for it with Harolds Club chips. They aren't legal tender, but they're as good as money. In a sense, then, we do sell money.

Our real merchandise is games of chance. In my club they include dice, roulette, chuck-a-luck, panguingui (commonly pangini or pan), hundreds of slot machines, racehorse Keno, baccarat and 21. We don't call it blackjack in a gambling house; blackjack is the game you play outside gaming clubs, where the deal and its risks and profits travel as a player turns ace-ten. I'll have more to say of it in my primer on gambling.

There are, to be sure, gambling games we don't offer at Harolds Club. Some we have tried and, for good reason, discontinued. We don't have a racing book any more; if you want to bet the horses or a sporting event, you'll have to go elsewhere. Klondike dice, or Ace-Away, a very popular game in the State of Washington, never caught on with our patrons so we dropped it. We also have discontinued poker, lo-ball and crapless craps, a game in which 2 and 12 are points to be made, rather than penalties that lose your bet. We found in crapless craps that the normal percentage of 1.41% against the player in a dice game rose abruptly to 4% against him, and we don't care to gouge our customers like that. We are, furthermore, one of the few gaming houses in the world which does not employ shills to pretend-play our games when it is quiet and hope, thereby, to inspire customer action.

It's in these intangibles, I would say, that Harolds Club is different. Ours is a gambling house, we like to believe, which attempts to make your Reno stopover fun, even though it can't always be profitable. Every girl making change in our club says "Good luck" when she opens your roll of coins. Attendants paying your jackpots exult with you and urge you to hit another. And why shouldn't they? As signs in the club proclaim, 99% of Harolds Club employees gamble here too. Looking at it from their purely personal standpoint, a given number of pulls of a slot machine handle are required to produce a jackpot. You're making some of those pulls for them while they work.

Yes, my employees do gamble in their off-duty hours. Their reasons are exactly the same as mine or yours—that undeniable thrill of offering a dollar to Lady Luck and having it return a hundred-fold. For many people, perhaps most, it is tension-breaking recreation.

Among my employees, like the general public, however, there are those who should not gamble. That is to be expected. I am thinking now of an otherwise sensible and attractive young lady who deals 21. For the game of 21 she couldn't care less. Baccarat or roulette leave her cold. She scarcely hears the rattling of nickel, dime and quarter slot machines. It is a dollar machine that raises its siren call for her. Not any dollar machine, either; there's a specific one. In fact, this young lady who earns her living dealing a gambling game goes regularly to a psychiatrist we all hope will break her of this crazy attachment for one inanimate bit of mechanism.

That isn't recreation. It is tragedy. I don't want the money of sick people or poor people, or even normal people whose emotions suddenly get away with them. I understand how it happens, God knows. For this girl, and others like her, troubled by whim-whams only a psychiatrist or padre can diagnose, we have signs posted prominently throughout the club. YOU CAN'T WIN ALL THE TIME. HAROLDS CLUB URGES YOU TO GAMBLE ONLY WHAT YOU CAN AFFORD.

Almost daily, however, my attention is called to the plight of some poor soul who has gambled away his last nickel. He hasn't even bus fare home. I have given him that and sometimes he will go right back to the tables and lose it too. Then there's nothing to do but send out an attendant to purchase the plane, bus or railroad ticket and escort our man to the depot. We've done it often.

Not long ago, in fact, a man trudged tearfully up to Daddy's office and blurted out a sad tale. With his wife in the hospital back home, rent and car payments due, and three children to feed, there just wasn't money enough in the bank for everything. So he'd come off to Reno in hopes of making a killing. He couldn't, of course, with that handicap—worried and playing needed money. He was bound to lose and he did. He was broke. Now Daddy and I have our differences, over club policy, investments and such, but not in things like this. It took only a few moments to check the man's story—you'd be surprised how dealers remember you and how much you have played. He ordered every cent of the man's money refunded. If I know my father, he added the few extra dollars the man needed in the first place.

I've done the same thing many times. There have been years, in fact, when Harolds Club has refunded up to half a million dollars, all of it *after* paying the state's take of 5.5% on our total handle. There's no business advantage there but we preach no sermons. We say just three things to the unfortunate loser: 1) Don't tell anyone Harolds Club gave you back this money. 2) You're over 21 or you wouldn't have been in the club, so we will not tell you never to gamble again. We do ask, though, if you come to Reno in the future to play, that you will give us your patronage. 3) Tell people that Harolds Club is an honest place to play. That's all. You would be surprised how this bread cast on water has returned. Daddy believes it has brought us more business in the long run than our familiar billboards, which now are spread clear across this country and onto every continent in the world, including Antarctica.

♣

We are realists above all. We realize that most of the million-plus people who come through our doors every year hope to win some of our money. Often enough, they do. Gaming tables can get just as unlucky as players. We had one dice table, for instance, that went 30 straight days without a winning shift. And how that word spread! However, with as many tables as we have, a loser like this usually is balanced off by a wining station. A big day's loss for the club would be $100,000, which isn't jelly beans, of course.

It can happen in so many ways. A classic true story involves the Reno man who found a dime on the floor as he strolled through the club one day. He played it in a dime machine and hit a $15 jackpot. Then he went to the quarter machine and hit it for a $35 jackpot; thence to the half-dollar and dollar machines, and finally a dice table. When he walked out some hours later, he was carrying $3000 of our money. I won't tell you his name or point him out, though I see him almost every day. It's a Harolds Club policy to keep it quiet when your luck is good. We don't want our customers becoming targets of any kind. If your win is very big, in fact, I may put my pistol in my pocket and drive you to the airport or at least walk you back to your hotel.

I can't say what Internal Revenue does about these wins. That is your responsibility. I do know they watch operators like me very closely. Only recently I had to try to explain an item of $8.20 spent three years ago in the Riverside Hotel, which I had claimed as business expense. Believe me, my memory was sorely taxed. I am careful to report accurately every penny of earnings though it is understood that as a professional gambler I have huge losses to match my big wins. (I was the one who ordered the sign that says YOU CAN'T WIN ALL THE TIME.)

I am not a completely free soul in this never-never land. Under the law, I may not make a bet in my own club—and that certainly has saved me money. I may not take one dollar off any table, not even to help a deserving down-and-outer or to buy a newspaper. I must keep track of all refunds in readable black and white, preferably ink. I may not loan money on your jewelry, your watch or your automobile. You will have to cross the street to the hock shop.

There's another thing I don't do, purely as a matter of personal policy. I never, never carry a playing card or die on my person. The reason should be obvious, but I will draw you a picture. Some people, when they lose, are quick to claim the house is cheating; others hang on our coat tails waiting an honest mistake. We watch the tools of our trade more closely than a doctor watches his instruments and when a carper raises a fuss I simply call a city detective as witness, take the complainant to our Vault and offer to let him caliper any dice or examine any deck of cards he choses. Supposing, then, I were to put a deck of cards in my pocket—perhaps to take home for a bridge game—then reached for a cigarette in the club and the cards spilled out. Someone would see and misconstrue it. Gossip is merciless. A little of Harolds Club's good reputation would vanish in that instant.

We casino operators must always think ahead. When you walk into Harolds Club, for instance, there's an air of festive excitement. The clank and clatter of slot machines—did you ever hear thirty silver dollars fall kerplunk into a metal tray?—the shriek of winners, the endless wisping of cards, the orgiastic pleas of dice players, the tolling of Keno numbers, announcements of floor shows, telephone calls, "Security officers come to Section 2" . . . "So and So, please report to the credit office" . . . "Long distance calling . . ." Your first impression might be one of great confusion. It isn't. There's studied order to it, I assure you, in which a little pocket of silence may mean the biggest game in the house and I will keep an eye on that.

We work hard to reach your physical senses. That is our intent and our need. We want your eyes to widen, your ears to perk up and a quiver of excitement to seize you. The only sense we don't appeal to is smell; you won't smell cigarettes in Harolds Club and smoke won't get in your eyes. We have air purifiers over every table to draw it off. Asthma sufferers say they find relief here and that makes Daddy beam. It was asthma that drove him off the Vermont farm and into the west many years ago.

Our motivations are clear. We like you. We want to keep you out of the clubs which surround us. Assuming you're over 21—and this you must prove to our satisfaction—we try to get you into Harolds Club and keep you here. We do have clocks on the wall but you have to look to see them. If we can keep you twenty-four hours, we're prepared to do so. Our public relations department issues printed news summaries to keep you in touch with the outside world; we have radio and television, including a big screen for life-sized reception of major sporting events. There are carpets on our floors for the long-run comfort of your feet. Should you get tired, our complimentary bus makes regular runs to Harolds Pony Express Lodge, where you can have an invigorating swim. Our restaurant never closes, and the coffee of which I drink at least twenty cups a day myself, is top-notch. So are our pastries. You have kiddies on your trip with you? They can't come into the club, of course, but we have a theater for them with a regular schedule of western movies. We also provide baby sitters. Is there something else you want?

A drink? Once Daddy wouldn't tolerate liquor on the premises but we found many of our customers like a libation now and then and would wander off to other clubs that offered it. Sometimes they didn't come back. So now we have seven bars operating day and night and we sell more whiskey than is sold under any other roof in the world. Our Silver Dollar Bar on the second floor is paved with 2141 real silver dollars; you can touch the money at least. We don't push our drinks, however, and it's a real occasion—such as my hitting a big dice game—when we buy drinks for the house. We have relatively little trouble with drinkers. I like to believe this is due chiefly to the type of clientele that comes to Harolds Club and to the fact people are having too much fun to blot it out with booze. When a customer does get too much—which can happen to any man, as I well know—we attempt to persuade him to stop gambling and let us hold his money for him. Not a few revelers have awakened next day, pockets empty, to learn with amazement they still have several hundred dollars in winnings with the cashier.

♥

We get some wonderful, funny people in here. I met one the other night when I stepped in to check a men's rest room. He was tipsy and had just withdrawn a $50 bill from the "bank" in his shoe; now he was doing the damnedest buck and wing you ever witnessed, trying to get back into his shoe without sitting down and without toppling into the urinal. All the time, oblivious of me, he was continuing to implore Lady Luck.

Then there was the intent player who had the dice when a defective flue fire broke out near our back bar. Flames were shooting three feet high around the dice table as firemen arrived and shouted for everyone to stand back. "Not now!" shrieked the player from the heart of the inferno, brandishing the dice overhead. "I've got a streak going. Come on eight!"

I have seen a pregnant woman stand at a 21 game, oblivious to labor pains, until we thought we were going to become midwives, and leave only when we summoned an ambulance. And I have seen death come to the gaming tables. One I will never forget. The gentleman keeled over after tossing the dice and I guess I glanced automatically at the play. A five and two. He had crapped out literally.

Our customers are everyone except, of course, honest objectors to gaming and out-and-out prudes. They are pensioners, merchants, housewives, millionaires, politicians and professional people. Soft-drawling Southerners who play the games as if the South will rise again, Aunt Ida tourists from the Midwest, sophisticated travelers from New York and grim-lipped Downeasters. I hear words in Yiddish which tell me how the game goes for this Momma or Poppa, a line of Spanish here, Greek there and Japanese. Winter weekends bring families of handsome young Chinese whose checks at the credit office tell me they are prosperous California ranchers. I know the faces of Piute and Washoe Indians from the nearby desert, playing side by side with a turbaned Indian from across the sea. Sometimes an excited player will rush up to say Bing Crosby is at a dice table. He is, but I don't bother him. Or it may be Ted Lewis dropping in for a little play between engagements at another club, or Milton Berle or Robert Mitchum. Jimmy Durante and Eddie Cantor have had their moments in Harolds Club, as have Charles Bickford and Edward G. Robinson, among many, many others. One big star, whose identity I shall not reveal, proved the most vulgar man ever to enter our doors. After winning pretty good, he had some losses that loosened his inhibitions and brought a torrent of talk we can't tolerate.

Human nature, as I say, invariably shows itself at the gaming table. Lily Pons, after her recital here, wanted to try her luck at the tables. I had just seen her as a great artist. Knowing gambling as I do, I knew I would now see her as a person. She went after the dice with all the serious intent of a woman out to break me at $1 a throw. There was nothing halfway about *ma petite femme*. She was tremendous.

Mice in the club don't bother us because even a poor little church mouse can't subsist on hard cold cash, but we have had our dog. A sweet old bloodhound attached himself to the place once, though he had a good home here in town. He would come every day, look the players over in his bleary way and find the most comfortable place to flop. It didn't matter to him if that happened to be in front of our busiest dice table. The funny thing was that the players didn't mind. They seemed to consider him as good luck and would rub his coat now and then between plays. He was a great dog. When he died, the Reno papers printed a solemn obituary for him.

One horse has visited the club. I rode him in myself one day when I was feeling good. I rode right up to the first floor bar, took off his bridle and ordered him a saucer of Coca Cola. This was Bobby Sox, my quarter horse palomino, a flashily beautiful animal. Someone phoned Daddy, of course, to report that Harold really was cowboying today and he came to look. "That's great!" he beamed. "Customers love the unusual." My daddy has always had a shrewd eye for gimmicks, including once a Lazy Susan bar in which your drinks came rolling around on miniature trains on a track. That almost made me, a real drinking man, take the cure.

The unusual has served us well, however. Thanks to another purchase by Daddy, we own one of the world's greatest gun collections and display it on our walls, between western paintings, murals and tableaux, from the sidewalks through the Roaring Camp and Covered Wagon rooms. There are derringers, rifles, cannon, Billy the Kid and Buffalo Bill models, even machine guns from World War I, and most have drawn blood. Should you run out of nickels or simply tire of the games, you could spend your entire vacation studying these guns or the pioneer stage-coaches and carriages suspended from the ceilings. In some ways, Harold's Club is a first-class western museum. Once we even had a real fountain of whiskey gushing from a mountain scene at the Silver Dollar Bar. It didn't last long. By the end of the first shift the bartender was tottering from the fumes and customers three tables away were spifflicated.

You will find the Smith family, in person or photograph, everywhere in this club at all times. Daddy's beaming countenance even confronts you from certain of the slot machines and if you can line up the right combination—photos of me, my brother Raymond, and my ex-wife Dorothy—in a row, you have our special Jackpot paying 1000 to 1. This may seem immodest but we are a family club and we want you to feel our presence. I am president, Daddy's general manager and treasurer, Raymond is vice president and secretary and my son Junior's a night boss. Every one of us is available to you. As our customers said, the day when a Smith isn't on the job at Harolds Club would be a sad day indeed.

This air of friendliness is, I believe, the prime ingredient of the club. All employees wear western clothes with name plates telling their Christian name and home town. Every employee, no matter how busy, is under orders to stop whatever he may be doing, when a customer asks, and explain carefully each phase of his game.

If you should go broke—and it does happen—or are just plain tired, you can take elevators to the Fun Room, where you don't even have to buy a beer to enjoy the show. I pick that entertainment myself. Looking in through the red plush drapes, as I did an hour ago, I can almost hear the trademark of some of our favorite performers; the plunking banjo of Eddy Peabody, the clear trumpet of Harry James, Carmen Cavallaro's tinkling piano, the jokes of the Wiere Brothers, Carl Ravazza's sweet tenor voice, and the lilting plunk-plunk of Rusty Draper's *Gambler's Guitar*. You will notice we don't attempt the lavish reviews of Las Vegas, which cost up to $60,000 a week. We'd rather give the customers at our tables a run for that money.

This is why I can say truthfully our slot machines are generous. Every club in Nevada, of course, has neon signs claiming this distinction. The simple truth is that volume of play will determine how low the operator may gear his machines. We have the volume and I have a favorite expression I found in my reading: *Quid pro quo*—something for something. Latin it may be, but it speaks plainly to me, the player as well as proprietor. A customer of ours once won a bet that Harolds Club paid more jackpots *in one day* than all of Las Vegas did in one year. To be sure that was ten years ago, when Vegas didn't have pure slot machine houses, but we still will top their best.

Our biggest day, incidentally, on which we might pay off 6,210 jackpots, would not, as you might suppose, be the Fourth of July. It is Labor Day, and for a very good reason. Most people with money in this country are over thirty years of age. They don't like to mingle with the multitudes on highways or beaches when the firecrackers are popping and the kids are howling. So they take their vacations in May or October and avoid the rush weekends. The only exception to this is Labor Day when their comings and goings overlap with the throng. That's when we hit our peak.

Quiet days here are determined by weather. The bulk of our customers come from California and a snow storm or threat of one can make the Sierra passes fearful, even for recreational gamblers with hot hunches. Sunday is always Sunday in a gambling club, a fairly nice business no matter what the weather. Monday is blue Monday, the same as in the entertainment business all the way to Manhattan. Tuesday, for some reason, brings good business. Wednesday is so-so. Thursday picks it up and Friday is quite big. Saturday, of course, is America's night of nights to play.

Perhaps the most convivial of all times in my club is the day we hold our employees Christmas party. To play it safe and not disturb the guests—since a lot of spirits are built up here over a year—we hold this shindig at the Harolds Club Gun Club out on the Pyramid Lake Road. I wish you could attend this little soiree, which starts at 1 PM on the designated day and continues uninterrupted for twenty-four hours so that all shifts of our round-the-clock operation may attend. There is dancing to a succession of orchestras, free drinks at a non-stop bar, and the best spread of food you would find this side of the Waldorf-Astoria. My personal recommendation for anyone who wants to attend, if the security force would even let you in, would be to arrive at about the halfway mark when the herring has really begun to marinate. This get-together of western style gambling club employees embodies all of the office parties in America thrown into one. I am glad I no longer am a drinking man.

Christmas Eve at Harolds Club isn't precisely Silent Night, Holy Night, though you'd be surprised at the ones who slip off to church for a little visit. The premises are decorated in tinsel and greens and the games all are going. But there's a different atmosphere to the place as folks drop in on their way from late Christmas shopping, or after dinner for a few hours of friendship. The play isn't heavy or loud. There's something nice about it. Then, a week later, New Years Eve kicks off with a bang. The past one was the biggest, businesswise, Reno has ever had.

During the holidays, I happened to be strolling through the club one evening when a certain man approached me with a request to cash his check for $200. I had known this gentleman for twenty years as a thorough eight ball, a man who would cheat you in any way that he could. I said no thanks.

"But Harold," he protested. "Did I ever give you a bum check?"

"No," I replied. "You never did. I have never let you give me any kind of check."

It didn't faze him at all. He came back to me again and again until I finally thought: What the hell. It's Christmas. This is only $200, not life or death. I told him I would keep track of that check. "If it bounces," I warned him, "you will pay if it kills you. You're just the type of schmuck who would go to any lengths to cheat me."

He did, too. The check bounced, of course, and I set out to find the gentleman. I found him in the mortuary, victim of a sudden heart attack, and without funds. So I chipped in a little more to help bury him. Maybe we'll meet again on the other side and he won't be such an eight-ball any more, though I find it hard to picture him with wings and a harp.

At least he went the whole route to beat me and there's a certain amount of class in that. Maybe, at that, this is an improbable game I'm in.

Never-Never Land

IMPROBABLE THINGS DO happen in Reno.

Consider, if you please, this painfully true tale of a young man who came to town a few years ago to establish the six weeks residence necessary for a divorce. Days passed without turning up a job and one afternoon he stood in front of Harolds Club with only four silver dollars in his pocket. Not enough for overdue room rent; not enough for a good steak dinner.

Consider now, if you will, how Lady Luck looked upon this forlorn gentleman when he was low and took him in her loving arms. He stepped in through our Virginia Street entrance where we have a bank of dollar slot machines. Perhaps he thought: *What the Hell, I might as well be broke as the way I am.* At any rate, it was a fateful moment for him and time plays a vital part in this story.

When you insert a coin in a dollar machine and pull the lever, the first of three wheels spins for three seconds, the second for four seconds and the third for five seconds. You get your answer in five seconds flat. Our man had chosen to make or break fast

41

and played two dollar machines simultaneously. He got his reply in ten seconds. On either his last, or next to last, dollar he hit a jackpot for $150.

Most people would have mopped the perspiration off their brow then and departed with the $150 to buy a meal and pay the room rent. Not our young man. He continued to play dollar machines and take jackpots. I learned later he won nearly $1000 that afternoon.

He was back that evening and, the dollar machines having gone through their cycle for him, turned to half-dollars. He still played two at a time. Several hundred dollars more fell for him. Now he had money enough to satisfy the landlady, pay off his attorney and keep himself for the remainder of his six weeks.

But our man was not stupid. He saw that he was into a fantastic lucky streak. He ventured on to the double-header slots, where you play two coins at a time with one pull of the lever; when a jackpot from one of these falls, it's a 1000-to-1 payoff. He was sticking to dollar and half-dollar machines and he won. He went on to four-bar machines, on which four jackpot bars must be lined in a row. They were lining all right for him.

Thus began one of the most fantastic lucky streaks I have ever witnessed. Our man was winning almost $500 a day and it went on for weeks. He simply couldn't lose. Now, of course, he didn't bother to seek work. No job could possibly provide the money he was getting for very short hours. Reno was his oyster and our machines his pearl. He put a down payment on a home in the Country Club district and soon owned it outright. I say "soon" because this gentleman was having an incredible streak. He would come in around 10 or 11 AM each day, play for a while and have a leisurely lunch, then go at it again in the afternoon or evening. Daddy was positive the man had a gimmick and you can believe we checked the machines thoroughly. Not a thing was amiss. It got so that customers and employees would gather the moment he arrived. He didn't disappoint them. He thoroughly enjoyed the attention he was getting.

A certain cockiness crept into his manner. One day he went to one of Reno's better stores, ordered $3425 worth of furnishings for his home and spurned the happy salesman's proffer of credit. "I will pay in cash," he said, "but first I must go over to Harolds

Club and win it." The salesman's chin hit the floor. Being a whilesome player himself, he knew you just can't do that. Our man did, though. In two days he was back with the cash. He did the same thing with an automobile agency, promising and giving $5000 cash on the day of delivery. That afternoon he worked us over good.

So it went, for week after week, until I estimated his total winnings at $70,000. Then, suddenly, his luck began to falter. So did his attitude. Now he played desperately and bitterly, for longer and longer hours, which is always an encouraging sign for an operator. I knew he wouldn't win any more. Lady Luck was drying up the well.

Let me interject here that I since have given this episode much thought. The man made the cardinal error, I am sure, of coming to believe Mother Providence owed him a living. He forgot, if indeed he ever knew, the most basic precept of gaming, that luck, good or bad, changes inevitably.

Losing steadily and swiftly, he complained to his lawyer, an old friend of ours, that the machines at Harolds Club had now been fixed. The attorney snorted. "If they were going to fix those machines," he asked, "why didn't they start long ago? Before you took them for $70,000?"

This the gentleman could not answer. He suddenly was disenchanted with Reno. Selling his house and furniture, he left town with approximately $50,000 of my money, all from that initial ten-second, make-or-break investment of four dollars.

I doubt that such a thing could happen in your home town. It doesn't happen too often in mine, fortunately, but when it does it adds to the legend of a never-never land.

♦

Many hundreds of thousands of people have passed under the bright-lighted arch proclaiming Reno "The Biggest Little City In The World." They come and go, most to remember only the convenient divorce court, marriage license bureau or gaming clubs. Few realize that these clubs occupy but a few blocks hard by the railroad tracks. Rarely do our visitors wander on up to the next block where the normal activities of a city of 60,000 begin. There, on any day, very normal inhabitants are being fitted to dresses or eyeglasses, to shoes or dentures, are having deeds of trust drawn or school clothes laid away for their children, are discovering they are pregnant or have cancer. Of course they know about double sixes and cutting a square deck, just as the residents of a Kansas farm community know about mash feeding and windmills.

None of us here are made of marble. We wouldn't live constantly in the high fever excitement of endless crap games. So it is that I leave Harolds Club for an hour or so every day to regain my perspective. There are plenty of places to go. I may stop in at a movie to see *Ben Hur* still another time, at St. Thomas Aquinas Cathedral for a moment of devotion, at my Daddy's lovely new home for an evening of bridge, or drop in at the Dominican Convent for quiet talk with the brothers. Perhaps I take flowers to a sick friend at St. Mary's Hospital, drive out to Pyramid Lake to view the pastel shifting of moods, or to Steamboat Springs to bake out a head cold. From the heart of the city to the growing suburbs, it's much like any town this size with its new high school, new markets, established residential districts and spreading tract homes.

Its gaming club employees live their private lives about as workers in an electronics plant do. One of our pretty blonde 21 dealers on the day shift, for instance, is married to a dice dealer and they have Wednesdays and Thursdays off. One week they work around their new little home or take their three children shopping. The next week they may tog out in Khakis and thermal underwear for the winter trout fishing on Pyramid Lake. Once a month, perhaps, they will have a night on the town and do a little conservative gaming. The same kind of people in your town would be playing bingo that night at a church social.

Reno has its particular flavor, to be sure. It's a western town and not too far removed from its cowboys and Indians. Just around the corner from us, on Commercial Row, is a saloon that caters to Indians exclusively. Talk about segregation! If you're not an Indian, stand back. I'll make it clearer. In my wildest drinking days, that was one saloon I did not enter. Every afternoon at three o'clock I hear the railroad crossing gates clang down across Virginia Street and traffic backs up all the way to the Riverside Hotel while a long freight crawls through with automobiles stacked three high. There will also be three or more cars of cattle or sheep in the train and they're off our Nevada ranches. Real cowboys with bowed legs and lean, leathery faces work out saddle kinks at my bars and dice tables. Only the other day I heard a horse whinny on Virginia Street and it sounded good. It was being towed on a trailer, to be sure, but it made Reno sound right again. When I came here twenty-five years ago, horses were rather common on our streets.

It's only a few moments from my baccarat table to the wide open spaces where coyotes and bobcats prowl and you can stand in magnificent solitude and look for two weeks in any direction. Once Daddy had some mines in the weird desert mountains to the east—he still dabbles in oil, his idea of a safe gamble as against my dice and cards—and I've had some of my grandest adventures out there.

Once, I recall, we were off on a cross-country ride. The first morning out, one of the wranglers, with characteristic cowboy humor, handed me a rawhide lariat and pointed to the corral. "Rope y'r hoss," he said. I caught his sly glance at the other cowboys and knew they'd studied my hands, soft and smooth from card dealing. But I'm a gambler. I took the rope impetuously and laid my coil the way I'd seen it done. There were thirty horses milling around the corral and I knew my chances of roping one, let alone my own were less than 30-1. I never changed expression, but stepped forward and threw the rope. Just as it happens for Keno players in rare moments, I fell into the right combination. The rope settled over my horse's neck and the cowboys nodded approval. Of course it was a fluke. The next morning I missed completely and my wrangler friends had their laugh.

The point I'm trying to make is that, close to the Old West as we are out here, a man soon can learn how much of a real man he is. There wouldn't be a privy here today with running water if tough men hadn't out-toughed this rugged land. It's flat and it's hot. (Or cold.) All Nevada once was the primeval bottom of Lake Lahontan, which also covered parts of California and Utah. The Great Salt Lake and Pyramid Lake are its remnants. I tell you this, not to demonstrate my erudition—after all, this is supposed to be a gambling book—but to show how geographical background is a consideration in the makeup of a never-never land.

Thirty years ago, Reno was just a prosperous market town for ranchers. Las Vegas was a steaming stopover in the desert 400 miles to the south. Today both are world-famous communities. Ask anyone about Reno. They'll tell you of its quick divorces (two Nevadans can argue at breakfast and be single for dinner) and the fact you can refinance your automobile faster here than you can wire for money. Who hasn't heard of Las Vegas' big-name casino shows in which, among other things, the female bosom proudly flaunts its bare maidenform? People who've never been in Nevada know all about these two communities but have never heard of Elko, one of my favorite towns up to the east, center of the richest cattle country in the United States, or Carson City, thirty-two miles south of us, the smallest state capital of the fifty. Tourists, of course, have read of Virginia City and the old Comstock Lode, whose silver established the elegant mansions on San Francisco's hills. Lately, however, they confuse quaint and legitimate old Virginia with Mister Lucius Beebe, a transplanted settler who's about as western as an Easter Parade on Fifth Avenue. On Mister Beebe I shall maintain a tight lip. I am not one of his subscribers.

My first visit to Vegas, incidentally, was to ride in a rodeo parade. It was just thirteen years ago and I stayed at the old Last Frontier where "Mr. Nevada," the late U.S. Senator Pat Mc-Carran, was also frequently in residence. No place on the Strip today, regardless of the millions spent, compares in style or quality, in my estimation, to the pioneer Last Frontier. Perhaps I am also prejudiced about the pre-Belden Kattleman El Rancho Vegas, which was there then, because it had the two sixes on me. I once won $12,000 at El Rancho, but usually I was consistently unlucky at its tables and helped pay its overhead with my losings. One by one the other name places came, the Thunderbird, which for personal reasons no longer gets any of my play, Desert Inn, the Sahara, which started first as a Bingo parlor, the Riviera, where Marlene Dietrich has really opened men's eyes to mature womanhood, the Sands, where my friend Joe E. Lewis wisecracks about his losses, and so on. It has been an incredible growth in thirteen years, from a water stop for freight trains to a bustling city with some ninety airplane flights arriving and departing daily. All of it has come about from gambling. In the early days I drove down leisurely by car, a matter of some 440 miles and eight hours, with sometimes a freak snowstorm to skid you about. Today I fly by Bonaza Air Lines jet prop in one hour and a half. There's good reason for my haste. I want to get out of Vegas fast—with my winnings intact or because I'm a loser.

♠

Las Vegas, as you must by now be aware, is far more improbable than Reno. Consider, if you please, the single matter of taxicabs. Down there in the sagebrush flats where burros wandered a few years ago, more taxis are whipping about between midnight and sunup than you would see in Times Square at the same hour. More toke money is passed to doormen, maitre d's and captains in an hour than the waiters at posh Chambord may see in a night. More cash is put out for show names than Broadway could afford to spend in a year. The reason is very simple. Las Vegas was built as a play pen for the Los Angeles-Hollywood crowd, among whom it is more important to show off than it is to have the money you are trying to show you have.

In Las Vegas you are encouraged subtly, as only gamblers can do that, to use chips instead of silver. Give a man one $5 chip instead of five silver dollars and he will tend to bet more. Five chips go into the pot silently; five jangling silver dollars can upset the nerves. Big betting, furthermore, has almost a mystical, epidemic quality. Let the bets get heavy at one table in a club and almost instantly they increase throughout the place. I have seen it in my baccarat room here. In baccarat, only currency is used. That green stuff is the most eye-catching thing there is; it will even take a man's eyes from the bare bosoms onstage. The moment play gets heavy at my baccarat table, I have observed, it also picks up the tempo and size of the bets at the nearby 21 and roulette tables. Las Vegas operators, working with the Southern California crowds, apply this psychology to the limit.

In Reno, however, we draw from Northern California. And if there is one person on the face of this earth you cannot distract with bosh, it is the San Franciscan. He is a hard player and a good player. He is not stupid. He will pay for what he wants, but he will not pay double for it. San Franciscans make up the bulk of our players and they set the example for others. They like silver dollars and our way of doing things.

There is generally a more substantial air to Reno. It was a natural center of trade, as I've noted, and it is on a main transcontinental road to the Coast, Highway 40. It has water, a major consideration on this side of the Sierra rampart; the Truckee River, where divorcees used to toss their wedding rings immediately upon getting the final decree, passes through the heart of town. On the south shore is the eight-story Riverside Hotel, where such names as Sarah Vaughn entertain, and on the north shore the eleven-story Mapes, tallest building in town. The billious pink State Building is nearby, with the Post Office, and two blocks downriver is the new Holiday, built by my good friend from Elko, Newt Crumley. We have a skyline, as you see, but you still can look up to the limitless blue of the desert sky and wild ducks still skim down to our river.

Some people even come to Reno for an education and can get a fine one especially in mining engineering, at the University of Nevada. The campus is less than half a mile north of my office and for years Harolds Club gave annual scholarships to deserving students. I never went near the school and one condition of our scholarships has been that students never come in the club. Why? It should be obvious. There is a stigma attached to professional gamblers. Neither I nor my family want any hint of a taint to spread to the young scholars out there.

In a way, this is ironical. No student on the campus is hungrier for knowledge than I. Whenever I hear or read a new word, I write it down. Then I look it up in at least two dictionaries and type out the definitions until I know the word and can use it. That is why, perhaps, my vocabulary is a little more fluid than you would expect of a gambler. I am determined not to be *esoteric*, and that's one of my newest finds. But back to the university. I made my first visit there only recently at the invitation of Hilary Sax, an instructor in tax accounting, who asked me to tell his students something of our business. I did not accept his invitation lightly after all my years of avoiding the academic halls; when I went finally it was only because he convinced me I had valid findings to offer the young men and women. I was a little surprised at the number of professors who turned out to listen. Some, I perceived, were not exactly on my side. But it came off satisfactorily and it was Mr. Sax subsequently who persuaded me to start tape-recording reminiscences for this book.

I believe a gambler has contributions to make to society just as Harolds Club contributes to every cause and charity in town. We're the first target for all drives. We give generously, too, and not just to grease our way or claim deductible expense. The things that are Caesar's, I give to Caesar, and I am hard-headed enough to know that it won't do the club a damned bit of practical good to brag to you about my charities. Those I can claim legitimately I tell to the Internal Revenue Service, not to you. But there are other things which are not Caesar's. I am proud to be asked to speak for an Israel Bond Drive, as I have with our Governor, handsome young Grant Sawyer, or to clown for a March of Dimes program. I want people to realize that Harold S. Smith, Sr. has more in his heart than the odds on chuck-a-luck. It isn't any picnic to be sick or down-and-out. That is elemental. If I am fortunate enough to be able to gamble a lot, it is only right I should help my fellow man where I can.

Just the other day a young woman came to Mrs. Mercedes Hoover, my confidential secretary, with a pitiful tale. Her husband had been stabbed to death in a barroom brawl. It would cost $150 to bury him and the woman was pregnant and broke. The local welfare agency could advance only $75 and must deduct that from any amount the woman raised elsewhere. The dead man had not been a customer of the club, the woman readily admitted. She'd come to us because she heard we're a soft-hearted lot and because it was the last resort. I gave her the $150 from my own pocket and will claim no deduction anywhere. What the Hell else could I do? Tell her to go out and bury her dead in the sagebrush like the pioneers did? I would hope for a little better than that if I were to lose my last dollar.

♣

But I was explaining Reno. The town would like to add small industries to its commercial assets and I wish them well. I have heard, however, that industry and gaming don't mix so well. Some say the gaming creates employee problems, which might be true. Maybe it's like the entertainment I seek for my Fun Room. I am intrigued with hypnotists, but I would never, never book one into the club. A hypnotist makes people uneasy. I am afraid they would troop up to see the show and not come back to the games. The basic psychology of a gaming house is, as I have indicated, to get you to play more. For that, there's nothing like laughs. Give me a comic making light of his losses, like Joe E. Lewis or Dean Martin, and the play increases. I have seen it happen a thousand times after I have cowboyed through the premises in my Gay 90s costume. You will note, too, that our farflung billboards never mention "Gambling." They all say "Harolds Club *For Fun.*"

There's another side to that coin too—happy players win more. Just a little while ago I noticed a bus boy from our restaurant with a big win going for him at Number Six 21 table. He had started with $10, I learned, and had run it up to $14,000. Naturally I stopped to ascertain if the game was on the up and up. It was and I got interested in him. He would bet $500 and double it on a 10 or 11 without any seeming concern for the value of money. Remember, if you please, here was a man earning, say, $11 or $12 a day and betting $1000 (when doubling) on the turn of a card. Think how long it would take him to save $1000 in wages. Yet his attitude was one of complete happiness. He'd been drinking a little, but not much, and he wasn't concerned with the price of the chips. He was living. His good luck had given him confidence.

The bus boy was, thereby, killing the "hidden percentage" that all gambling houses have in human nature. It is an absolute finding that most people will stand longer at the tables when they're losing than they will when they win. When losing, they're desperate to get their money back. Winning, they only want to get out with the boodle before the house's luck returns. I will go down to the club again pretty soon to see how the bus boy is doing. It wouldn't surprise me if he cashes in a $25,000 winner. Not at all. This chap either will win $25,000, as I see it, or he'll go broke. If he breaks, he'll feel a little unhappy with himself for a week or so, but that's not the point. The point lies in how he played $10 up to $14,000. What was his attitude? How did he handle the money? Was he afraid to throw the house's money back at them? These are the vital questions whenever we talk about gaming clubs and the people in them. Particularly those who are capable of winning a lot of money.

With such goings-on occurring somewhere in Nevada daily, there must be controls. We have them through our State Gaming Control Board, which is headed by an ex-FBI man. Regulations reach from the finger-printing of all employees, even stenographers, to a rule against any operator licensed here holding so much as a hidden interest in gaming elsewhere. To show you how absolute it is, the casino boss from a prominent hotel disappeared recently. Investigating the case, agents found he once had been arrested in Oklahoma for possession of crooked gambling devices. It was a misdemeanor there but his Nevada license was lifted immediately. Our dice and cards must be available for an agent's inspection at any time of his choosing and sometimes the State Control men do move in to look at our paraphernalia. I will tell you something about that and then I will tell you something else. We could cheat all the time and they would never know it. We're far more expert at this business than they are. Now I'll tell you the other thing.

Nevada is a place where you can be certain that the dice and cards and dealers are honest for a simple economic reason. No man is going to be such a damn fool as to risk a gambling casino license in which the investment is anywhere from $5,000,000 to $25,000,000 for the few dollars to be made dishonestly. Furthermore, the "weight," as we call any unnatural advantage, must be manipulated most cleverly. Therefore it gets in the way. A casino with a large volume of traffic can make all the money it cares to by playing honestly.

Now let's look elsewhere. I have never visited a city of any size in which, if I were looking for a dice or poker game, I couldn't find action with very little effort. On one of my trips to New York City, I was approached about the possibility of attending a dice game. It was merely a notification that some rounders were getting together for serious gambling. No one urged me to go; nobody twisted my arm. I merely was told there would be a big game, bring your money if you want to play, or stay home if you don't because we haven't room for kibitzers. In this case I went. I know that when I get into a game with other operators their reputations are at stake.

In any city outside Nevada you take a very big risk getting into casual games unless you know the operators and other players and can determine that the dice aren't loaded or the cards marked. In a typical "friendly" crap game, for instance, the operator has little to lose. If he were to use some form of weight, what could you do? I would never, therefore, get into such a game outside Nevada unless the other players were known to me or known to have interests in a casino. I would not get into a large game with a wealthy oil man, rancher or industrialist unless I knew him very well for many years. What does he risk if he gets caught using weight? With me, the name of Harolds Club goes wherever I go. I must never, under any condition, get involved in any transaction or game that could damage the reputation of my business. Other casino operators feel exactly the same as I. For this reason alone I know it's as safe to play with them as to put your money in the Bank of England.

Oh we keep an eye on each other. Make no mistake about that. My neighbor, Mr. Harrah, has for twenty years had a man who comes through my club at least four times a day to count the house. That's business; that's the competition. I don't hire such a person to go through Mr. Harrah's club. I do it myself because I believe my own eyes.

I would like, in this connection, to give you my findings on Las Vegas, which I have studied as a scholar might. Any time a group of men puts up $11,000,000 or more to build a hotel-gambling club, I study it from one end to the other. In the first place, I have never seen one thing dishonest in any shape or form in Las Vegas, and I can smell fish before most people's noses would quiver.

Las Vegas is a big money operation and you frequently hear the criticism: "All they want is our money." They do want your money, of course, but so does the hospital where you go to have your appendix out. Las Vegas is selling a commodity, entertainment, with all the trimmings. They have a terrific overhead and they have to make it back on the gaming table. When Marlene Dietrich appears twice nightly at her reported pay of $30,000 a week, plus X dollars for a line of chorus girls and X dollars for a top-notch orchestra, no nickel slot machine player is going to crack the nut. Add to that some fine dining rooms with well trained waiters and a corps of captains to back up the maitre d'. The casual tourist doesn't pay for this.

We hear the word "sucker" used carelessly in this country. A sucker actually is someone looking for something for nothing. He's the square who turns up at the door to one of the big Vegas entertainment rooms expecting to be ushered to a ringside seat. Particularly if he's first in the line and the president of a bottling works somewhere in Ohio, who doesn't gamble, really, but is accustomed to every courtesy at mention of his name. Well, Mr. President, I will tell you something. The maitre d' and those captains don't give a damn about your bottling works. (They probably also know you wouldn't tip $5 for a seat in the chorus girls' laps). Actually, they wait on word from the casino boss that so-and-so, someone who plays in terms of $10,000 and upwards— a Live One, in other words—would like to see the show. This man pays those big bills. There is always a table for him. I have one open in my own Fun Room at all shows because there is just no way to say no to a player like this. And you should know something further. This man may be walking in his own blood, be losers $40,000-50,000 when he goes in to see the show. But he will tip that maitre d' and those captains as though they personally had brought the show to him. That's why he's known as a "live one".

Speaking of shows, I am right back to the matter of Nevada being a never-never land. Not long ago Daddy sent girls around to the people in our Fun Room with a questionnaire which asked: "Did you come into Harolds Club because of the entertainment?" When I heard about it, I blew my top. It is one of the areas in which Daddy and I tangle like a couple of lions. "People," I told Daddy with some asperity, "do not come all the way over those big Sierra mountains from San Francisco to see the brown bears out in Idlewild Zoo Park. They do not ride a Greyhound bus for 240 miles to go to the Majestic Theater to see a motion picture they could see in their own home town. They do not drive all the way to Reno to hear a comic or musician in our Fun Room or to sit in our bar when they have bars in their own home town. So, obviously, the very simple reason they come up here is to gamble."

I told that to Daddy and I tell it to you.

Just recently, an encampment community called Jackpot has sprung up on the Nevada side of the Idaho border. It started as a 100% gambling community to attract players from Idaho. Someday it may become a small city like Vegas or Reno. Gaming, after all, is more profitable and pleasurable than raising cattle or alfalfa. So what's so improbable? Of course it isn't easy to get started in the gaming business, and we'll come to that too.

♠ ♠ ♠ ♠

Who Plays To Lose?

SOMEONE WITH A sinful sense of distortion has blasted Nevada as the Sodom and Gomorrah of the Twentieth Century. Oh, bless me, and pass the succotash. Of course there's sin here. There's sin in every town, sin in Harolds Club and sin in me. Sin, unfortunately, is ever with us. But Sodom and Gomorrah! I protest.

Is it the gambling that's sinful? I point out, as I have before, we all gamble—with our lives if not our money. There are definite odds against our accomplishing most of the things we try, yet we gamble every day of our lives on our ability to beat these odds. And I don't propose to expand on that now. Having introduced myself, my club and our environment, I want to discuss people who play at gaming and explain why they do.

It is very simple. They play to win money.

Bring any man into my club from any corner of the world. Any kind of man from any walk of life. He plays to win. Regardless of whatever deeper quirks he may have (such as my always carrying a bar of soap in my pocket), he wants to take more money away from the table than he brought, be it dimes, dollars, rubles, yen or pounds sterling. In a club across the street, if you please, there's a row of slot machines on which you may even play pennies and there are people who play them quite eagerly.

It's human nature to hope. It's even more in human nature to hope to acquire something for nothing. Call it greed, if you will, avarice or acquisitiveness. Say the player merely is reassuring himself that Lady Luck likes him. Search his ego for flaws, death wishes or father hatreds. The man still is here to win if he can.

Now it is true that some people do play for fun. It is very, very true. My dear old Aunt Ella from Vergennes, Vermont, who is seventy-five and about as sinfully disposed as Dr. Schweitzer, was visiting us last year. She played the nickel slot machines. Since she would take only $1 in nickels—at most $2 a night—she couldn't get hurt financially or in any other way. She thoroughly enjoyed herself and I am sure did no harm to her imperishable soul. But she wanted to win. Basically, she was playing for the jackpot.

I know I sure as Hell don't gamble for the gay, mad ecstasy of it. I want to win and I expect to win. Being somewhat of a contradiction, of course, I admit I'm the only person I've ever known who would play dice for nothing and get a kick out of it. Even then I had a reason, an avenue to financial gain. It was in the early days of the club when I shilled here, pretending to be a player so others would stop and we'd build up a crap game. I would start game after game and leave when they flourished. I got a terrific kick out of every roll of the cubes. The fun I get now from gaming for money usually is rather excruciating.

Any player will understand that. The bigger the gamble the greater the agony and the sweeter the win. That's true of most things in life. What farmer, planting and cultivating with a wary eye to the weather, doesn't rejoice when a bountiful crop's in the barn? What young doctor, staking his knowledge, skills and perceptions against a dread disease, doesn't thrill when the patient pulls through? What evangelist, for that matter, after talking, praying and persuading, hasn't known elation when his prodigal turns about? When you lay your talents or your money on the line in anything and reach over that vague horizon where success or failure lies, there's an exquisite sense of adventure.

The amount of the stake doesn't matter. People playing the penny slots across the street know identical apprehensions and hopes with those yanking on the dollar machines. Make no mistake about it. We have one Harolds Club customer who owns a tremendous distributing business in California. He comes regularly to play 21 and roulette, but always with a quota on what he may lose. If it goes, he drops immediately to $2 bets. I have noticed he plays the game just as intently, just as eagerly, for $2 as $200. To him, gambling is pure recreation, though he hopes to win. He can afford it and he enjoys it. Later I'll discuss some who can't afford to play. For them gambling is a mistake, though not necessarily a sin, my clerical friends to the contrary.

There are many, many facets to gaming beyond the obvious ones. Gaming can emphasize the quality in people as quickly as their defects. It will, for one thing, demonstrate an acumen you might never discover by counting a man's money or studying the financial statements of his company. It sometimes even shows his perception in choosing a wife.

I remember such a man. He was already a big winner when I came into the club that evening. A crowd had gathered, always a sure sign someone has a large stack of money or is betting big. I stopped to scrutinize the game, which was 21, and learned that the gentleman, a middle-aged businessman, had run ten silver dollars up to $50,000. He gambled very quietly, I saw, and did not drink, but concentrated deeply on his cards. When he stopped a few moments later, having dropped three hands in a row, he left most of his money with our cashier. This is a service we offer customers who don't wish to carry large sums. You sign your name in a register, the cash is put in an envelope and you are given a receipt. When you want the money again, you simply present the receipt and duplicate your signature. No fuss, no delay.

This man was back at noon the next day for his money and began to play 21 again. I now discerned that the quiet, graying lady watching from a few feet away was his wife. She was watching but not kibitzing. She did not interfere even when he played three hands at $300 each and doubled down on 10 or 11 for a total bet of $900 to $1200. A lot of money can change hands fast at those amounts and it took just an hour and forty-five minutes for him to lose back the $50,000. That was when the quality showed. As he stood up from the table, stunned and crestfallen, I heard the wife say: "I am glad you lost. If you hadn't, you might have kept on gambling all the rest of your life."

What a rare and wonderful person. You knew he didn't win her with green trading stamps. Most women would have called a husband stupid for dropping $50,000. Why, they would have moaned, couldn't he at least have saved $5000? They would never comprehend that it takes something special just to run $10 up to $50,000 in the first place.

This reminds me of James Stewart's wife when the actor was in Reno to receive the Silver Spurs award given annually by the city to the best western picture star of the year. We had a cocktail party at Harolds Club as part of the festivities and that was where Mrs. Stewart showed herself to me as a tremendous lady. I mean in the essence of the word "lady." She knew that females would be swarming about Mr. James Stewart at the party, just to touch him, get his autograph or peck him on the cheek, and she could have been a sopping wet blanket. What did she do? She went over to a 21 table and passed the time playing cards, completely happy and at ease. She knew her man; she demonstrated no doubt about it. I can't say as much for the wife of another famous star who visited the club. In fact I wasn't at all surprised to read later that they were getting a divorce.

A celebrity, incidentally, is no more able to disguise his true nature at the gaming tables than you are. He's there to win, just as everyone else is, and whether he realizes it or not, the dice don't distinguish one man from another. I have had occasion to observe Bing Crosby a number of times over the past twenty years and particularly when he had extensive ranching interests in Elko County. He is a most unpretentious man and a very conservative gambler. Usually he was dressed in western clothes because he was coming straight from the ranch and he wore dark glasses to conceal his identity. He approached the dice table as quiet as a mouse. Never, never did he grab the cubes, wave them and whoop in the melodious voice that would tell everyone who he was. He would stand to lose maybe $300 or $400, which to a big, monied man like him is very small money. Then he would leave as quietly as he came. The dealers all liked him.

One day it was Charles Bickford who came in and I will tell

you how he played. I remember accurately how much he won: $300. He was very much like the parts he played so successfully in motion pictures—all man and no silliness. He played the three-to-one odds on 12 in the field and the two-to-one odds on 3, 4, 9, 10 and 11. He won, as he intended to, went to the bar and had a drink, all most unobtrusively, cashed in his $300 and left the club. The same was true of Robert Mitchum, who appeared to enjoy playing dice and was considerate in every way. He played for nominal money, considering his reported income, and left a winner. Had either of these men been a loser, we would have had no scenes, no arguments. A quality of character shows in that.

Which reminds me again of the lady who rejoiced when her husband dropped the $50,000 he'd won. With 5000 or more persons in this club at a time and all wanting to win, we see many wives not at their best. I remember one customer's sad story distinctly.

"What happened?" the 21 dealer asked as he sat down to her table. "Your jaw's all swollen."

The man shrugged. "I was sitting at the bar," he replied, "when, with no warning, a woman came up and gave me a terrific belt on the jaw." He made a wry face. "Then she said, 'Oh, excuse me. I thought you were my husband'."

I can guess what happened. Her husband was losing money when she, naturally, expected him to win or not play. Perhaps he was fighting out a little losing streak and had indeed been at the bar moments before the man she clouted. Now, perhaps he was back at a table trying for his win. It happens very often that you must lose a while before you win.

♥

Since you do come to the tables to win, and for no other purpose, let me relate a little anecdote Daddy tells on my brother Raymond. He took boxing lessons, as I did, and used to fight as an amateur. Twenty years ago, when he still was young enough for such exertions, Raymond fought in a Reno tournament. He did very well through the first two nights of eliminations. The third night was not so good. While he did knock the other man down once, he was knocked down six times himself and they stopped the fight.

Daddy remembers how we waited anxiously for Raymond to come to the club and the calm way he answered our questions. "No, I'm not hurt," he said matter of factly. "They shouldn't have stopped the fight. I was in condition and could take it. The other fellow was not and he would have gotten tired out knocking me down. I would have got up and licked him."

That is precisely the way you must think if you're going to be a successful gambler, whether with cards or your career. You must train yourself thoroughly and know yourself and the other fellow. You may not win the game in the first ten hands. You *can* win, and win big, if you know how to play the last five hands and are in position to continue the struggle. Many a time I have been loser in a game for amounts from $5000 to $14,000 and come out even or on top. I, of course, have long since accepted that I am gaming to win and therefore have studied myself and arrived at some definite policies of conduct.

One important one covers this very matter of getting behind and then recouping. It is this: When you have managed to get even after a loss, quit. Don't procrastinate. Don't temporize. Don't kid yourself. Pick up your money and leave the game. You have had a marvelous stroke of luck in getting your money back. You can't win all the time. Quit now.

Hard to do? It is harder to do than quitting drinking or quitting cigarettes. In gaming, that desire to win is so strong you're up against yourself in the hardest battle you've ever fought. It reminds me of another of Daddy's stories.

We had the first escalators in the State of Nevada and, with them, some misgivings. Win-minded people pressing their way from floor to floor aren't always observant. One night, in fact, Daddy was sitting at the top looking down when he saw a young man with about three sheets to the wind sizing up the Down escalator. Sure enough, he gathered himself deliberately, got a Hell of a head of steam on and came scrambling up the wrong way. At the top, puffing hard, he turned to Daddy and said: "Now ain't that a Hell of a way to have to get upstairs?" It's the same exactly trying to play your way out of a loss and into a winner. It's a Hell of a way to get up.

Wanting to win so badly, some people just can't accept the facts of losing. Out come all the fears and frustrations. I've seen this in high school principals given to long harangues about self control and self discipline and in a coach who swears idealistically it isn't whether you win or lose that counts, but how you play the game. (If there's one place that maxim doesn't pay off, it's in a gambling house.) One man loses and impetuously tries to tip over the table, which is, of course, securely anchored to the floor. Another hurls his drink across the room. Others have gone out and thrown rocks through our doors, windows and neon signs.

Gaming causes you to reveal yourself in myriad ways. At 21, for instance, when a player has a 14 or 15—what we call a "stiff" hand—he must decide whether to draw another card or stand on these and hope the dealer goes broke. The practice, when you want to draw, is to scratch the table with your cards. On 14 or 15, naturally, a player wants a 6 or less. He reveals this fact very clearly to the dealer by a tiny little scratch. If, on the other hand, he scratches vigorously for a hit, the dealer knows he has 10 or under and wants a face card. Long before she has to deal to herself, she has a pretty good idea of the hands she must beat.

One of our girls dealers called me over in tears one night. She said that a man playing at her table—whose name, I will never forget, was Harold—was having a terrible losing streak. She, on the other hand, was being unusually lucky. Now he threatened to hit her if she won another hand.

This was back in the days when I did a lot of physical training. "Instead of hitting her," I said to the gentleman, "I would suggest that you hit me." He turned to measure me and I continued: "This is silly. How can you blame the dealer when you lose your bet? She's just like a human slot machine dealing the cards, however they come out. If she gives herself 20 and you 18, for instance, she has no control over it. So how can you possibly talk of hitting this girl if you lose the next bet? Instead of hitting her, hit me. I guarantee I'll give you a receipt for it." Naturally he didn't hit me. A man so intent on winning doesn't want people to know he can't or didn't win.

There are some people, on the other hand, who lose every time they play and blame it squarely on bad luck. They are not the type to blame themselves, although some handle their money so foolishly and play so badly they seem to defy my theory that everyone basically wants ot win. Most of these players don't realize they're going to continue as consistent losers until they change their mental attitudes, their way of thinking about gambling, and their playing technique.

Luck brings winning hands, no doubt of it, and entire nights of won money. But being a consistent winner is far from a matter of luck. By the same token, the winning gambler must be a good businessman at the table, but it doesn't follow that a good business-man elsewhere will be a winner at gaming. The fact is it's often just the reverse. Some men who are expert in their own lines should never touch cards or dice just as some men who can mix a good martini should never touch liquor.

A winning gambler has an alert, agile and analytical mind. He gets a complete and thorough picture of a situation quickly and makes decisions promptly and instinctively. So does a good businessman, you say, but I would ask you to consider again, if you please. I have seen too many successful businessmen lose their touch when it's a cards or dice situation they must assess. The good gambler's an expert in applied psychology. He understands himself thoroughly. Does your successful businessman really understand himself? Does he have the self control necessary when the cards tell him flatly this isn't his night? A winning gambler never lets emotions carry him away. His heart and mind always are completely disciplined. These are most important considerations.

A successful businessman usually is inclined to scoff at nebulous things like extrasensory perception or luck. Isn't it interesting then that with no practice he should attempt to employ these two things accurately when he turns to gambling? I don't mean to say that professional gamblers are scholars on such matters as extra-sensory perception. The truth is most of them think of ESP only as their hunches. They will, however, work hard to distinguish between this hunch drive and wishful thinking. It is more impor-tant to the gambler's business than money or a college education. I know. I've been in casinos with my pockets full of money for playing when my hunch suddenly said: *That dealer's going to have a bad run of luck!* I obeyed the hunch instantly and won money. In business, on the other hand, I prefer facts and findings over hunches every time.

There's another curious thing that sets me apart from the

average businessman who gambles. One or two drinks, I have observed, seem to sharpen my perception for hunches. More than two drinks can induce false bravado and a thoroughly stupid losing streak. As a non-drinker now, in fact, I am reshaping my mental radar to pick up hunches as clearly when sober as I once did with drinks. I still want to be a winner. One way to accomplish that is to walk swiftly in the opposite direction when I sense the dice are cold.

What about the system players? You see these men and women at every table, each with a pad of paper on which to record the order the cards have taken, and complicated charts telling just when to bet ten more or withdraw three. These are people who want to take the risk out of gambling and play sure things. (A nice way indeed to amass money.) The only trouble is I've never seen the system that works. Gambling, by its definition, means games of chance. Nothing has occurred to change it. For this reason, I consider every system player as money in the bank. When he comes to me with his system, any system, I know he's going to lose. If not this time, then later.

Don't misunderstand me, please. Most gamblers have their pet ways of attacking a game. Nick the Greek, for example, is an inveterate Don't Side player. By this I mean he invariably bets against the shooter in a dice game; he bets the shooter will not make his point. This isn't what we mean by a system, however, and I will come later to a discussion of systems.

♦

Right here I should introduce you to Nick the Greek who, in the public mind, is undoubtedly the living prototype of all professional gamblers. I have known Nick these many years and confess that he is not a man I would nominate for the United States Senate, despite his college education. Stocky and handsome, with slightly wavy, graying hair, he is suave with intent. Conscious of his public image, he dresses tastefully. In fact he puts me in mind of Polonius' instructions to his son Laertes: "Dress rich but not gaudy for the attire oft proclaims the man." It does with Nick and so be it. He is the prototype of the professional gambler and conscious of it. He says nothing while he is playing. Nothing. Should anything arise that requires comment, he will direct it to the boxman or dealer. Yet you cannot fault him. His casino demeanor is faultless. Let a little old lady walk up while he is concentrating on the play and ask: "Aren't you the famous Nick the Greek?" He will turn to her most genteelly and graciously. "Yes, madam," he will say. "I am." Seemingly he has the will power to make himself be nice even though it might be annoying when he's playing heavily. Obviously he takes into consideration the fact he is a nationally known figure and the only people he wishes to impress favorably are the majority.

Nick the Greek is a celebrity and it's part of the game to be nice to the little old ladies. Even so, you don't get dull with him when he is shooting dice. It is just not advisable. If the lady from Namesville, Ohio, goes home and tells her friends she saw Nick the Greek in Las Vegas—"I walked right up to him and said you're the fabulous Nick the Greek and he was so gracious and so nice to me"—it doesn't interefere with his game at all. Nick, remember, is a Don't Side player, and to me this is a breed apart.

I have studied the Don't Side player for a quarter of a century and I believe they have a predominance of cynicism in their makeup. I looked up the word *cynicism.* One definition is "misanthropy," which also means, of course, hatred of mankind. Don't Side players don't like people. That is, they don't genuinely like people. The cynic, remember, says he does, but his mouth does not speak the inner soul. He plays at gaming to win, but he always loses. Always, as you know, is quite a word.

Now when a man always loses, there has to be a reason. I have looked for this reason in my friend Jack Filtzer, who has lost at crap games for forty years, and Al Wolfe, who says he loves horse races but couldn't win a bet on one if they let him shoot all the other horses. Both of these gentlemen are, I am convinced, John Philip Sousa cynics.

Not long ago, in fact, I staked Al to $1000 to bet at the opening of a new California racetrack. It was pure philanthropy. "Go on down and enjoy yourself," I told him, "but you know you're going to lose. I would sooner take a seven-year-old child to the track and ask him what horse he liked. If he said Number 1, I'd say:

'That's good enough for me.' But you—you're cynical, Al, when you say you expect to win. You know damned well you can't pick a winner." Naturally he resented it. And he lost. He came home Single-O, broke. The man cannot win at the racetrack. It is impossible, and that's quite a word, too.

The Don't Side player, I would add, lacks confidence. You can't even teach him. Another friend of mine who has been a Don't Side player all his life, and always a loser, came to me for some coaching once. I took him up to my office and explained the odds against him on the Don't Side, the cynicism in his nature which made Don't Side betting such a passion with him, and the fact I would guarantee he would only blow his money. I thought I had talked him into playing the Do Side, or betting with the shooter to make his point. He went down to the club and placed his bet on the Do Side. The shooter made five straight passes. That is to say he made 7 or 11 on his first throw or his point when he had to, five times in a row. What about my student? He couldn't resist himself. After the five passes, his negative thinking urged him to get back on the familiar Don't Side. The shooter went on to make five more passes and our friend lost every bet. He might have won $1000 by following my counsel. I can say truthfully I have never been successful in teaching gaming to an innate Don't Sider.

There are, of course, exceptions to every rule. I recall a Chinese businessman from Hawaii who won $16,800 betting the Don't Side at Harolds Club. He made just one bet, for the limit, and laid the maximum odds. (On the Don't Side, you give odds, rather than get them. The gentleman picked up his winnings and deposited them with the cashier after that one play. But, then, Chinese are like no one else in the world when it comes to gambling.

Please do not attempt to compare yourself or your neighbor with any Chinese when it comes to gambling. No other gambler is even similar to them. With the Chinese, gambling is almost like a religion that is handed down from generation to generation. Jewish people, I have found, are second only to the Chinese in this. To them, there are no social or religious tabus associated with gaming. They come in as families, youngsters of 21 to oldsters who speak no English, and they play with zest.

Never in my life have I seen an Oriental out of line around an amusement park, carnival or gaming club. They bet heavily and fast and win or lose in large amounts. If they lose, it invariably is with a big grin or inscrutable Oriental calm. They are just as courteous as they are when winning. They never forget to tip the dealer who brings them good fortune.

A Chinese will gamble on anything if he gambles at all. Even at Faro Bank, which is the only even-money game there is and, incredibly, an all but unbeatable one. We don't have it in Harolds Club and Jack Sullivan of the Bank Club, which does have it, once told me: "That Faro Bank son-of-a-bitch is no damned good. It keeps everybody broke and I don't make a dime." Nevertheless, the Chinese play it and seem to have some sort of a system. A Chinese will be playing alone until he thinks his condition is about to come. He bursts some chatter over his shoulder and in five minutes six other Chinese are there chunking out their dough to catch on his condition.

They're the most inscrutable of all the thousands who come to win at our tables. Perhaps because they know the facts about games of chance and never forget what they came for. Perhaps because, while they hope to win, they don't forget that in gaming the house has the best odds going for it most of the time.

5

♣ ♣ ♣ ♣

You Can't Win

All The Time

THERE ARE TIMES when you positively will not win.

These days come to us all. They are bleak, they are empty and they are frustrating. They are also impossible to avoid. No matter how skillful a gambler you are, you will have such days. The better the gambler, in fact, the sooner you perceive on such a day you aren't going to win. You don't waste money and short-circut your nervous system trying.

I have never known the gambler who didn't have such days. Nor have I ever known a gambler, once into such a day, who could change his luck. I have known any number who tried and walked in their blood and anguish.

Need I say it more clearly?

Accept the facts and remain solvent to play another day. Reject them and pour your money into gambling club vaults. I am convinced Mother providence sets aside these extremely unlucky days for us individually just as she sets aside days when our luck will be unbeatable.

At first you may not even recognize what is happening to you. Slowly, though, the play takes a pattern that follows to every table you try and every game, dice or cards, that you buck. Either you're getting "stiff" hands that require decisions every time or you're constantly just being beaten out.

Say you're playing 21. You're getting pat hands of 20 while the dealer has to hit each time. Somehow, though, she does hit. As she does, hand after hand, your stack steadily dwindles. Maybe you get an 11, with the dealer showing a 7, so you go down for double, doubling your bet and hoping for a 10 or face card that will give you 21 and beat the 17 you suspect she has. You get a 9, which usually is adequate. But not this ill-starred day. You're not casing her hole cards correctly. She has a 4 under that 7, it turns out, which gives her a nice fat 11 to hit and she does. She draws the 10 that edges you again.

"But it was a good bet," you protest, "even if I lost. I *had* to double down and try for a 10." If you please, my friend, there is no such thing as "a good bet even if I lost". There's only one good bet—the one you win.

When you repeatedly get stiff hands in 21, repeatedly seven-out at dice, just miss your number at roulette or the third bar on the slot machine, I say it's one of those days. They're weird, they're eerie and they're unexplainable. But when you see the pattern, quit for that day. Quit fast. Go see a movie or the show in the Fun Room. Mother Providence has sent up her order you are to win nothing this day.

I haven't come easily to this conclusion, you understand. I have come to it many times after finding my back to the wall. Many, many, many times, to my great sorrow, I've had to go back afterward and make good the markers other operators granted me. They are most happy to extend credit on my blindly losing days, just as automobile agencies are delighted to take my signature on the day I am determined to buy an expensive automobile. The difference is, of course, that I have the car afterward even though I'm still paying on it. Repaying $200 or $25,000 you've gambled away is like buying a dead horse or paying the bill for liquor you consumed last year.

Yes, I've known losing days, and no one on the face of this spinning globe can be sicker than I am when I have lost my bankroll. I trudge out of the casino feeling ninety-two years old, and perhaps my eye falls on a passing Cadillac. *Ten minutes ago, I think ruefully, I could have owned that beautiful mechanical contrivance with all appliances. Now I must watch my expenses again.* (Contrary to what you may think, the owner of a successful gaming house like Harolds Club does not have unlimited funds to gamble away. Definitely not.) A friend of mine who's in the mattress business in Southern California tells me he has the same thoughts after losing. *There went so many hundreds of mattresses,* he admonishes himself. The story of losing days is as soul-wrenching for us as it is for the clerk or cowboy who shoots his paycheck in one losing day.

Herein lies the one danger of gaming for otherwise normal people. And maybe you think I'm silly to bring this up when I operate a club with full credit and check-cashing facilities for people who can't guess what their luck is going to be when they set out over the mountains for Reno. Let us not be foolish. I tell you all this because I promised you a book worth your while and because I do not expect to change human nature.

I will even be more candid with you and recall the two most horrible results of gaming I have ever seen. The first was not our customer because her passion was Faro Bank and we don't have the game. This was nearly twenty-four years ago and I don't know how the lady got hooked on Faro originally. She was a rather nice-looking person in her thirties with natural red hair; she was married to a man who owned a string of stores in California. She wasn't just mildly interested in the game, as I say. She was hooked, and no nit-picking. She bet $100 bills on a turn of the cards.

Faro is a Hell of a game to get in your blood like that. I know. I had it in mine. (Yes, I've had all these gaming diseases.) I finally quit it because I never saw anyone make a big scratch. I never saw a big win. I once heard of a jockey in Miami who won $5000 and I've seen the Chinamen pick up a few dollars here and there. Nothing great. I also saw Carl Laemmle, the famous movie producer, stake Nick the Greek to three months of Faro play in Reno with a special condition of $50-100 limits. They lost. As I say,

Faro is an absolutely even-money game and the only one in which there's no percentage against you. Yet you still don't win.

So this was the game the California lady was bucking. She came to Reno every weekend, then was staying through the week. When her husband finally divorced her, she took an apartment here and did nothing but play Faro. She was the kind of player who would sit at a table for eleven or twelve hours straight without going to the powder room. It didn't take long to go through her $50,000 divorce settlement and she had to work. But a job took time from Faro Bank.

Here, then, is the end to her horrible obsession. She turned prostitute to get Faro money. She went out into Douglas Alley and offered herself to passing men. That isn't the most degrading part of it either. Our former housewife had suffered a lot of wear and tear in the process of gambling away $50,000. (It's not exactly easy on the constitution). She wasn't any bargain beauty and the Line was open in Reno then with attractive young women selling for $3. Our woman had to offer cut rates and take what she could get. She sold herself for 50¢ an act. Fifty cents—the minimum bet on the Faro table, which—if it won—would pay exactly fifty cents.

♠

My second horrible example, also a woman, was about thirty, and a 21 bug. She was married to a miner and had two children, a boy of nine and a girl seven. Now I appreciate that some people love to play cards. I do myself; it's a minor addiction and no obsession. But this woman was not one of your inveterate card players. She never got excited and she didn't have brains enough to worry. I was dealing the 10¢ 21 game at the time. She would waddle in and flop on a stool the moment I opened and would stay there for twelve solid hours watching the cards turn. Oh she bet every hand, but not like a real player. And she never won. The truth is, as a real player knows, you won't win when you stay in a game that long. The odds will eat you up. Anyway, her kids would turn up at the club door as soon as school was out; she'd send them off to a movie, sometimes to two movies a night.

One night, in fact, I blew my top when they turned up at 11.30 pleading with her to come home. "Get your ass off that stool," I roared, "and take those children home!" She did, but she was back next morning. Eventually the authorities moved in and took the children. Her husband divorced her. It was then she went out to the alley. Only she didn't have too much going for her. She was fat as a pig and had to undercut the Faro Bank woman. Yes, her price for an act with a man was 25¢. There's only one bright point to this story—her little daughter grew up to graduate from the university and become a fine wife for a young man who must never know the whole story.

Now let's not pounce on these horrible examples as though they happen every day around gambling casinos. They don't. I just looked out in Douglas Alley and didn't see one prostitute. Of course, I don't know them all. The two women were isolated instances.

They met their downfall a long time ago, when I didn't know very much about gaming myself. Just the year before I came to Reno, in fact, I heard the "0" and "00" on a roulette wheel called "house numbers" and didn't realize the customer could bet them. I had been quick to learn about the stated percentages in favor of the house in most gambling games but I still didn't know about that hidden percentage of human nature, the fact we'll stand longer losing than winning. Contracting the gaming diseases one by one, and since having been cured of some, I now find myself seeking immunities to the others and offer my findings to those who will listen.

That's why I harp on this business of a losing day. I now can recognize quickly the symptoms of an addictive player on this day Mother Providence has allotted him. He keeps bobbing up at our credit office for a marker or to cash another check. He's wiring for money, borrowing or running out to refinance his car. He keeps needing bigger money and that, if nothing else, should be his tipoff that he's having a very bad day. When you need more and more money, my friend, you're probably not winning.

No two persons will gamble alike, of course, or are in the same circumstances. A big winning day to one of your friends may be $5; to another, $10,000. Still another man may set his sights on winning $20,000. My long-time gambling buddy Eddie Sahati only wanted to win the club. To most people, though, a win of $110-120 makes a great day. Now let's say this caliber player picks up his $120 in the first hour; he feels on top of the world and leaves the winning table to stroll around, perhaps to eat, play a slot machine or two, try the dice, reveling in his good fortune and, he thinks, delaying the moment of further pleasure. He feels very secure, though in truth it may be that moment that Mother Providence has waggled her finger. He should have stayed at the table while the game was going for him and chunked in the house's money in bigger and better amounts. But he didn't. Now he ambles back to the table and wins maybe $40 more. But it's over. In a disastrous twenty minutes, he drops it all. And there's some herring to chew upon.

Why is it, you ask, that you always lose it so much faster than you won it? Human nature again. Most people double or triple their bets on the theory the losing streak will stop and the money will come back twice as fast. What if the losing streak doesn't stop? Why should it? You say it *has* to sometime? And mumble something about the law of averages? Well kiss me and pass the succotash. If you please, my friend, quote me that law while I take your silver dollars two at a time, instead of one, and stack them in neat little piles for the vault. If this is your losing day and you have the resources, we may just be hauling your cash back there all afternoon. The law of averages, eh?

But losing money isn't a laughing matter. I don't think I ever saw anyone enjoy losing his money, although some folks can cover it better than others. Why, then, do people bet larger and larger amounts when they're not winning? I've shown that it isn't logical. I think there are several things involved. I believe it's human nature not to want to lose and subconsciously it may be akin to the fact we want to stay alive. I suspect we have a little greed, a degree of impatience, resentment, impetuosity. Probably there's an association of maybe three or four basic characteristics that all normal human beings have.

The Bible, for instance, seems to have been written for he and thee but never me. Most people know, when they gamble, that they are bucking a mathematical percentage against them. They also know that with a little good going in their direction—call it Lady Luck—they can overcome that percentage and win more than 50% of their bets. You must win more than 50%, of course, if you bet the same amount, to come out ahead. It becomes a challenge, as I see it, and the American people are stubborn and tenacious when it comes to challenges. They are also great ones to consider the Bible as for he and thee.

Personally, I'm becoming more and more intrigued with the supernatural. Particularly with these losing days and the mysterious things that beat you. Take roulette, for instance. It pays 35 to 1, as we know, if you play it straight and your number hits. In other words, if you put $1 on number 14 and the ball drops there the dealer will hand you back your dollar bet plus $35. Now here's just one of the crazy things that happens in a losing streak. You play number 14 for hours and the ball rolls into every slot but 14. Finally you move your bet to another number. On the very next roll, the ball falls into 14. I'll give you my teeth if you can explain why that happens. You could tear the table apart with your hands. I know I've had the urge. Countless people have told me how it happened to them and I've seen it so often I recognize it as a recurring phenomenon. Yet I've never heard a satisfactory explanation except that Lady Luck just loves to tweak your whiskers at times.

It's the sort of thing that seems destined to happen on a losing day and it causes people to lose more money than they meant to. I remember a man I watched playing number 21. He stayed with it for hours and it simply would not come up. In his mind he probably felt: *If I give up that number once, it'll hit.* He didn't dare leave it though it was bleeding him white. This is one of the strangest intangibles in the gaming business. We all recognize it. It's the same attraction that keeps a person glued to a slot machine too long. He's sure the next pull will bring the jackpot. Oddly enough, it often does. A lady plays a machine for two hours and turns to get change or go to the rest room. Someone else steps up with a nickel or dollar and cracks the jackpot. (Some of these creeps, in fact, are like patient vultures standing off clanking their coins, just waiting the chance). They have caused hair pulling and fights in the club. For that reason, when you play a machine in Harolds Club for a reasonable period of time and wish to leave temporarily for a sandwich or whatnot, we will cap the machine and reserve it for your return.

♣

This eerie business of the next roll or next turn of the cards runs all through the losing day. Nothing falls the way you expect it. I think of a situation that has dogged me at 21 for a year and a half. It comes about like this. I've doubled down on 11 and won. If the bet was very large, I usually cut back before the next hand. And now what? The next hand invariably brings a blackjack which pays 3-to-2—$300 for a $200 bet. After several such experiences, I get cagey. I may have occasion again to double down on a large bet. I win and remember that the blackjack follows invariably. So I leave my big bet intact. The blackjack fails to appear. In fact I lose the bet, which now includes my earlier bet and the double down. I now have lost a whopper. When Lady Luck's tampering with a man's cards he can't win. When she's with him, he guesses correctly and has the right bet down every time. That is my finding.

Right here I would like to interject something about losing days that everyone who is going to gamble his money should know. Don't whine. You bet your money and you lost. You were ready to gloat if you won. Don't belabor your friends with a running account of your woes—how, *if* the dealer hadn't done this and *if* the lady on the end hadn't done that—your friends don't care. I like to believe I have a reasonable compassion for my fellow man, and certainly I hear enough of his troubles when he comes to ask that his money be refunded. I may be sitting there in my own gore after a tremendous loss across the street. As a professional gambler, I can't gloat if I win big and I can't bellyache when I lose big. I respect the man who comes to me and says simply: "I bet and lost $5000 that I should not have. I need a refund." This man I respect.

We collect the bellyachers in a gambling house, believe me. Every day is a losing day to them, even if they win money. "My God, it's hot!" they complain. Or: "It's so cold." Or: "Everything seems to go wrong with George—" Or: "It's too bad people have so much money to throw away." I walk away when I hear this talk.

I know we're all human and we all must blow off steam. But whining flips me. I heard enough of it back in the days of my mother's rooming house in Cleveland, Ohio, to last me the rest of my life. Once, to get away from it, I attended Good Friday services at Loews State Theater and heard a handsome young man—I never knew his religious denomination—speak on why it is important for people to be happy. Too many, he said, get up complaining: "My God, I wonder where I'm gonna ache today." He was trying, of course, to bring out the point that we should develop the habit of blessing each day we live and trying to live happily. I never forgot that sermon. How in Hell are people around you going to be happy when you're always singing the blues? And how, may I ask, are you going to break a losing streak or start a winning streak at cards if you're beating your own subconscious into defeat? It's like people wishing they were millionaires. I like to tell them being a millionaire might be their complete ruination. Think of how much more money you could drop, and how much more misery you could buy, in one of these weird, flim-flammed losing streaks I've been talking about.

I'm not looking down my bent nose at anybody when I speak this way. I believe I have made every mistake a man can make in fifty years. There have been many, many, many disappointments in the past forty years. Many of them I still don't understand. We're only human, all of us. We get to feeling sorry for ourselves, which is human again. We do a bit of cussing, maybe some heavy drinking and—speaking for me—this is no damned good at all. Oh, dear God, the things that can happen amongst your immediate associates and especially your family when you're in trouble and drinking heavily. I've thought about it. I know it's human nature to kick a crumbling wall. But, if you please, don't whine about it. No two days are even similar. Accept today as your loser, if it's that. Quit the game early and maybe you won't wake up aching tomorrow.

♥

One thing I know from operating a gambling club for twenty-five years. Alibis come easier to most people than the facts. The sad loser invariably had bad luck (never bad play), the employee never feels the blame should be on his own shoulders for a serious mistake. I even have had entertainers whose songs or comic material failed to go over and who swore the entire problem lay with a spotlight that was orange rather than yellow. As I reach my mellower years I don't argue. I simply accept bad luck and responsibility for the mistake and change the spotlight to yellow. Then, perhaps, I go out and do a little violent gambling.

But I was speaking about those isolated can't-win days Mother Providence allots us. In a later chapter I will outline my system for managing your money through temporary losing streaks so you'll be around when the tide turns. At this point I believe I should point out to you some of the percentages you buck in various types of gambling.

Let's make some comparisons with horse racing, which is legal in many states. The odds against the bettor at legal horse tracks are of course much greater than the odds the player must overcome in a gambling casino. In the first place, race track operators must pay a very high tax on the *gross amount* which has been bet; the state usually takes about 9%, and the track itself about 6%. The rates vary from state to state, but the total bite is approximately 15% at any track in the country. Thus, out of the total pool bet by the players, the first 15% goes to taxes and the player must overcome this 15% before he can win. Contrast this with the legal dice games in Nevada, where the odds against the player are 1.41% on a Line bet. The 21 player has about 2.5% odds against him and the roulette player about 5.2%. Remember, if you please, the player in a casino is paid 100% on the amount he has bet. The casino pays taxes to the state, local and Federal governments only out of *its own share* of the gross profits. (Plus some substantial license fees.) The casino does not pass these taxes on to the player and, since he is not burdened with that overhead, he definitely has a much greater chance of coming out ahead on his betting than he would if he played consistently at the race track.

Nevertheless, I do not believe that anyone should play steadily at either a casino or track, except in moderation. Gambling, whether with big winning or big losing, can be like drinking and

I know that no man or woman should drink alcoholic beverages if he can't control himself and drink in moderation. It's yourself you have to contend with in both pursuits. Yourself is always a pretty big order.

Never, therefore, have I suggested to anyone that he should gamble. I never will. I find fun at the tables myself and enjoy the challenge of risking big money. But I also know what a struggle it is to keep my emotions under control and make thinking dominate my actions. A good gambler must master emotions as I've tried to indicate in this explanation of losing days.

Gambling in any of its forms creates thrills. It is wired with tension. The sex act itself can never be as thrilling to some people as the sensation of winning, of making just the right decision, exercising just the proper extrasensory perception and lubricating the ego with a big stack of chips. It isn't difficult to gear one's living to such pleasures; to feel the need for a success charge every day just as the heroin addict must have his belt of narcotic. This is the danger area in which the thrills, emotions and tensions of gambling turn into obsessions. Invariably it becomes expensive for someone.

Just from a practical standpoint, I should point out that such a person is no longer a good gambler. You just can't play cards as well, or gamble as expertly in any way, when you are torn by your feelings. You might, for example, lose a few dollars you can easily afford. Suddenly, though, you're emotionally upset. You're mad about it. You have become "too human," I say, and you're no longer playing for fun or recreation. Oh, you may say you're now playing to get even again, but I think I know better, and you're going to have a lot of losing days. Your nerves are playing your hands. You're like the alcoholic who must have the drink early in the morning, late at night and at regular intervals in between, but who actually cannot enjoy the taste or tingle of one drink he absorbs. The fun of it's gone for you and you lose.

I've had such periods in my life. There have been times when the urge to gamble was so strong I felt nothing else could calm me. *Why,* I asked over and over, *why should this urge be so strong in me?* It was vital to me to know because I had long since learned that if I let myself play then my wishes and emotions would jam extrasensory perceptions and kill hunches. Loving gambling, charged with emotions, I wage a daily battle to remain captain of my ego. One of my disciplines is to deny myself the pleasure of gambling on the very days I am driven strongest toward it. The thrills, tensions and emotions of gambling, as I say, can come with any form of gambling, including betting the horses at the track or through bookies. When they become an obsession, all other interests must go. I remind you of the two women who sold themselves in the alley.

I would suggest there's a difference in the games that will attract you. Card players, for instance, are usually people who like to hold and fondle the cards. If they weren't playing 21 in Reno, they'd be bent over a whist or bridge table in San Francisco, or playing pinochle in the kitchen. Cards are a pastime; they're slower paced than other games. I find I can control myself and manage my money much easier at 21 than dice; it is easier to leave the game when I am behind. Curiously, though, if anyone plays or deals 21 long enough, it gets under his skin. We find we have to transfer 21 dealers to other games at regular intervals. It is, for one thing, our hardest game to deal, both physically and mentally, because the dealer never rests. She either is shuffling or dealing cards, paying or collecting bets, or lighting a cigarette for the customer.

Dice is a far faster game and tugs at the restless, impetuous individual like me. When I get into a dice game, I can't wait to get those Mississippi marbles in my hands and defeat that game. Maybe this is because I know one good hand will win a lot of money. For the dealers, it's an easier game to work than 21. There are two men to a table and moments of relaxation for each. The last time I went over to the Horseshoe with that big money glow in my mind, I didn't even look at the 21 tables. I wanted to take money out with me. By the same token, I can't quit a dice game as early as I should sometimes.

Roulette is still another kettle of emotions. The player knows he only has to hit once at the 35-to-1 odds to be even. It's not so hectic as dice. Professional men particularly enjoy playing it. One of our local doctors, for instance, has been playing roulette regularly for twenty years that I know of. He is always very quiet and serious, almost introspective as he counts the times the ball has passed his number. Like most roulette players, he probably has his private system in the back of his head.

It's from the roulette table very often that someone looks up and utters what I consider his famous last words: "Harold, how are you going to like working for me?" I look again and see he's got perhaps $40,000 or $50,000 in winnings stacked in front of him. He is implying that very shortly he will have won control of Harolds Club and I'll be working for him. To this very familiar query I simply smile my Mona Lisa smile and shrug. His question is music to my ears because I know he's about to start losing.

Why am I so confident? Well, first of all, this is an old established casino now and a loss of $50,000 or $100,000 won't make much of a dent in our capital. More important, I have observed that when a player talks this way he has begun to unchain his ego. Greed is stifling judgment. He's not concentrating on the game any longer. Perhaps he feels the risks have been eliminated from gambling.

He's going for larger and larger stakes with every whirl of the wheel. His pride's involved now. I notice he isn't as sharp as he has been; instead of making correct decisions quickly and accurately, he's beginning to stumble. All this while that patiently spinning wheel grinds on. It doesn't know he's holding $50,000 of our money; it doesn't know anything. Not even the house odds grinding relentlessly with it. It has no emotions. Soon Lady Luck will reach out and tweak my man's whiskers real hard.

She's a spiteful hag, this Lady Luck, or a softly curved beauty, and faint heart never won her favors. Maybe that's why I like to gamble so. I can't be halfway about anything, and particularly a lady. She's either all for me or she's against me. If she's with me, I'll go the whole route; if she's not, I pass. I'm getting a little elderly for weekend romances.

I'm still speaking of Lady Luck, of course. One of the quickest ways to lose your money, I learned long ago, is to try to have your mind on gaming and sex at the same time. But now let's join the ladies. We have all types around a gambling house, from those who enjoy going to balls to those who enjoy funerals.

♦ ♦ ♦ ♦

God Love Our Queens

ONCE UPON A time I contended that women should not be around a gambling club in any capacity. This was some years ago, before I operated Bingo games at the Russian River, in California, and discovered I'd better have women players if I hoped to be successful. Any lingering doubts have since been dispelled. Women, for one thing, control the bulk of money in this country. For another, as Kay Starr has proclaimed in song, *Papa Can't Go Where Mama Don't Go.*

You see their influence wherever you turn in Nevada's legal gaming establishments. And I don't mean the bare-chested women bit at Las Vegas. That is superfluous, if you ask me. We were getting along nicely without it and, if anything, it hurts the gaming industry. I'm not a prude, mind you; I have looked. But when I speak of the fair sex's influence on gaming I mean our lady customers. The truth is that the hand that rocks the cradle also occasionally rattles the dice.

Harolds Club would not be the biggest gambling club in the world today if it weren't a fact that ladies—any lady—can walk through our doors and wager her money without risking her reputation. There isn't a game under this roof, from baccarat to 21, women don't play. The female of the species is our most avid slot machine player. Rather than coarsening themselves in the process, they make the games more genteel. And, though they spend but 20% of what our male customers do, we work harder for the ladies' trade than we do for the men's.

Maybe you think I'm kidding so let's look at it another way. If Nevada gaming was restricted to men only, the famous casinos would have none of the refinements that have made them world famous. They would not have floor shows. Their bartenders would not have to serve delicate liqueurs or know how to make daiquiris or pink ladies. There would be no carpets on the floors. The talk would be loud and vulgar. And there wouldn't be much you could do about it.

Right here I'd like to say something about cussing and/or vulgarity. When a man has $500 riding on a turn of the cards and his card doesn't turn, he's apt to say something. It simply pops out. No one takes offense. I have witnessed this phenomenon again and again. The word sort of slips out under his breath and even in mixed company people realize he isn't trying to be crude. They understand exactly how he feels.

Now let's consider the ubiquitous phrase, *son-of-a-bitch*. Owen Wister showed in *The Virginian* why, at certain times, you'd better smile when you say it. Harry Truman, for instance, was not smiling when he used it on one notable occasion that made headlines. Furthermore, he was President of the United States and a large part of his audience was in the eastern section of our country where *son-of-a-bitch* is always a dirty word.

I am sorry but this just isn't true in the West. Semantics are different out here. And we don't dilute the language with a weak substitute like "S-O-B". We say "son-of-a-bitch" (accent on first or last word indicating intent) right out loud. It can be the very vicious insult Mister Wister implied, and you'd better smile, or it can be just a figure of speech somewhat stronger than shucks. Men from the mining, logging and cattle towns have always understood this and refer to each other affectionately, or even admiringly, as "that son-of-a-bitch." It has many complimentary usages: "He's a *big* son-of-a-bitch." "A *riding* son-of-a-bitch."

"The luckiest son-of-a-bitch I ever saw" or "the smartest etc." It can be deflating, too, like "the stupidest son-of-a-bitch," but still without insult. Naturally, over the years, Western women have heard their menfolk use the term. They wouldn't use it themselves, but they don't swoon in its presence.

I tell you all this not so I can write dirty words on paper or imply that you must wear cotton in your ears if you visit a gambling club. I'm merely trying to show you folkways that happen to apply in an area and activity where men and women come together. In a high-rolling crap game, for instance, you might hear a worse word. A man with $2 on the Line, losers by $800, and eight his point, may toss the seven that craps him out. A blunt four-letter word rarely heard in the home might slip from his lips. Again, I have noticed, people aren't offended. They understand.

The veneer of society, as you see, rubs a little thin around a gambling house. Sometimes inhibitions do slip momentarily. If it weren't for the ladies, it could get rough. Their presence helps us all maintain our perspective.

I learned some of this, as I say, from my Bingo days thirty years ago. Most Bingo players then, as now, were women. I still believed, however, that a real gaming house would operate better without females and it took my Daddy and several further experiences to show me how hopelessly wrong I was. We didn't have lady customers when we first opened Harolds Club. We didn't have too many customers of any sex and we couldn't go out on the street and drag them in. One day as Daddy stood near the doorway, a woman came in, took two or three hesitant steps toward the first game and stopped short. "There are no women here!" she almost shrieked as she fled.

Out of that episode, Daddy got the idea of lady dealers at our tables. He broached it to me. Apprised of the woman who had fled, I readily agreed to try . Soon afterwards *The Saturday Evening Post* published a story on our lady dealers. That gave us the publicity break we needed and overnight the atmosphere of the club was changed by the presence of women at our tables. Then came World War II and the manpower shortage; we had to use women for everything but bouncers and they saved our business. Reno has always had a small manpower pool. It has long had attractive young ladies in residence while waiting out their divorces. Most need to earn money. Now, with the high cost of living what it is, many housewives are working in order to supplement their husband's salaries and give their children advantages they wouldn't otherwise have. Harolds Club paychecks don't all come sliding back over the gaming tables; our employees do gamble, but they also are buying homes, boats, appliances, life insurance and orthodontia. I have seen so many of my lady dealers assume complete responsibility for supporting children I am reminded constantly of the brave pioneer women who came out here by prairie schooner originally to develop this wonderful West.

♦

If the ladies help themselves by working for us, God knows they help us. No man could possibly be as charming and pleasant as a kind and gracious woman. A man customer may be walking knee deep in his own blood after losing a substantial amount of money. A courteous dealer can ease his loss. I have seen it again and again as dealers apologize when winning a close 21 hand or reluctantly take the money when a man loses at dice. It seems to come easy to our women dealers to show that they hope the player will win. I have seen them bawl out a player for throwing a seven and losing his bet when he appeared to have a winning streak going. I have watched from our supersecret security catwalk as a 21 dealer muttered under her breath at a man: *"Hit 14!"* I didn't fire her. The man was an inexperienced card player. He didn't comprehend, as the girl did, that small cards were running and in this cycle he would enjoy the game more if he tried to improve his hand.

I have seen a woman dice dealer say petulantly to a man who sevened-out: "Why did you do that? I thought you were going to have a hot hand and you disappointed me!" Did it drive the player away from the game? It did not. He grinned and tried again. Another player in that game dropped $1000 and still gave the girl a toke for her kindness. No one enjoys losing his money, as I have pointed out, but even the loser responds to sympathetic understanding. Need I point out that this is good for business?

The player who tokes a dealer after losing is trying to show that he appreciates her working so hard for him to win. This man will be a gentleman wherever his wanderings take him. Compare him, if you please, with a gentleman who was in the club just the other night. He started with $100 in chips and won $6000 within three hours. He gave the dealer a $4 tip.

Our employees all wear a badge with their first name and home town so the player will feel at home with them. It doesn't take more than a few minutes, usually, for the dealers and players to get acquainted. Before the evening is over, the player may open his wallet and show the dealer snapshots of his wife and children. Still later, perhaps, he returns with his wife and she becomes part of a congenial playing group. Very often she will invite the dealer to visit them at their home. There is a lot more good to this than the immediately obvious social benefits.

A dealer soon learns what a man can or cannot afford. My women dealers are the only dealers in any casino with which I am familiar who will encourage a man *not to gamble*. They will, at times, even insist that he quit because his luck is bad and tell him bluntly he won't win this evening. Short of twisting his arm, or actually barring him from the table, they will do everything humanly possible to keep the customer from going overboard. I am glad to say that they succeed, too, almost every night in the week.

Similarly, and for the same reasons, we have women working in our credit office. In fact our oldest employee, from standpoint of service, is a woman, Eddie Grisham, who started when we first opened an office and even served as floorman when I was away in the service. Credit is a touchy area in a gaming house. We have to extend it and yet we mustn't overextend it—both for our welfare and the customer's. To establish credit with us, you go to the office on the first floor and state your need, showing your driver's license or a good air travel or bank credit card. (We will also check with your bank in a prudent way.) You *set your own top limit* on the amount of the checks we will cash for you. It might be $50 in any one day or it might be $5000. The girls, after examination of your credentials, will approve limits up to $5000. At $5000 or higher, the potential customer is referred to me. I can tell you now that there are very few people with limits of

$10,000 or higher.

When a man has set a limit for himself of, say, $200, and loses it, no one in that credit office will cash another check for him that day. It isn't that we don't think he's good for it; it's just that we don't want him to lose more money than he estimated he should. (Estimates can change radically when the gambling fever's on you.) Here is where our women do such a magnificent job for us. We'll say a man has cashed and lost his $200 for today. Perhaps he has had a few drinks before he storms back to attempt to raise his limit. A male behind the wicket, telling him he can't have more money, might well provoke a punch in the jaw, but a woman's voice seems to get through the alcoholic haze. I'm not sure, of course, but it might just remind him of a wife waiting at home. Of course there *is* the boorish male who tries to bulldoze over ladies, so we always have a man on duty at the credit office too. One way or another, we keep you from overextending yourself.

We have never, incidentally, been sorry for this policy. I think now of a very wealthy player who comes in several times a year. His limit is $200 a day, though he can afford to lose much more than that. This gentleman likes to play 21 and quaff highballs, which he must purchase himself because another of our policies is not to encourage customers to drink while gambling. This man, when drinking and losing, has tried any number of times to cash another check. He has even come to me and called me every filthy name there is because I also refused to let him exceed his limit. I've laughed off his barbs and tried to explain we don't want an advantage while he's drinking and having a run of bad luck. Our day of justification was to come. He had set similar limits at certain Vegas casinos. On this day the bourbon was flowing and he needed more money. They cashed checks far beyond his limit. He lost $15,000, in fact, and when he sobered up and looked at the wreckage he was furious. He stopped payment on the checks. The casinos sued. His defense was that they breached an agreement not to exceed stated limits, and while they did so at his insistence, it was when he obviously was under the influence of alcohol. The casinos had to settle for a very minor sum.

Another of our customers, one of the few with a $10,000 limit, went through a bad night and wanted to cash another check. He was drinking; his luck was very bad. I refused the increase. Again I was called every name in the book and he stomped out. The next day, however, he was back to apologize. When he left Harolds Club, he related, he went to another casino and dropped $50,000. He thought they took unfair advantage of his condition. He paid, but he's never entered the other club again. How many times some pleasant little woman, who is also a lady, has saved men this embarrassment with her quiet: "I am very sorry but the regulations of the club do not permit me to cash a check for you."

♠

Certain of the Strip hotels in Las Vegas are known to be more successful than others and my findings show it's the women who make this so. It may lie in such simple things as the location of the registration desk. At Casino One, for instance, the desk is to one side of the main entrance as you come in. At Casino Two, the desk is at the opposite end of the long room. Casino One returns much more on its investment than Casino Two. Why?

Consider some facts, if you will. It is almost 300 miles, much of it over desert, from Los Angeles to Las Vegas. This makes for a hot and dusty trip. No woman cares to appear before other ladies looking anything but her best. If she can register immediately upon reaching her hotel, go to her room and take a bath, she has a chance to freshen up and make herself appealing before she enters the casino. I know my wife feels this way. With this in mind, and watching the arrivals at Casino One, I saw that many more couples registered there than at Casino Two, where the ladies had to cross the casino before getting to the desk. Casino Two, in fact, seemed to draw most of its feminine guests from the airport; they flew in and had only a short cab ride to the hotel. One beautiful red-haired lady proved my point. She had come with her husband by automobile. They stopped at Casino Two and I saw the look on her face as she was confronted by the glances of other women while she walked the entire length of the casino. She was only slightly disheveled but she was most uncomfortable. It was obvious she was not going to enjoy herself.

That, I knew, would make it all but impossible for her husband to enjoy himself.

An operator with half his wits about him knows he must please the women first and the men will follow. Kay Starr has told me frankly she sings the songs that will please the ladies and she dresses primarily to please them. I know from bitter experience that I can't determine whether I've booked a good show in my Fun Room until I get the reaction of the women in the audience. If they like it, they will want their husbands to take them to it. If they don't like it—well, as Miss Starr puts it, *Papa Can't Go Where Mama Don't Go.*

So now you know about the sexes in gaming clubs and now you want to know about sex and gambling. Frankly, there's damned little sex around a gaming table. The other emotions prevail. Of course, with so many attractive ladies and gentlemen about, there's bound to be a little he'n and she'n.

In fact I will tell you of such a case because it is the only time it has ever happened around Harolds Club in just this way. One of my lady dealers came to me one morning just after breakfast when the club was quiet. I have always respected this girl, a quiet, unattractive spinster well over forty. Her lip quivered just a trifle as she asked if I could hear her for a moment. She was, I saw, most ill at ease.

"I always have time to listen to you, honey," I assured her.

She told it straightaway. She was pregnant. She had thought the man was in love with her; it had never happened before. She did not want an abortion. She did not want money. She intended to have the child and to love it and care for it. She was trying to ask me if she would have a job after the baby was born. What she was asking really was: "Will they laugh at me?"

Well I like to think I'm a sophisticated man, but this one stopped me cold. *Harolds Club never had a baby before,* I heard my mind say. *But with all the he's and she's who work here there's bound to be a slip somewhere. So far as the outside world is concerned, it is certainly not anything nonpareil. A child is on the way. It should be welcomed graciously as the Big Gent must have meant.* Would the others laugh at her? I was preparing the answer for that already. They would treat her like a lady and they would not censure her. I would see to that if it meant the most abrupt burst of firings ever known in the club. I would set the example myself. And I did. I threw my arms around her and said: "Honey, congratulations! I am happy for you as only a father and grandfather can be." Perhaps you played some 21 with her in the months that followed. You saw only a radiant, slowly-filling woman who was ever so gentle with you when your luck turned a little bad.

That was a situation that could happen in any office at any time. The fact it happened in a gambling house makes little difference. But I won't kid you. Professional prostitutes, hustlers, do come in from time to time. If they have any finesse, I do not harass them. After all, they may be there only to gamble and may conduct themselves like perfect ladies. I know they're there and they know I know. They do exist. So long as there are no scenes, no overt acts, I find them to be less trouble than the little chippy who's from every strata of society. She's the one who's liable to be showy, vulgar and very possibly infected with venereal disease. A professional can't afford to be so careless.

I am reminded again of the Line, or "cribs", as we called them, where prostitutes were cloistered and tolerated until World War II brought an ambitious district attorney and the armed forces. I do not intimate that the Line was a good thing to have in the city. I am, after all, a family man with sons and daughters and a religion that does not condone prostitution. But as an observing man, whose round blue eyes see a good deal more of my city than most people's, I will say there are tremendous problems here, now that the Line is closed. The cribs at least kept free lance amateurs under control; if a chippy or semi-pro got to flouncing around, her established sisters would howl to the police: "Make her get her license and get in here." A lady could walk down Douglas Alley at any hour of the night and not be accosted or whistled at— there being a place for that—and that isn't the condition now. I offer no solutions. Our city fathers must, as the gambler says, play them as they lay.

I have heard more than one gambler, incidentally, say when he goes for big money at the gaming table he likes a good-looking woman, most particularly a red-headed prostitute, sitting beside him. It's a superstition, of course, for he's not interested in her wares. You simply can't have sex on your mind when you're gambling. It's better, in fact, that you don't have anybody with you that you know. If an attractive girl is nearby, and you feel emotions of any kind toward her, you may be trifling with Lady Luck. It would be hard to win under those circumstances, I think, though I don't say impossible, for there are always exceptions. And I don't think exceptions ever prove a rule. The only thing they prove, so far as I can see, is that exceptions do occur.

These are matters I know you expect me to discuss. There are others involving the female of our species in or about the gaming house. Are there, for instance, any famous lady gamblers corresponding to Nick the Greek? There are not. Over-all, women are not tenacious in this competitive sense. They are quite conservative, preferring 21, roulette or even Bingo to the fast-hopping dice.

The one exception I know certainly doesn't prove any rules. She's a local woman, about fifty, sharp as a tack, and married to a man who can afford her play. She has that quality you don't ascribe to ladies, but which a player must have: guts. She bets to win and when a streak is going for her she can pile up $10,000 in no time at all. Please don't mistake me, though. She's all woman. When she's not at the dice table, she has a whale of a time at the slot machines, yakking with the change girls, floormen and anyone else who may be around. The other day, when I heard she was in the club, I took my violin down and followed her up and down the rows of slot machines soulfully bowing *Kiss Me Again*. She loved it. She didn't miss a note, or a symbol on the turning wheels, and she didn't stop yakking. This lady has lost big—as much as $25,000 at a setting—and she has won big. Once when she won $25,000 she blew it all on a wardrobe of lovely clothes and a high-living trip around the world.

I think of one big-playing woman 21 player. But she's different too. She's from Texas and she's one of our dealers. When you hear wild shrieks of "San Antone!" ringing through the club, you know she's pushing her pile of chips up to $2500.

Another little lady comes quickly to mind. She is mousy, nameless, faceless and always lurking where she can ruin my game. I saw her just the other day when I was trying to make the 21 cards run coherently for a while. Suddenly I had the rhythm of the game just right. There was only a dealer and me. I was hitting everything right and the dealer was breaking. Now I was betting $160 a hand. The little PTA lady flounced up and took a seat to my right. You think this won't change a game? Well look at it this way. Now the little lady is getting my hands and I'm getting the ones that were breaking the dealer.

That wasn't the worst of it. She was betting one silver dollar. One shiny cartwheel that could kill my $160 on every turn. And that wasn't the worst of it either. This lady would split a pair of 10s. You have a very good hand in 20, of course; split it and you may well have two bad hands. I wanted to speak to her. I wanted to lean over in my most patient way and say: "Honey, if you don't split that, I will pay you $2." But I knew better. She would have snapped: "Who's *playing* this, anyway?" So there lay my $160, waiting for the executioner, while she split a solid 20, which might have won her $1 she could have played for an hour in the slot machines. Counting that dollar and the one she had bet, as a matter of fact, she was blowing $2 while killing me. Oh, kiss me, and pass the succotash. Have you ever seen a dealer split 20? Of course not. Ask any 21 player who splits face cards or 10s if he would do so if his bet was $500 or $1000. "Of course not!" he will tell you with great scorn. Then why, why, will he do it on a $2 bet? So my lady split hers and stripped off all the small cards. She couldn't leave a 10 to break the dealer. These 10-splitters never do. She managed only to break me and lose my $160. You can take my teeth if you can explain why this always happens.

I remember once when I visited Cuba I saw a lot of this. There was an excursion of merchandisers on a cruise ship down from New York, mostly women and the smartest ladies from the big city. I was surprised at how many of them would split 10s. When, I wondered, did money get that cheap? Of course I shouldn't censure women too hard for this. I've seen men do it too, poor things.

The vast majority of ladies who come into gaming clubs are, of course, well-mannered, self-contained and out for nothing but a little pleasure. A few are lonely and come in because they are lonely. I think of one sweet 68-year-old lady who comes into Harolds Club every day of her life and sits quietly by the roulette wheel. I gave her $25 to play just the other day. I'll give her another little "refund" in a few more days. I don't watch her play because I know she always loses. With her, there just aren't enough numbers on the wheel. But roulette is the only interest she has in the world; she'll sit and play it mentally when she hasn't any money. Her sweet, solemn little face is one of the finest assets Harolds Club has.

The ladies, God bless them, do us a favor when they come in with their husbands but the husbands would be doing themselves a favor if they arranged to play just beyond their wives' range of vision. Not all ladies, unfortunately, can be as philosophical as the one who watched her man win, and then drop, $50,000. Femininity being what it is, a man must always represent a winner to his woman. He mustn't show her weakness, particularly where the family finances are at stake. I believe women generally prefer the winner and haven't too much time for losers. To be sure, a wife must feel needed. But don't, I urge you men, don't let her feel so needed she's got to botch you up with her wifely position and insist upon splitting your 10s.

My second wife Lois, by the way, is the only person I know with a system that works every time for betting the horses successfully. Since we've been talking of women and gambling here, I shall give you her system. She lets me pick all the horses, buy the pari-mutuel tickets and pay for them. If one of the horses wins, she takes the ticket to the window and cashes it. If none of our selections wins, she simply doesn't go near a window. You can win a little that way and you can't lose. It's what you might call a woman's parlay.

7

♥ ♥ ♥ ♥

Just Hit Me Easy

AN INTERESTING, THOUGH not precisely unheard-of thing occurred here the other evening. A beautiful woman made a play for me.

When I say beautiful, I say it all. She was like a page from *Esquire* or *Playboy* in full, living color. A Petty drawing, if you please, or a Varga, come to life at my elbow—and very much at my elbow—with long, coppery hair, ivory skin and a voice that would dim the lights. Actually they were already pretty dim since this was the Harolds Club Fun Room where I had just emceed the 11 o'clock floor show. The evening was young and so was the doll.

"Oh, Mr. Smith," she cooed, closing in on me like a scented sunset, "I thought you were just wonderful." Her tremendous, luminous blue eyes seemed to bear out the statement. They were brimful of admiration.

Now I did cut quite a figure of manhood at the moment. Dressed to the teeth in white stetson, boots and one of my tailored white cowboy suits, with not even a wallet to bulge my hips, I wasn't displeased at all with my appearance.

"You're pretty wonderful yourself, honey," I said, and got out of there like a striped-assed ape. I mean I departed.

Why, Mister Smith! you're probably saying. *You, a sophisticate and rounder—you'd have us believe you flee the attentions of beautiful dolls?*

Oui, monsieur.

As the proprietor of a gaming house, I am a target for all manner of cute tricks. I'm a target for fights, lawsuits, crossroaders, con games and conniving females. If I knew a way to flee a situation like this any faster, I would employ it. When I don't like the odds or conditions of a game, when I can't possibly win, I'm sorry, but I have to pass.

I'm not being coy. A woman who is soft and curvy and feminine is a joy to my round blue eyes. But when they took in this doll and her curves I saw danger signs. In the shadows just beyond was a large gentleman, all smiles and white teeth, like a big, bad wolf waiting for me to fall for his little Red Riding Hood. I had been looking for him, as a matter of fact, from the moment her alabaster bosom quivered against my elbow. I was sure he would be there.

I am not, as I have said, made of marble. Neither are my brains made of dull Washoe adobe. I know I'm no Apollo, even in tailored cowboy duds, with my ruddy cheeks aglow and eyes sparkling. I'm fifty-one years of age and I wear bi-focals. The arthritis in my back bends me over like a clam digger some days. A gorgeous young creature like this can estimate the mileage. She knows it's too late for us to grow old and gray together.

Quite clearly, then, there are other considerations to her game. I saw dolls like this bucking for colonels and generals when I was lonesome Harold Stewart Smith, Pfc, in the khaki of Uncle Sam. They didn't give me a second look. Why should they now, then, when I'm no handsomer and considerably older?

They're going for the dough, as we say in the gambling profession. Cash; money; COD. In post-war Reno I am Harold S. Smith, Sr., president of Harolds Club, with access (or so they assume) to a very large bankroll. Another objective might be position in the club. A girl wants to better her lot. The boss is a male and she has certain feminine attributes. I don't need to draw a picture. You can add two and two.

I don't really blame the girls. What the hell. There aren't any depletion allowances on beauty. Everyone is going for the dough in one way or another. I accept the condition and the challenge. You will get the name you earn, I find, whether you like it or not. Occasionally, of course, I do point out to over-aggressive females that they aren't as irresistible as they think. "I've never seen one of you," I tell them, "who didn't think she had just a little different twist to the age-old bait. You don't honey."

In my own club, a pretty girl with a pretty body will get ahead swiftly—if she has common sense, intelligence, skill at her job and a good head for the rules. None ever got a job here with her body and none has to hold her job that way. I can be most severe with a floor boss who forgets that fact, although this doesn't always take us off the firing line. Whenever I must upbraid a girl dealer for disregarding regulations, for example, I always have a floor boss in as witness, just as a doctor has his nurse stand by when he's with a woman patient. Even so, the girl may dash down to the club and spread the word she was fired "because I wouldn't lay him." My only hole card in such a situation is an adage I treasure: *The truth will sustain.*

Usually it does, but as an operator I must wear propriety and prudence like a chastity belt. I cannot be interested in dames. I cannot afford incidents. My behavior must be circumspect as a preacher's whether in church, at a baseball game, in a saloon or the opera house.

This, I assure you, involves alertness to details the average man never notices. Take mirrors for instance. I am most interested in mirrors; in a new hotel room I examine them before I test the mattress. Remember, if you please, we have several miles of mirrors in Harolds Club. They're all two-way glass. You look up from your play at a table and see only your reflection. Beyond your reflection, though, there are eyes peering down on you and the play at the table. This is one of our defenses against chicanery. If we use mirrors defensively, other people can use them for ulterior purposes. I won't stay at one world-famous hotel in San Francisco or at several in Las Vegas because I've learned certain things about their mirrors. I also check a room carefully for bugs, recording devices, and I don't hold court with strangers or make a club of my room. Being an operator and acknowledged target, I move about a city restlessly, changing from hotel to hotel like a bird in a tree or a wise old wolf in the north woods.

Even so, strange things happen. I was in Dayton, Ohio, a few years ago to take part in a big trapshoot and had a suite at one of the largest hotels. There were two bedrooms and parlor with a common vestibule. Junior occupied one of the bedrooms, which led to a little more traffic and a little more laxity with keys than I care for. One afternoon I came back to find a doll sitting in the parlor.

"Could I have a cigarette?" she asked.

"Certainly," I replied. I offered her a pack, thinking I could be wrong about the green light look in her eyes. She might be a trapshooter's lady or a friend of Junior's.

"Wouldn't you like to come over to my room?" she asked cordially. "I have some bourbon and scotch—"

"No, thank you, honey," I said, mentally tightening the chastity belt. "I don't drink."

"I was watching your television set while you were out," she said, apparently in explanation of her presence there.

I shrugged. "Watch it some more, if you like."

I'm sure she read me loud and clear. A woman can tell when you're not interested. A man strolled in. He was rather a pretty boy but muscular under his impeccable suit. *Here it comes,* I thought, *and I need witnesses.* Maybe if I invited them to dinner they would go along, hoping to trap me later. I tried and they accepted. They pardoned themselves to go clean up; they stayed gone. Obviously they had had a little shake-down to deal until I cut the cards. They decided not to play when they saw I recognized the game.

♣

I wasn't always so astute. Years ago, as a teen-ager in Cleveland, I happened to stop one day at a hock shop where a real hustling auctioneer was performing. Every word he shouted was a $3 one, utterly counterfeit, and with forty people looking on he aimed his pitch at me, the kid. That night I described the episode

I rarely show so much of the rule of my life.

Our road signs, clear to Antarctica, made us famous.

Pre-war Harolds Club—still a hole-in-the-wall.

Today it's a towering giant by day—

And a gaudy blaze of light by night.

The big wagon train mural out front. That's me "up" on Bobby Sox.

Pappy (right) contracts with an old-timer for more guns.

HAROLDS CLUB
AND RADIO STATION
KDOT
present the...
...LATEST NEWS...

TUESDAY, February 28, 1961: GOOD AFTERNOON

PRESIDENT KENNEDY plans to send a special message on highway construction to Congress today--which will set forth his proposals to finance the nation's giant interstate highway network.

NEW THUNDERSHOWERS forecast for today are adding to the hardships in flood-stricken areas of Georgia, Mississippi and Alabama.

KING MOHAMMED, the Fifth, is being buried today. Heads of State and diplomats stand with mountain tribesmen on foot and in primitive carts before the pink gates of Morocco's Royal Palace. The 51-year-old Monarch died Sunday.

SECRETARY OF STATE Dean Rusk faces questioning by Senators today. They will ask him about published reports that he has proposed putting less reliance on nuclear weapons in plans for defending Europe.

A HOUSE LABOR SUBCOMMITTEE today is expected to give final approval to an amended version of the Administration's minimum wage hike proposal.

WEATHER IN BRIEF: FAIR TODAY WITH LITTLE CHANGE IN TEMPERATURE. THE LOW THIS A.M. WAS: 18. HIGH EXPECTED TODAY: 58.

ENTERTAINMENT NOTE: OPENING TONIGHT.......RUSTY DRAPER and THE JUDY LYNN SHOW. SHOWS AT 9-11-1 IN HAROLDS 7TH FLOOR FUN ROOM.....NO MINIMUM OR COVER CHARGE. RESERVATIONS ARE RECOMMENDED.

When I was "cowboying," my horse visited the club.

Our "newspaper." You're never out of touch.

On really crowded days you can hardly move about here.

The Roaring Camp Room's rarely as quiet as this.

Not even a Marine band (rear) disturbs slot players.

Some of my Nevada neighbors pass in parade.

Camp collection from 1949 to 1959 but never advertised the petitioner.

The petitioner and Harolds Club entered into a contract in 1950 whereby Harolds Club agreed to pay to the petitioner $19,000 a year for 10 years for the use of the items in the Roaring Camp collection and to reimburse the petitioner for its payments to the Staggs under the advertising contract.

Most of the guns, shields, and some of the old pianos, music boxes and wagons in the collection were displayed in Harolds Club during the taxable years and at the sides of various highways throughout Nevada and other western states.

The petitioner established a reserve of $10,000 at the end of 1950 for payments on the purchase price of the collection. It was also required to expend an additional $4,000 to cover insurance, taxes and miscellaneous expenses.

Option to buy Harold's stock in Harolds Club

Raymond I. Smith became greatly distressed and worried when his son Harold, upset by his divorce, took to drinking and gambling excessively. He was able to persuade Harold on four occasions to stop gambling in other clubs, but Harold returned each time to his heavy drinking and gambling. He gambled for very high stakes and in unwise fashion. He was encouraged to do this by rival gambling establishments which gave him unlimited credit. He thus lost practically everything he had saved in prior years. His father feared that rival gambling establishments might be able to acquire from Harold some or all of Harold's stock in Harolds Club. The father and the other directors of the petitioner felt that it would be necessary that the petitioner control that stock for its own protection so that if Harold had to sell it for some reason in connection with his wild gambling it would not get into unfriendly hands. Harold's gambling was mostly with competitors either in Reno or Las Vegas, and the directors felt that if any of the stock of Harolds Club got into the hands of such persons they would interfere with the petitioner's operation of the bars in Harolds Club. Smith felt that it would be better to have the petitioner take the option rather than take it himself because of the advantages of corporate ownership. The petitioner acquired on September 6, 1949, a first refusal option on the stock in Harolds Club owned by Harold S. Smith, entitling the petitioner to buy the stock for $500,000 if Harold S. Smith should offer it for sale during the next 5 years. The directors of the petitioner felt that there was real danger, that the option was necessary and that it might have to be exercised. They had the petitioner set up a reserve of $25,000 in 1950 to support the option. The option expired in September 1954 without having been exercised.

Moana Motel

Most of the patrons of Harolds Club came from other cities and many of them called Harolds Club in advance for lodging reservations. These had to be obtained from Reno hotels, most of which operat competing gambling establishments. T officers and directors of Harolds Club a of the petitioner felt the need for attracti comfortable accommodations under th control where out-of-town patrons Harolds Club could be housed at reasonal rates and with ready access to Harol Club, but without being guests of con petitors. Harolds Club purchased a mo in December 1951 for $205,671.28. It w enlarged to accommodate 100 person Harolds Club in December 1951 had pu chased at $120,000 a ranch west of Reno f protection of its business in case "st operations" were started in that vicini it had purchased in 1950 and 1951 f $420,000 property next door to the Club f current expansion at that location, planned to make improvements and ad tions at its motel, it needed cash for all those purposes and was not in position purchase another motel.

The petitioner therefore purchased t Moana Auto Apartments on December 1951, in order to improve its business alo with that of Harolds Club. It was motel on the southern outskirts of Re near the airport. It is on the main ro to Reno from Los Angeles, Carson Ci and the south end of Lake Tahoe. It w in an excellent location where it might desirable to add a hotel later. The cost w $200,000 of which $121,169.06 was paid cash and the balance was evidenced by note payable during 6½ years and secur by a mortgage.

Harolds Club established schedul limousine service between the Club and t two motels. The petitioner changed the i terior of its motel to accommodate a tot of 76 persons at a time. The petitione purchased the land and buildings of t Moana Coffee Shop in September 1953. Th purchase price was $25,233.30, of whic $12,200 was deferred, payable at the ra of $150 a month, plus interest. Th restaurant was needed in order to feed t guests at the motel and also because of i location at the entrance to the motel prop erty. The petitioner planned to put a b in the Coffee Shop as soon as the existin lease expired and it planned to acqui additional property in order to increase t size of the motel. However, the price the adjoining property needed for t planned expansion became excessive wh the owners learned that Harolds Club ar the petitioner wanted the additional groun Also, the operation of two motels Harolds Club and the petitioner, in con petition with other motel operators in th vicinity, created ill will, whereas Harol Club and the petitioner needed the goo will of the other landlords in the vicini who frequently housed patrons which Ha olds Club attracted to Reno. The Moar Motel was not first class, was not ad quately furnished and proved unpopula with the patrons of Harolds Club. T petitioner, for the foregoing reasons, de cided to sell it and thus obtain fund needed for the purchase of another pie of property hereafter described. The mot and the Coffee Shop were sold during 19 for a net gain of $39,462.54.

to a city detective who lived at my mother's rooming house. He smiled. "When they play you for a sucker," he said, "the advantage is all with you. Learn to sit back and beat them at their own game." It was sound advice for the future gambler though it took many years and many incidents to get it through my thick skull.

There was, for example, one day when I should not have encouraged a fight. At that time I had a body guard, Kenny LaSalle, a former professional fighter who had had three bouts with Fritzie Zivic; his job was not so much to protect me as to be a witness. I was drinking heavily and cowboying around at the time and one of my standing orders to Kenny was to keep women away. If I wanted female companionship, I would make my wants known.

We were having a little fun this day at a place out on Airport Road. We were having a lot of fun, in fact. I had sent a cab thirty-two miles to Carson City to bring back a Hawaiian quartet I liked and, while they played, I ate a platter of chicken and talked with the proprietress. This lady seemed to have an endless supply of daughters whom she insisted on introducing to me. One, however, started to make a play without introductions.

Kenny warned her. "Harold doesn't want girls bothering him when he's drinking."

She turned like a wounded lioness. "Who's a whore?" she demanded in a voice that could be heard all the way to Tahoe. That, of course, brought up the inevitable big male—this time he really was her husband—declaring: "No one's gonna call my wife a whore!"

No one had, but she was profoundly indignant. Kenny got her away from the table but she kept up her shrieks. And kept them up. So did the husband. "If they're bothering you," I told Kenny facetiously, "take them outside." It was most indiscreet. Kenny, an ex-pro, should have known better. The husband threw a punch which Kenny slipped. Kenny threw two punches and the fisticuffs were over, though the trouble wasn't.

They went for the dough. The husband sued me and Harolds Club for $25,000, alleging among other things that I kicked him three times while he was down. That was ridiculous. I was standing twenty feet away holding Kenny's coat. The man who fought Zivic, furthermore, needed no help from me. However, wise Mister Diskin, our attorney, decided to settle and avoid publicity. It cost us $6000.

That was one type of incident. There are others. We once had a girl dealer from a local family I wouldn't have trusted with wild horses, let alone money. She'd been fired once, but Daddy, with his big, soft heart, had taken her back. (She could cry tears in a volume to equal a melting iceberg.) One night I was called to pay off $1200 she had lost to a man at her roulette table. "Oh, Mr. Smith," she bawled, "I'm sorry—"

I looked the situation over and was satisfied. The man had been around the club often. He was a big chap, about thirty-three, always in lumberjack shirt and leather gloves, who played heavily. He had every license to win $1200.

"But all that money!" the girl blubbered.

"Don't feel too badly, honey," I told her. "It's only money."

Several nights later, however, another of our dealers chanced to drop in at a gambling house on Center Street. The man in leather gloves was there and propositioned this girl to let him win a big bet—"shove over some money," we call it. He had dropped $8000, he said, was trying to get even, and would split whatever she gave him. "But," he warned, "if you tell Harold Smith about this I'll kick your teeth in."

Well this girl is one of the loyal employees still with us. She came and told me immediately. I recalled the $1200 I'd given this gentleman in my innocence. Suddenly I had a homicidal urge to get my hands on him. (Despite the fact he was big and burly, while I weighed 150 pounds; in those days I was boxing a lot and in good shape.) I brought tennis shoes and a boxer's protective cup and put them in the vault, and warned Jack Shaver, one of our floor bosses, not to let this glove-man near a wheel. "Notify me immediately if he shows," I ordered. Two weeks passed.

On a Saturday night, which is always our busiest and usually the time for chicanery, I came to the club after dinner. Jack met me at the door. "He got to us," he said. The man had tamed another girl pigeon and was waiting even then for an $1100 payoff. I won't trouble you with what I said to Jack Shaver. When I went to the vault for the money I put on my cup and tennis shoes. I personally handed the $1100 to the man. "From now on," I said frigidly, "your money is no good in here." A gambler knows what that means. He's barred from the club. I might add that the word gets around.

"I'll take you out in the alley!" he roared.

The club dumped. I mean everyone poured out to see the fight, among them the Smith family and customers. The leather-gloved gentleman looked about uneasily. "Hey," he protested, "you've got all your friends here."

"With you," I retorted, "I don't need friends. I'll meet you in the YMCA gym at 2 PM tomorrow." I grabbed his plaid shirt and shook him. "If you don't show, you stink."

He showed. So did Daddy, my brother Raymond and half the town. They weren't too happy about the difference in our weights. In fact, Jack Shaver was so damned nervous he couldn't locate my mouthpiece. Actually I never needed it in this fight to the finish. It lasted two rounds. The man hadn't trained. I had. Artie McCann, a former lightweight boxer who refereed, deliberately stalled the clinches so I could chop home heart blows, which I did with delight. The big man was getting clobbered and knew it. He quit. There were no silly epithets. I congratulated him for showing up. I congratulated him for having the good sense to quit when he couldn't win and reminded him he had brought it on himself. I like to think I made a believer of him. To my knowledge, he never tried to cheat another operator.

At other times, to be sure, I have not been so brave. I will never forget the surly voice that stopped me one night. "Hey, give me a thousand on this." I turned to confront a young man who was trouble in spades, doubled and redoubled. He was a narcotics user from San Francisco and always traveled with a retinue of six tough pals. Having lost at a crap table, he wanted to hock his watch, a beautiful, diamond-studded timepiece with knife and chain attached.

I did not signal the bouncers. We were on the first floor, surrounded by customers; the young man was a little edgy for want of his drug. There would be no fisticuffs with him. It would be a knife or a gun. I had long since learned that it takes brains to stand behind a gun; you are going to lose any way you play it. I slowly edged out of the stream of customers and into a passageway to one side, hoping my brawny bouncers, Jim Slattery—now a distinguished Nevada State Senator—and Jack Filtzer wouldn't see the play. As luck would have it, Filtzer ambled in the other end of the passageway.

"I am sorry," I was telling the young man in my most courteous way, "but the city council just passed an ordinance which prevents us from loaning money on jewelry."

"I want a thousand on this watch," he repeated. He had one hand in his pocket, where something bulged. I was not looking into the eyes of a sane man.

"I can't give it to you," I repeated as softly as I could speak. "I would lose my license."

His eyes narrowed. His lip curled. His pals crowded up behind him so no one beyond would see the action. He glared at me like a cobra hypnotizing a bird. He all but spat in my face. "F - - - you." It was cold, crisp, venomous and to the point. I could almost feel the nasty words drip off my face.

"And you, too —" this into the very teeth of big Jack Filtzer. To his everlasting credit, he held his temper. Perhaps he, too, sensed the finality in the words. The business discussion was ended. Now either we got out of there gracefully or a murder might start. I touched Jack's arm and we got. The young man had told me to my kisser what he thought of me. Presumably he could get his money elsewhere. Months later I read how FBI agents moved in on his San Francisco apartment to take him on a narcotics charge. He shot himself dead and I knew I"d not judged him wrong. When he made his move, whatever it might be, he meant business. Even my gambler's nerves couldn't take many episodes like that.

♥

Quite often it's litigation for which we're the target. Sometimes, in fact, I look out to see if there isn't a line of lawyers two blocks long waiting to file suits in the Washoe County Courthouse against Harolds Club. With all our naked cash lying about, you know people are going to sue us. At times it's legitimate, like the day a workman trying to take rubber matting from the catwalks unscrewed bolts he supposed held the matting. They didn't. Those bolts secured the cluster of lights over a pan table and when he released them he dropped a heavy cluster of lights and metal frame on an unsuspecting group of players. No one was hurt seriously, thank God, but there were hospital bills to pay.

Gambling house lawsuits can start from the damndest things you ever heard of. There was one involving a little chap named Sam and our dime crap game. The dealer, incidentally, was one of those gentlemen who cultivate a hairline mustache, which, as I have pointed out, is one of my pet annoyances. He demonstrated why it is—the thinking that goes with hairline mustaches—when Sam asked to see all the dice on the table. This is something every customer in Harolds Club has a right to do. The dice were about to be changed and he wanted to select the ones they would play with next.

"You will shoot these," said the hairline-mustached dealer, and tossed two dice to Sam.

"I want to see them all," Sam argued.

"You are going to shoot these," repeated the dealer.

The argument got hot and loud. It reached me when Jack Filtzer came towing Sam. Sam had a copy of the United States Constitution imprinted on his brain and was reading section and paragraph at the top of his voice. The moment to mollify him and admit our dealer's fault was passed. Sam was swearing and belligerent. I told him he would have to leave. Under his version of the Constitution, he didn't have to. That was when we sent for the cops.

Having called on them for assistance, we had to back their play. We signed a complaint charging Sam with disturbing the peace. Then, unfortunately, our police department went as blank as our dime crap dealer. They failed to bring Sam before a magistrate within the required forty-eight hours. He sued the two arresting officers for $25,000, charging false arrest, etc. and etc. He sued Harolds Club for another $25,000, charging everything but restraint of trade and piracy on the high seas. We won after a battle that took us through the Nevada Supreme Court but it cost us $10,000 in legal time, fees etc. to win. Many suits like this, based as they are on a series of human failures, take much of the profit from gaming.

There are, on the other hand, a vast majority of customers who wouldn't think of suing. I remember a miner who had come to town for a weekend, gotten himself properly drunk, gambled away his money and then fell down the escalator. All he wanted when he came to me was a grubstake of $8. He rubbed his bruises gingerly and stared at the escalator. "All my life," he grumbled,

"I've climbed up and down mine shafts and never got hurt. Then one of them durned stairways runs out from under me." The humiliation of his tumble far out-weighed any avarice he might have had. He didn't even consider a lawsuit.

Mostly, I should say, I am a target for handouts. Sympathy money. I don't complain about this a bit. In fact I'm proud of the saying around Nevada that Harolds Club has to win its money six times before we get it to the vault. This refers, of course, to our little black refund book and our policy of refunding all or part of the losings of players who shouldn't have lost as much as they did. No other club has such a book. Certainly you don't find any such thing at the racetracks, where they have two kinds of windows, SELLER and CASHIER, but no SYMPATHY WINDOW. The fact we have one costs more than half a million dollars some years. Yet no policy we have has profited us more in the long run.

When I walk into the club in the morning people actually are lined up to ask me for refunds. The floor bosses are empowered to make them, but people have found through the years that they get more if they can bend my ear. Why? Well, I know for one thing what it is to have nothing. I know, for instance, what it is to be a desperately yearning teen-ager and to lack the few dollars that could get me started toward the thing I wanted. I also know what it is to walk out of a game flat broke. It makes no difference whether you dropped $40 or $40,000. You suddenly are broke. A broke man, as I see it, can be a potential killer, a potential robber, a troublemaker of some sort. I would much rather see him walk out of my club jingling a cheerful $3-4 in silver. If this policy costs us money and benefits the entire gambling fraternity, I am glad. It benefits me too, inside.

I feel that I—the whole Smith family—we're all most fortunate to be able to be generous. Someone upstairs has been generous with us, I honestly believe this. I have all I need. How much more can you expect to take from this game of life?

Naturally this policy doesn't always bring happy endings. In fact it rarely does. I am thinking now of a big game prizefight promoter who was my good friend for many years. At 3:30 one morning I had a telephone call from him. He had to have a serious emergency operation and he needed money. Of course I sent it. I walked right around the corner to Western Union and put it on the wire. I was honored, if you want to know the truth. Of all the big men this old-timer knew—all the fighters and promoters and rich gentlemen to whom he had given ringside seats— he had called on me in his need. The operation was successful from a physical standpoint, too. But it had taken something from our friendship. We would sit down to coffee and things were different. Instead of fights and fighters, the lore that I love, all he could talk about now was the money he owed me. I tried again and again to tell him, when I stopped in for a visit: "I just came to say hello, my friend, not to collect money." One Christmas Eve, finally, I telephoned him. "Look, pardner, I want to give you that $2500 as a gift—your Christmas present from me. Come New Years, maybe, we can have a cup of coffee together and some friendship again." You know how it worked. He was embarrassed. I had lost a friend.

◆

A gaming house proprietor is a very lonely man for these and many other reasons. He loses real friends in about the same proportion that he wins money. He becomes a target for all the insincerity this world can generate. I am thinking right now of a bartender in this club who starts almost every conversation with "Now look, Harold, it's not because you're Harold Smith, but—." His subservience is sticking out like the horn on a bull elk. Probably he goes on to say: "It's not because you own Harolds Club, either, but I wanna tell you one thing: you've got the nicest club in this area." Now isn't that something? He wants to be acknowledged, to be heard; he wants to be a big deal and he's using me for consideration. Supposing you and I were to go in to see President Kennedy and I said: "Now, Mr. President, I want it clearly understood—not because you're President of the United States—but I like you personally." This is bosh and some men must live with bosh—or live without the company of their fellow man. That's why theirs is a lonely job.

I would like people to like me for me. I have long since seen that is impossible when I am in a position to give them a job, feather their beds with my greenbacks, or make a simple refund of their gaming losses. Life is so short—though a man lives a hundred years, it is only a day. So why do we make each other miserable? Why is simple honesty such an elusive gem?

Don't misunderstand me, please. I see examples of honesty and integrity every day. They're so unusual, though, I invariably notice them. There was, for instance, a little girl working down in the club who got a divorce from her man. "I decided to make a lot of men happy," she said frankly, "rather than keep one man miserable." She meant just what she said. She hadn't been happy with this man; she couldn't be happy with any one man. So, instead of living unhappily and making him unhappy, she decided to scatter her play. She did, too, for quite a while. Then she got married again and now she has a lovely child about eight years of age. Society must frown on her attitude, but it was honest.

Society, of course, is your constant critic, in the gaming business or out of it, and society doesn't trouble itself to be always well informed. Just the other evening I was feeling jam-up. The world was rosy. Laughter was in the air. I dressed up in my striped jacket and straw skimmer, put on my enormous spectacles and went over to the club to stir up the play. Within minutes, the grapevine was buzzing: "Harold's drunk again." I wasn't; not on liquor anyway. I simply was intoxicated with happy feelings and they didn't last long enough.

Another time I took a man friend on a cowboying tour of the country. We had some wonderful times until I got home. Then I began to hear the stories. How I got so drunk in Las Vegas I was throwing $100 bills at the ceiling. It was utterly, bitterly untrue. I just don't throw money around. I spend it freely but I also pick pennies off the floor. Why, I wondered, had this man spread such a tale when I had done my best to show him a good time? You can see the answer quite clearly, I'm sure. It suited his ego. By making me a legend and himself a witness, he became part of the legend too. And that is another way in which I have become a target.

It is another reason, too, why I often think of the words of that detective at my mother's rooming house in Cleveland. *When they are playing you for a sucker, sit back and beat them at their own game.* Establish a policy for yourself. If you are doing well in your game, you will be propositioned just as I was in my Fun Room. I thought of this when we learned how young Professor Van Doren had accepted the "fix" in a television quiz show. He was young and inexperienced; he hadn't been coached by a wise detective on how to play the sucker. He isn't the only man who's been propositioned. Ask any doctor who has been offered many times his daily income to perform an abortion; ask any lawyer who's been offered $5000 to drop a lawsuit. It happens every day to men who are not professional gamblers. It just happens more often to men who are in the gaming business.

As my old rancher friend Early Prunty says, it's a condition. "If you've never missed an easy shot," he contends, "you've never hunted. If you've never been thrown by a horse, you've never ridden." To which I would add: If you've never been a target, you haven't gambled successfully.

I can tell you all this philosophically because I have established my own policy long since. Actually I am not quite so philosophical. I have a son. There are times when I go into my office sanctuary, turn up the hi-fi behind the double-locked doors and simply stare at the wall as I think of him and his future. Junior is young, handsome, well-heeled and inexperienced. He didn't come to a position of responsibility in Harolds Club the hard way, as I did. He didn't break in behind amusement park wheels under Daddy with wise advice from a city detective lodged away in his mind. Only the other day a man I recognized instantly as a cold-blooded crossroader bobbed up in a shooting jacket at our gun club, where Junior was conducting a trapshoot. "It's not just because you're Harold Smith Junior," I heard him say, preparatory to laying out a gin rummy game, "but you shoot a mean gun." I watched my son beam and wag his tail. Bless me, I thought, and pass the succotash. This boy is such a vulnerable target. He hasn't learned yet how the sharpies work on an ego. But he will learn—for that I can vouch—and I must pray he doesn't lose a share of the club in the process.

This game of targets never ends, of course. It will go on just as long as we operate a gaming club and show our money nakedly to the public, just as long as there are avaricious people and predatory dames. It goes on in slightly different ways in your office, the schools and in world politics. If you can't accept the challenge and condition, better to cash in your chips and get out of the game.

I do when I can. This is precisely why I slip off to the convent some evenings to have dinner with the priests, learned and humble men who, while not as worldly wise as I now am, can at least help me regain perspective. That growing perspective is what leads me away more and more from the gaming house's rattle of mammon to the concert hall, theater, my books and Shakespearian recordings. A target I am, but I don't want to be utterly cynical, completely skeptical, or the victim of my own ego. A professional gambler I must remain, wary of my fellow man, looking to the marrow of his bones, judging his motives and gauging his movements. But I was a human being before I was a gambler and I can see now where twenty more years will bring me to ripe old age. That is a condition of the game also. So I think of the famous Edwin Markham quatrain I read recently:

> They drew a circle that shut us out,
> Rebel, heretic, a thing to flout.
> But love and I had the wit to win;
> We drew a circle that took them in.

Isn't that, really, just another way of saying what the detective taught me years ago in Cleveland? When you're a target, when they're playing you for a sucker, the advantage is all yours. Sit back and beat them at their own game.

♠ ♠ ♠ ♠

Twenty-four Hour

Shift

Periodically, as in any store, the gambling casino organization gets a little lax and we bring in efficiency experts to take a look. This is to be expected, I suppose, where cash money is the chief merchandise and a steady flow of it comes through seven doorways by day and by night. The efficiency expert, however, always reminds me that I earn my daily bread like no other man on earth.

We have in Harolds Club, of course, the usual operational mechanics of any commercial enterprise. There are regular corporation board meetings with our lawyers and daily conferences between me, Junior, Daddy and big Jim Hunter. There are routine personnel changes, tax forms to file, vacations to schedule. With this, any businessman or efficiency expert is familiar.

At precisely this point, though, the action changes. We receive correspondence, for instance, unlike the letters written to any other business firm. "Enclosed is $1.50," says a scrawled epistle from Arkansas. "Will you please play it carefully on a roulette table and run it up to $500 so I can buy a farm?" We must direct that letter *and the money* back to the sender posthaste. We're not a mail order firm.

Or I may take one of my casual strolls through the club, as I did the other morning, and come back to write an impassioned notice for the employees' bulletin board. Daddy, it seems, had grown tired of the happy music we play from recordings on the public address system and had substituted his own favorites like *Somewhere In the West* and *Silver Threads Among The Gold*. (On an organ yet!) The club sounded like the repose room in a mortuary as customers gloomily stared into space and played picayunish bets. I had tried classical music some years ago and found it hurt the play. I removed it immediately. But Daddy was stubborn. So I asked the employees in my note to belabor him with complaints. We soon got rid of the organ music. But did you ever hear of a corporation president making such an appeal to the employees over his general manager's head? Neither had the efficiency experts.

Now I am aware, of course, that these experts are like mothers-in-law. Everyone laughs at them. It is particularly easy to do so in a gaming club where more cash is retrieved from the floor than some businesses ever save. The wonder to me is that any of our experts ever leaves Harolds Club still in command of his senses.

The last one we had, for instance, recommended that we keep a performance chart on dealers. Every girl would be rated on things like politeness, patience, friendliness, dexterity and earnings for the house. On the face of it, it seemed quite intelligent. After a month or so, we would know which girls to keep, which to dismiss, and would have only super-courteous dealers making loads of money for the club.

The trouble was our expert had never dealt a gambling game of any kind and I told him so. His business engineering tables just didn't include intangible factors like the sudden, inexplicable runs of luck any player, or the house, might have. They didn't allow for very tangible situations like the tourist lady who can't count cards under pressure and holds up the game, or the virile dandy upsetting our lady dealer's equilibrium with goo-goo eyes. I have dealt every game we have and know how human nature changes all conditions from day to day. And how do you meter that?

Most of our experts have looked a little bewildered when I, the president, put on my striped blazer and comedy spectacles to wander through the club getting laughs. They're inclined to agree with a local codger who called out: "What the hell's eating you, Harold?" Nothing was, of course. Though I haven't a card file to prove that a laughing player gambles more than a pensive one, I am convinced, after twenty-five years at the business, that a little laugh that breaks the ice of inhibitions is dollars and cents to us.

Efficiency experts, furthermore, invariably protest my generosity with the little old lady who plays roulette with our money. They don't know the lady, of course; they only see the $25 I slip her for a weekend at the wheel. I could argue that she really likes the game and is, in reality, an unpaid, *interested* shill working on her own time. (Harolds Club hires no shills to stimulate play). I know, where the expert doesn't, that other customers constantly are watching and weighing. They see me being sweet to a little old lady and are more comfortable gambling here.

It's not exactly efficient, perhaps, to hand another old-timer $25 from the refund book when a floor boss has already turned him down. Conceivably, with a run of luck, he could run the $25 into $10,000 in winnings. I know he won't. I have known this man for years; his luck is all run out. Ultimately his $25, like the roulette lady's $25, will find its way back to the vault. These are considerations that prompt me to reject many of the experts' recommendations.

I make no jokes about efficiency experts, however. We must have these killjoys in occasionally. Among other things, they prevent floor bosses from hiring extra dealers they don't need just now. All bosses have cronies in Reno who need work and it's human nature to help your friends. An actual count of customers, table by table and shift by shift, tells us the facts of life. Let the eager beaver prowl and snoop and make his report. I, the boss, will sift his findings in the light of my own experience. This, I assure you, gets richer with every passing year.

♠

My working day, spotted over twenty-four hours, can be like no other man's. I can have no regular hours, no scheduled comings or goings, no routine or close friends. My daily life is, in fact, a mess of irregularities. I may go home for a late dinner with guests and be summoned back twenty minutes later to deal with a temperamental entertainer. A series of minor emergencies may then keep me at the club until I fall into bed in my hideaway room at 8 AM, only to be awakened at 11 by word that a crossroader is in the house. I may start to drive up to Lake Tahoe for a breath of air only to be stopped by the jangle of my car telephone; a floor boss needs my OK on higher bet limits and credit for big-play spenders just in from Las Vegas. I drink quarts of black coffee, sleep as I can, in snatches, and work without any regular flight plan. I don't even get uninterrupted holidays.

One day, for example, I was taking a breather in San Francisco when Daddy telephoned. "We have important papers to sign," he said. "You'll have to be in Reno at 3 PM." It was then 12 noon and Reno is at least a four-hour drive. However, when Daddy calls, I try. This time I would be trying for a new trans-Sierra driving record. Hitting every traffic signal and doing 80-90 miles an hour, I managed to reach Sacramento in one hour, twenty minutes. More than a hundred miles remained, most of it through the mountains. I knew I couldn't make it by three, so I called Daddy. "Oh well," he said, "the papers can wait a day or so." That day I could have hired an efficiency expert for him.

Our floor bosses, unfortunately, aren't always so quick to call me. The times they haven't when they should have, have cost this club, in the aggregate, probably $300,000, and there's something for an efficiency expert to chew on. When should a floor boss be in doubt? Let me give an example.

I learned through the grapevine one day that a gambler named Joe Bernstein had just romanced the Sahara Club in Vegas for

$75,000 and was headed our way. I knew Joe well, a shrewd, hard player who may have $300,000 today and be broke tomorrow. When he comes to your club, it is not a time to be dull. This I had told all floor bosses. That evening, however, I walked in and found Joe at a 21 table with $14,000 of our money in front of him. He was "counting aces," as we say in the trade, and had played undisturbed through three shifts.

Counting aces is not, of itself, a crime. Not if the house lets you get away with it. It involves an excellent memory for cards and crafty betting. Joe was giving us the classic example. He was playing all seven hands at a table, betting $5 on each hand as the deal went around, determining where the aces were. Aces, of course, mean blackjacks, which pay off three-to-two on your bet. When Joe could see that four aces should come up on the next go-round, he would raise his bet from $5 a hand to $500. Then if he got the four blackjacks on his $500 bets, he cleaned up $3500 per deal. The miracle was he didn't have more than $14,000 after three shifts. I stopped that pitch in two seconds with the house rule that a dealer breaks open a new pack of cards for each go-round when $500 or more is bet. "You can't count aces on me, Joe," I said. He shrugged. "You'll have to admit I was doing it pretty good," he observed. I did admit it.

In a gambling house, unlike a regular business, it's the smallest things usually that cost the biggest money. An efficiency expert might never spot them and I spend my working day watching for them. It takes experience, an eagle eye and a sixth sense for the trivial. As a case in point, I was on the catwalk over Table 2 one afternoon, idly watching a dice game through the mirror while I talked to my wife on the telephone. The dealer, I had noticed, was having nose trouble. She kept dabbing with Kleenex. It wasn't that, however, that alerted me. It was something else, something I couldn't quite pinpoint. It was more like a hunch until I finally saw it. "Oh, oh, honey," I said to my wife, "I've got to hang up. A queen down there is about to steal." A dice dealer normally is just as interested in the bounce of the cubes as the player. This girl wasn't. She kept glancing about the room as she dabbed her nose. I did not actually see her take chips from the rack; yet I knew she had. I called a floor boss and took her off. As she came into the office I noticed the tuft of Kleenex in her apron pocket. I reached in and took out two $100 chips.

"How much have you stolen?" I demanded.

"I swear on my mother's grave—"

That did it. I discharged her forthwith. She was through in Nevada's legal gaming industry and it was a shame. She was young, attractive and a good dealer, but she couldn't distinguish between the boss' bankroll and her own. A dealer is the steward of your money when she's working: it can leak out fast enough without thievery. A look at this girl's record should have tipped off our personnel office. Prior to coming to Harolds Club, she had worked here and there, usually in a store or shop dealing in money or valuables, and she never stayed long in one place. As an employer of thirty years, I would have spotted that instantly. I will say for the girl that she didn't stoop to stealing silver dollars or $5 chips. She went for the big ones, C-markers, and she didn't cut anyone else in on the act. She was a loner and therefore more dangerous. When I checked her out and she started to leave, I said, "Now, honey, don't slam the door." She looked at me with utter scorn. "I *never* slam doors," she replied. She didn't, either. They just closed firmly behind her.

Maybe it's the twenty or more cups of coffee I drink each irregular day that keeps me alert to little things. Maybe it's the fact I have learned to sleep fast when I do sleep. In the Army I was assigned to drive my commanding officer, who told me just once he didn't tolerate drivers who had to be awakened every time he wanted to move. "You won't have any trouble with me, sir," I assured him. "In civilian life I own a gambling house. I can't afford to sleep much." He didn't quite believe it so we made a standing bet of one cigar. Any time he caught me asleep, I would pay; every time he found me awake and ready to go, he would pay. I smoked his cigars throughout that tour of duty and paid him only once.

At home in the post-war world I'm not playing for cigars. I

must recognize instantly when someone is taking an advantage. Every day, all day, as a result, I am watching for the little telltale signs. I caught one the other day when I noticed a girl leaning on her elbow while dealing cards. When the players left, I went to her table, took the cards and dealt a few hands to show how she had looked.

"Oh I wasn't *that* bad," she retorted.

There was, I observed, no concern in her voice. Another sign. "Are you tired?" I asked.

"Yes," she said, too hastily. "I am, as a matter of fact."

"Haven't you had your rest period each hour?"

She said she had, though still quite airy about it all. This girl, incidentally, had dealt for us four and a half years and it was the first time I'd had occasion to correct her. Sometimes this means a man has started telling a woman how wonderful she is. I suggested she take off the rest of the shift and go home.

"If you're sending me home," she snapped, "I quit."

"No." I told her. "Now you're fired."

She flounced out the door and, sure enough, was met by a gentleman. I could not take her back no matter how good an efficiency expert's rating card might have shown her to be. If I did, she, not I, would be running this business. This is a very subtle fact about women employees. I don't fire many and I almost never hire back the ones I do. That is my policy and I carry it over to my personal life. When I make a decision, I stick with it. My first wife Dorothy, for instance, ended a discussion one day with the statement, "Maybe you ought to give me a divorce." I didn't hesitate. I gave it to her. If I tell a woman I love her, I mean it, and if the game is over, I cash in my chips. When I tell a man I am going to fight him, I will fight. When I fire an employee, it has to stick. The elbow-leaning dealer demonstrated clearly she was going to work on her terms. not mine. There simply isn't room for that in a business where the money flows both ways so swiftly.

Every woman employee of a gaming house is a dangerous employee simply because she's a woman. Though it would be most difficult to show this fact on rating cards, it gets a great deal of attention from me. I make a point of speaking to our classes for new dealers. I particularly warn the girls against men who become overly friendly or complimentary, or who like to lean across the table. "He's either after the money in your rack," I tell them bluntly, "or he wants to get into your bed. Given his choice, I believe, he probably would go for the money. So let's both play it safe and sane. Discourage romancers." The talk helps some, though not nearly so much as my unexpected appearance on the premises at any hour of the day or night.

Usually, to make my presence known, I can find reason for an announcement over the PA system, which reaches to every room and floor in the club. On a winter's day, for instance, when there aren't many tourists in town and the play is quiet, I may blast out with something like: "This is Harold Smith, Sr., the only operator in Reno today with more employees than patrons . . . So let's cheer things up . . . Bartenders, buy everyone in the house a drink." (I know this will wake up Daddy because he owns the liquor concession). An effiiciency expert also might cringe at the expenditure, but the announcement serves a double purpose. The help knows the boss is present and aware of business conditions; the free drink helps keep our handful of customers from drifting over to Mister Harrah's club.

At any hour of the day or night I may take the microphone to plug the show in our Fun Room. "Make your reservations with any floor boss," I urge. "If you don't know a floor boss when you see one, just look for an intelligent, handsome gentleman with a name badge on his chest who seems to be quietly musing on conditions of the world today." This, I have reason to believe, generates a certain activity among floormen. Sometimes it also provokes a chuckle or two.

Over-all, actually, we've managed to maintain pretty wonderful crews at this club and all they need is an occasional jogging. It is part of my improbable job to see that they get it, always remembering they're laymen, really, whom we are teaching to be gambling club workers. Not every operator has been as lucky at this as we. I remember only too well one man who tried to open a club in Nevada. He had been highly successful in business in another line outside the state and sank $5,000,000 in this venture. I took one look on opening day and saw the inevitable result: F-L-O-P. Intelligent and shrewd though he was in his own line, his money was going to go out every door. He lost one million between April 1 and December 1 and ended up in a sanitarium. As we say in the trade, he got romanced.

I recall another instance. The owner of an established casino died and his brother attempted to continue the operation. Suddenly a rush of applicants for employment came from every corner of the globe. Every thief in the business wanted a job with this pigeon. Many got jobs because he didn't know how to screen gaming employees. And he didn't know how to watch them. While he stood in one room counting nickels—literally—they carried currency out through the doors. I would defy a non-gaming efficiency expert, furthermore, to detect the leakage.

There are many, many ways in which your money can leak accidentally. Dealers can and do make physical mistakes. They miscount cards or misdeal, in which case we must order a redeal or pay, ever mindful they must not offend the customer. A girl in a blank moment may start paying off with $20 chips instead of 5's, and in no time has given away several thousands of dollars. (Some players call her attention to the mistake; some don't.) Actually, mistakes like this are of little consequence in the over-all picture. I have made them myself as a dealer. I know too well those crazy moments when you just can't think straight. Only the other night, in Mister Harrah's club—where I was having a nice run of luck at 21—the dealer suddenly couldn't count. His mind simply saw the numbers out of pattern. When I tried to point it out to him, he insisted he was right. That will happen to some employee in your club every day or so and I know it will. One of our cashiers overpaid a customer $5000 once by just such an accident. She still works here.

Some people in this world, of course, are constantly on the search for such mental lapses. They capitalize on mistakes. I am thinking now of a millionaire whose name I must withhold because of the laws of libel. At the moment, anyway, he's having financial troubles of another sort with Uncle Sam. When this man first came to town, Daddy cottoned to him like a kid to Santa Claus. He wanted him for a Harolds Club customer and told every employee personally to do everything possible to make this man happy. I was not so impressed although I couldn't say why. Perhaps the man was just too casual, too nicely humble. At any rate, he established his credit and limits with us and deposited $10,000 in an envelope with the cashier. The next day he was back to get his envelope, only—and he searched every pocket so convincingly—he had just happened to forget his wallet with the receipt. Remembering Daddy's buildup, the girl handed over the envelope without a receipt and the man went away, so humbly grateful, to gamble. A week later, however, he was back *with* the receipt. Now we were in a quandary. That receipt says we must hand over the amount marked on it— $10,000 in this case—and no arguments. We paid him and he went away again, still nicely humble.

A man like that is out to steal your bankroll and you know it. It's part of the challenge and condition that you match wits with him. My pet peeve, however, is the very, very correct dealer I see every day in my rounds. She would rate well on the efficiency cards, she follows the rules exactingly, and yet I can't call her my ideal dealer. We have a rule in the crap games, for instance, that you must throw the dice hard enough to hit the other end of the table. This, obviously, is to prevent dice manipulators from controlling their throws. We know that if the dice bounce off the end the control is broken. Now along comes a little old lady who actually is barely physically able to get the dice up to the end. The exacting dealer makes her throw over, and over, until the game is ruined. The dealer is correct, of course; painfully so. She is following instructions to the letter. Somehow, though, I must step in and correct this particular situation. I must do it with a very soft pedal so the old lady still can play, the other customers understand clearly, and the dealer isn't embarrassed. It isn't easy, believe me. Not when I have seen this same exacting dealer let a real crossroader "kill the dice" on her, or hold up the 5 so he makes his point every time. I can't embarrass her then, either. I can only take the cheater aside and tell him to be on his way.

♥

But I've forgotten our efficiency expert making his rounds. He's up in the Fun Room now, counting the bar tabs to see if the entertainment is an effiicient gambit. Anyone can count bar tabs. They don't measure the success of the Fun Room, for which I am the impresario. The expert, for instance, might never notice the two ladies who got up in the middle of the floor show the other evening and walked out to the powder room. I noticed and I think I know why they took a powder at that moment. A beautiful young blonde girl was singing. The ladies' gentlemen escorts had eyes only for her. The ladies didn't like the competition; it wasn't as if the pretty young blonde was laying a bomb and they could criticize her. Then they would have stayed. No, she was outshining them, so they got away for a moment. This is human nature again and the reason I hire no beauty contest winners as cocktail hostesses. It is why I instruct all hostesses to be most considerate of men customers but to concentrate on the ladies. (That distaff side of the business again.) And while you're digesting that I must sneak some corn chips up to the fourth floor storeroom of our office building, where some pigeons found an open window and are nesting. Part of my daily mess of irregularities is to bring them a snack so their young will hatch out happy and healthy.

Little handouts like that do not contribute to financial success or failure in a business, as I well know. They merely provoke the grimness in efficiency experts. Daddy has a habit they would like to stop too. Almost every day, if it's even halfway quiet, he strolls through the club in his shirtsleeves and July 4 necktie greeting folks. He stops at every table and welcomes the players to Harolds Club, instructing the dealer to double their bets if they win the next hand. This is the damndest phenomenon I have ever seen in a gambling house. If I, for instance, were to step up to a dice table where the play is hot and stop proceedings to make a hayshaker speech, there would be a riot. Daddy does it in that slow Vermont twang and they love him. Selah. No efficiency expert dares to suggest he stop that giveaway.

But there we are again. How could any outsider come in and expect to judge efficiency at games they've never dealt? I, for instance, want to hate the dealer I'm playing with. I have a feeling that's the only way I will win. Any time a dealer seems to be in sympathy with me, I blow my money. A gambler's superstition, perhaps, but in rating my dealers I must consider superstitions.

They help to bring in our customers. By the same token, I know that a dealer, to be any good at all, must basically want to win. Not for the house necessarily, but for her own pride. She can't help but be pleased when she hits a sequence of six cards into 21 and rakes in the money. Maybe she likes you, maybe she dislikes you, but she has won. This leads to another little-known—I doubt, in fact, if most dealers realize it themselves—habit they have. If you've been cutting the deck lucky for the dealer, she will return it to you again and again for the cut. I can't make a rule that everyone at the table must have a chance to cut during each go-round. Many players superstitiously don't want to cut at all. The basic truth is that we just can't have too many rules to any game. It's confusing and leads to dispute, just as too many laws make crimes more numerous.

Another thing an efficiency expert would never recognize in dealers is toke hustling—favoring the customer she knows will tip her. It doesn't take much for a dealer, subconsciously or otherwise, to prostitute herself in this subtle matter. In 21, for instance, if she has a pat hand she can indicate in ever so many ways and with ever so many small remarks to her favored player that he should take a card. Wandering about the club, or looking down from the mirrored catwalk, I spot this instantly. I must stop it and prevent it from happening in the future. It isn't fair to other customers. If it is at all obvious to the others, I must take the girl off the table immediately. The more subtle it is, of course, the more serious it may be. The player may be romancing the dealer and she may now be responding. I will send for a cup of coffee and watch this a while. How long has it been going on? How expensive is it getting?

◆

I listen carefully to the small talk of the dealers. I never want them discussing any player and how much he won or lost. I never, never want to hear one say: "I *took* him for this much." I hate even to write the expression in this book. With so many people working in the club, of course, it's impossible to stop all the yakking. I simply try to keep it to a minimum.

Similarly, in watching a dealer, I am interested if she seems to keep count of the currency she deposits in her table. In Harolds Club, as in most in Nevada, we play our games (except baccarat) with silver dollars or chips. It is neater and more efficient; a breeze stirred by a passer-by can't blow the bets around. When you tender currency, then, for your chips or silver, the dealer places it across a tiny slot in the table and presses it through with a plexiglass pusher. The currency falls into a box securely mounted underneath the table. Now if I notice a girl giving that currency much attention when she presses it through, as though she is counting it, I am most interested. It may be a tipoff that she is going to steal. She may be estimating the take at her table on a slow day as against a fat day. The fat day would, of course, be the time to take some since it would not be missed so easily. Again, I realize, I am suggesting my employees are potential thieves. I am not. I simply know that money is the most tempting commodity there is and a lot of it must pass through the hands of these stewards.

Finishing my coffee, I wander on, greeting old friends from Russian River bingo days, making Fun Room reservations and refunds, watching here, listening there. I hear the PA dispatching security officers—our internal police force—here and there to settle a card argument, remove a pesty drunk or help with a lady who has fainted. Few players are aware of the nature of these emergencies; the announcement says merely: "Security officer to Desk One" or "Security officer to Section Two." Even our "panic button," which is a particularly shrill, klaxon-like sound that means serious trouble to us, causes no ripple among the constant other noises in the customers' ears. We have three shifts of security officers, all big, burly men who can handle themselves in trouble or be gentle as St. Bernards. When they're not on a mission, I want them in the area of the credit office and cashier booths. I want their big, uniformed chests looming up there to discourage anyone who might be thinking of making off with the bankroll or any man who might tend to get rough if a girl won't cash his check. Their job is to prevent trouble, which we simply can't have in a gaming casino.

Perhaps I hear my own name on the PA system with a request to call a certain extension. I take the nearest phone and learn, perhaps, that two heavy players are in the house and want a marker for $5000. A gentleman from another club, of whom I don't think too highly, has assured the floor boss these men are good for the marker. That isn't quite good enough for me. There is real money, or chips that represent money, in the racks at the tables where these men will be playing. If money is taken from those racks, I don't want hot air or bad checks put back. I tell the gentleman that his OK doesn't stand the mint. They confer at the other end of the line and put another man on. Him I know to be a hoodlum, but no welsher. He says they are good for $4000 and that is good enough for me. I know he will make it good if they don't. I approve $4000 for them.

Now, perhaps, it is 3 AM and I notice heavy play at a roulette wheel. I know I had better give that a closer look. The other day, on this shift, the dealer needed an extra racker to help with the chips. One was standing eighteen feet away doing nothing, but the floor boss failed to send her to help. (This is a business, as I've tried to indicate, that can put you in the nervous ward fast. I'm just letting you try to wiggle your toe in my shoe for a moment.) In roulette, we use blue, red, orange, yellow and white chips simultaneously. When play is heavy, 400 chips of various colors may be spread over a table with every play. After the play, while the winners are being paid, the checks must be raked to the apron and racked. I constantly remind the floor bosses to watch for this and send help if a dealer is swamped. Send two check rackers if she needs them; it takes two when the play's that heavy. This day, in spite of my orders, I found play suddenly had boomed on Table 3 while the regular racker was away at the rest room. The floor boss hadn't noticed, so I summoned a helper from another table. Woman, as they say, works from sun to sun, but the gaming boss' day is never done.

I stay out of the restaurant's affairs because I can't even boil a hot dog, but there's not another part of this building, from slot machine repair to plumbing, that I don't watch. When we first presented Jan Peerce, the great tenor, in concert at Bishop Manogue High School auditorium, I had to insist at the last moment that carpeting be laid in the aisles so the ladies in their fine gowns wouldn't be self-conscious of their own heel-clicking. When Harry James was to play our Fun Room, I personally had to supervise laying of plywood-carpet layers under the drum platform so the room wouldn't sound like a big drum. I've had to step into a game to quiet men players who were getting rough with the dealer. I could write another book just on the employees' troubles I've listened to and tried to help with.

In the early days of the club, before we could afford efficiency experts, I performed every chore in the place. That's precisely where I learned how things should be done. I dealt and helped customers, explained games, made refunds and watched over the whole operation. I counted money out to the tables and counted it back into the vault. I doubt, in fact, if anyone in this world has ever counted as much cash money, piece by piece, as I have. One shift might add up to $150,000 on a busy day and you didn't count it once. You counted three times to be accurate. If a bundle of $10,000 was to go out to a cashier, it must be accurate. Discrepancies could jeopardize someone's job. When I went into the Army in World War II, Daddy had to take over my tasks and he needed a full-time helper.

It was then that the praise-pinching old Yankee paid me the highest compliment I've ever had. "I just don't know how you did all that work," he said. With Daddy, of course, hard work is the greatest of all virtues. I smiled a wry smile. I never expected to be doing all this. I meant to be a concert violinist.

♣ ♣ ♣ ♣

"Tag Up And Run"

IN EVERY PERSON's life, I suppose, there's a moment to which he can look back and say: *"That* was when I became aware of myself, my circumstances, surroundings and family, and saw they weren't like other people's." It was the moment perhaps when you realized you wouldn't just drift along forever as a child, from chores to school to play, but would require an identity, recognition, maybe even justification for being here, and somehow you, and you alone, must find the way. This happened to me in Cleveland, Ohio, in about 1920, when I was ten years of age.

It was not a happy period of my life. I discovered that too. I was lonely, confused, frustrated. Up to that moment I accepted it as a condition that some people had money, talent, education and two parents for love and affection; some didn't. It hadn't occurred to me before to question our circumstances. You never miss fine food until you've learned to eat well.

Mama, Raymond and I lived then at 1919 East 55th Street, in what had once been Cleveland's fashionable East Side. It wasn't fashionable any longer; it was survival. Mama and Daddy were divorced and he was off in the West in his dogged pursuit of the amusement park dollar. To keep us, she leased the old three-story mansion and rented its twenty-three once-elegant, gaslit rooms to lodgers. Raymond and I shared a double bed in a lightless closet that had been the butler's pantry. I was Number One boy for housework.

I washed windows, scrubbed floors, mowed lawns, raked leaves, swept and dusted. In those days, you used a carpet sweeper which raised clouds of dust that settled quickly on the knobby old furniture and you took after it with cloth or turkey wing duster. I remember well these tasks I performed, and thoroughly, because Mama was as meticulous in housekeeping as she was in her person. Raymond, three years older than I, did little. In a vague way, I understood he was sickly from chronic ear trouble, though he played a pretty fair game of football, and I sensed that Mama favored him over me. "Mama," I finally protested, "I don't mind helping, but why doesn't Raymond do his share?" "Raymond," she replied tartly, "can't do a good job." It was not a satisfactory answer. I commenced to resent menial chores. Perhaps that was the beginning of my awareness.

Or maybe it had been festering in me for some time, like the splinter I ran in my bare foot one summer and discovered weeks later when it worked to the surface in a yellow pustule. I wasn't comfortable in Cleveland and that old rooming house, or with the handsome man with the Star car who seemed to be Mama's husband and yet wasn't quite our father. We hadn't come there as other families did, with moving vans piled high and whoops of excitement for a new old house to explore. Mama had run away with the handsome man. Daddy, in his laconic way, gathered up Raymond and me and deposited us on her doorstep like some baggage she'd overlooked.

It still isn't easy to face. I attempt it only from maturity, when I've had two families myself and am more sophisticated in the ways of men and women. As I hunt for the words to set it down candidly, Mama and Daddy still are alive, in Reno, living only a few blocks from me and each other. Each has married four more times. Daddy has sired three more children. As I track back on their ill-starred relationship, I see two adamantly opposite personalities who chanced for a while—she at sixteen and he at nineteen —to be man and wife.

I am a product of this union but, please, do not mistake me. I have always acknowledged there is no other man I should rather have had for a father. Squabble though we have, I've never worked for another man. Similarly, no other woman could have been so perfectly my mother. My restless, sensitive nature is straight from her. Individually, each of them has tremendous human qualities. But there are combinations in life, just as in cards or dice, that are never compatible. Take sixes. Toss a six with a five and you have eleven, a winner. Toss six with a one, seven, and you win. Six in most combinations is a good number. But on the first throw, when it lands with another six, you lose. Daddy and Mama were like that, two sixes on their first throw.

♠

Always, as gamblers know, there are considerations. Daddy, who can josh as he doubles bets for a houseful of players today, was a perfect symbol of the rocky Vermont soil that spawned him; a tough, undemonstrative, self-sufficient Protestant farm boy who got a minimum of love and attention and didn't miss it. Hard work was his key to life's problems. When he was seven, his father died; he had to quit school with somewhat less than a rudimentary education to help support his widowed mother, then ventured off the farm to try his hand running wheel games at the county fairs. Sixty-odd years and several millions of dollars haven't changed his basic nature. Dora May Pigeon, who was to be my mother, was the very antithesis of Daddy. Though a Vermonter too, by birth, she was of French-Canadian stock, small and dark, petitely pretty, warm-tempered and demonstratively Catholic. Her mother died before she was two and her father a year later. She grew into her teens in the home of my great grandmother, Delia Danyow, who had ten children, endless chores and little time for humoring a would-be princess. Mama should have been an only child in a rich household. She was to spend her life flitting from one hard rock of reality to another in search of love and attention. She found precious little of either with Raymond I. Smith.

For a time she worked hard at her marriage and Daddy. She got him into her church temporarily and went out on the road to help him at the fairs, amusement parks and carnivals. Daddy's gimmick in those days was always a wheel game, sort of a farmer's roulette in which you bought a chance and might win a pocket knife, which he would buy back for cash. He and Mama traveled the country like gypsies from fair to fair and dollar to dollar. Raymond was born at Burlington, Vt., in 1907, then Daddy was off as peanut butcher on the *Denver & Rio Grande,* selling newspapers, refreshments and gewgaws, and I was born February 23, 1910, in Denver, Colorado. There is nothing to indicate he celebrated the occasion by getting drunk or giving away cigars. Daddy never drank and never smoked. He was to be all his life the proudest of teetotallers and on joyful occasions the most aloof of men.

Raymond's and my boyhood was a series of migrations from school to school. I started kindergarten in Albany, N.Y., but didn't finish the year because Daddy was off to the carnivals. Mama took us to live with Great Grandmother Delia at Vergennes, Vt., where I started first grade in September. I was withdrawn November 11, 1918, Armistice Day. We were shuffling off to Buffalo.

Two very special moments occurred there. My demonstratively religious mother personally took me to enroll in St. Thomas Parochial School. I should mention here that in Vergennes my great grandmother had shown me more of religion than any person before or since and for her I light a candle every time I enter a church. Love and obedience she taught, and especially that spiritual love the Lord finds pleasing. She taught it and demonstrated with her hard-bitten husband, ten children and assorted waifs like us. Honor your father and mother, she preached, for mothers are only a little less than the holy angels. My mother somehow embraced the form and missed the essence. Less than a year after she enrolled me at St. Thomas, with admonitions about the higher life, I saw her kiss a man who was not my father.

I remember that moment as though it were only five minutes ago. I walked in from the hallway and he was kissing her ardently, right there in our home, and Mama didn't protest. She saw me. She kissed him back, hard, on the lips. At eight years of age you react more from sensation than judgment. I felt an agony of protest, a helplessness so deep I was limp. Yet I couldn't cry out. Something in me wilted. I had been aware of this handsome new face about the house when Daddy was away. I had seen and resented the fact that he did many nice little things Daddy didn't do. Hating him, realizing suddenly Mama was not an angel, though I didn't know just why, I stumbled from the room. I told no one, not even Raymond. It was something, somehow, I could talk about with no one. Jack Dempsey became my hero that July when he won the world's heavyweight boxing title, so I talked about him. Dempsey, I read in the newspapers, had fought his way out of the West with his fists and could beat down with those same fists any obstacle that stood before him. His lean brown physique weaved and bobbed through all my daydreams. In my wildest fancy, however, I could not have believed that one day Jack Dempsey and I, good friends, would walk down South Virginia Street in a small Nevada city, clowning together. Or that I would ever come near things like a rifle or pistol or horse with silver saddle mountings.

The life of a man, I have found, is twisted this way and that by the many decisions he alone can make. The first decisive one of my life, and this is the other memorable moment of that period, was made there in Buffalo. In my second year of grade school, knowing all that an eight-year-old could, I abandoned angels. I informed the good sisters I was leaving St. Thomas because they taught far too much religion and not enough arithmetic. Perhaps it only proves how you never know what you'll need most in this life. I successfully affected the transfer to public school and found I didn't care too much for arithmetic anyway.

We were still in Buffalo and it was still 1918 when I awakened one morning with a choking chest cold. I called for Mama. No reply. I called again, hoarsely, and Daddy shuffled in. Mama was gone, he said in his poker-faced way. She'd left during the night. Blown town, I believe he said, with the handsome man. Fighting back the terror in my chest and trying to be manly, I asked him what to do for my cold. He told me to take some cough drops. So I did.

If I ached to ask how he felt and what we were going to do without Mama, I held my tongue. He wouldn't show his feelings, I knew, and I couldn't let him see mine. Maybe I acquired a philosophy there. There are far more women than angels on this earth. When a woman looks at another man, you might as well pass. Count up your chips. You're out of the game. Daddy knew the truth of that then. I was to have it proved to me forcefully later.

Daddy's immediate problem, of course, was what to do with two children. He had to be free to travel where the dollars were; boys eight and eleven would only be excess baggage. Being resourceful, he located Mama quickly enough in Cleveland, bundled up Raymond and me and we boarded a train. I don't recall Daddy saying a hundred words between Buffalo and Cleveland. I listened to the clickety-clack of the wheels and prayed everything would be right again when we got to Mama. It wasn't. Daddy rang the bell and the door opened. She didn't catch us into her arms for a hug and kiss. She simply burst into tears while Raymond and I stood awkwardly on one foot and the other. Finally Daddy asked: "Can we come in?" She stood back and we entered the old mansion. There we stood some more. Then Daddy turned and left. The baggage was delivered.

That was our introduction to Cleveland. I will always remember it as a bleak, cold place where the warmest of hopes shrivel quickly. Surely they did for one eight-year-old in the months that followed. A big city rooming house in that time and location was not a nursery school; the innocence or naivete of a child vanished swiftly. Mopping stairways, I couldn't help but witness the angry fights between drunken men and women in which the vileness of words was only a little less shocking than the hatred laid bare; hatred seemed to me to hang permanently in those dark corridors. Lying in my bed at night, with Raymond snoring beside me, I heard men do things I had never imagined. Cleaning up after them, I had an overpowering impulse to wash and that was when I began carrying soap in my pocket. Watching Mama cling to the handsome man who promised love and attention, while I performed chores, I felt more and more my alone-ness. She got a divorce from Daddy, legally abandoning that hard rock of reality, though he had to pay $5 a week for support of Raymond and me. Daddy also sent $5 for our spending money, which Mama kept. The handsome man, it turned out, couldn't marry her because he already had a wife and family in England. One day he kissed her, not so ardently, and drove away in the Star car. Life went on with its window washing, scrubbing and carpet sweeping.

The sliver in my foot was festering. I was thinking. Dream I might, of titans like Jack Dempsey and Tris Speaker, but my world of reality was closing tighter about me. I only needed to step out of the house to be reminded of it. "Hey, Four Eyes!" came the cry from the street. I had had to wear glasses since my bout with German measles in Buffalo. "Come on out, Flycatcher!" came another taunt. I breathed with my mouth open because I had adenoids. Kids were rough on me, none more so than my brother who, with a buddy, once tried to make me swallow hen manure. Already I had taken a secret vow to defeat him with my fists by my twenty-first birthday. But I didn't cry then and I'm not crying now.

Many a man before me—I think specifically of Eddie Cantor, Georgie Jessel and Walter Winchell—was to discover the *quid pro quo,* the something for something you acquired by growing up in a tough city neighborhood. You learned among other things, that you can only be driven so far; when your back's to the wall, that's as far as you go. East 55th was that kind of neighborhood. It was a year before I even understood some of the names they called me. Most of the neighbors were Jewish, many of them immigrants; down through the ages, there has never been an easy way for Jews. They, however, have accepted the condition and challenge and gone on to win. From them I learned to play the game, any game, thoroughly, tenaciously and with victory in mind. Many of those kids with whom I went to Central High School in Cleveland were determined to battle their way up to professions like law, medicine, dentistry and the arts and learned to play the game right there on the corner lots. Troubles you might have, more troubles in fact than a kid should carry, but now you're on third base with the tying run and a long fly ball drifts out toward center field. "Tag up and run, you schmuckhead!" I still hear the angry, imploring call crying down through the years. They woke you from your blues. They made you play the game. They weren't halfway competitors. From them, too, I learned chess, a great game of discipline for an impetuous boy, and once, with their driving, got so far as to give a fairly good account of myself against the Cleveland city champion.

I was dreaming, too, and assaying that awareness of myself, make no mistake about it. I was aware now that Raymond— Mama would always speak of him as "my poor boy"—could come and go at will while I hurried home from school to start my chores. I would find my way. For some time, I realized, I had been growing fonder of music. Not piano music, not trumpets with their harsh blaring, absolutely not the sobbing saxophone so popular in the '20s. It was the violin that caught my ear and seemed to bring the great longing inside me almost to the bursting point. This is it, I finally told myself. Somehow, sometime, I will be a concert violinist and will make such great music the vast hall will grow still and people will never know I once was an open-mouthed, adenoidal four-eyes whose angel mother had feet of clay and a tireless carpet sweeper. The dream, as it grew, began to include a girl who would be an angel on earth. She would have all the spiritual beauty of sainted Grandmother Delia and the physical beauty of a princess. At the age of ten, dreams satisfy where prayer fails.

I knew about prayer, of course. Mama made us go to church every Sunday and some of it penetrated my growing discontent. I recall distinctly the Good Friday night I heard a Jesuit drive home the message of the 8th Commandment. *Thou shalt not bear false witness* . . . "You will surely burn in Hell if you violate this commandment," he admonished. I hasten now, therefore, to complete the record on Mama. Feet of clay she may have had, and I feel the clods in my own toes when I say it, but she did her best once she had sole responsibility for her two boys. An outcast herself, with almost no education and an all but unquenchable thirst for affection, she tried to raise us to be decent. I finished grade school and entered high school under her prodding, though I was an indifferent student. We never again got cough drops when a doctor's ministrations were needed. We ate three square meals a day, regardless of finances. Mama may have hated hard work as thoroughly as Daddy loved it, but she did it all those years in

Cleveland. She worked like Hell on that dreary old house and she turned up neat as a pin for dinner. In any criticism of her for what I may have felt, these facts must be a consideration. I should be the last to fault her for flights into fantasyland.

My own fantasy of the violin was to occupy my mind for several years. And, in spite of my playmates' examples, I simply was not aggressive enough to enlist the help I might have had at Central High. It is difficult when you're young, for one thing, to describe how much you appreciate an intangible thing like music. I couldn't even say where I had gotten the inspiration. So I couldn't presume to ask at school for one of the loaner instruments they had. Finally, when I was fourteen, I poured out my hopes in a letter to, of all people, crusty old Daddy, and asked for $150 to buy a violin. It is a strange fact of my life that every productive quality I have developed, from self-confidence to decisiveness, has come from trying to please him. By 1924, Daddy was established with his wheels at Chutes-at-the-Beach in San Francisco and was well fixed. He didn't think $150 for a violin was frivolous. He sent it immediately. Later, when he learned that I was studying hard and practicing hard, he was pleased. Daddy could always appreciate something if you did it by hard work.

The money came to Mama, however, and she was most reluctant to invest it in a violin. By the time I managed to wheedle it out of her, in fact, only $100 was left. I fairly flew with it to Mister Fred Hicks, a music teacher in our neighborhood. He was much more than a music teacher really. He was a poor man in money but a man of great elegance in manner and belief. He lived religion, all Ten Commandments and every dram of love his fellow man might need, though I couldn't tell you which denomination he favored. Years later I was to find another, Phil Spitalney of the all-girl orchestra fame, who knew the old man and revered his memory. On that glowing day of memory, Mister Hicks bundled himself quickly into his greatcoat and escorted me down to Superior Avenue to select just the violin for his new pupil. He pressed it up under the Van Dyke beard at his chin and drew back the bow. The angels themselves have never heard such an instrument, I'm sure. I still have it, with its original case, though the music is never so great when I bow out a tune for my slot machine-playing lady friend.

If practice, a loving teacher and a dream could make a musician, I should be the Fritz Kreisler of my day. I ran home from school gladly to get the chores finished so I could practice. My own pantry room was too dark to read music so I would go to one of the vacant rooms, if we had any; if not, to the room of a tenant who liked me. Either way, I worked at it two hours a day. Talent? Who needed talent when you had desire and a hundred-dollar violin? Wonderful Mister Hicks charged $1.50 a lesson, which I wheedled out of Mama, each lesson to last 45 minutes. He saw what was in my heart and gave me two to three hours when he could. I may not have done well in school or at baseball and I still couldn't lick brother Raymond, but at last I was finding the one thing I believed I did well. One day I put it all to the test. I tried out for concertmaster of the Central High School orchestra. The teacher asked each of us to play the violin, without vibrato. At last my turn came, the first great test of my life. I started to play and suddenly the violin was a thing alive. "Mr. Smith!" the teacher shouted. "I told you to play without vibrato!" I gulped. "I'm sorry," I said. "That wasn't vibrato. I'm so nervous my hand is shaking." I didn't get the position. Many years later, shaking one dice for an amount of money that could have cost me my gaming club, I chanced to glance at that same hand. It was steady as the Rock of Gibraltar. In all truth, that long ago concert-mastership had meant more to me than a $25,000,000 business.

Daddy sent for Raymond and me in the summer of 1924 to come to San Francisco and help with his games. Operating several concessions as he was, he could use two hustling teenagers. He got one eager one, I know; anything to my mind was better than Cleveland. I started by stacking leather bottles in pyramids for the customers to knock down with baseballs. I piled them quickly and deftly for I had a goal. If perfection is necessary to become a great violinist, I told myself, then everything I do must be perfectly executed; to be slovenly in one performance would mean imperfection in the other. No amusement park ball piler ever was driven by such lofty ambition. Daddy ambled by and beamed.

He was to have Raymond and me back four summers. I loved

it. Raymond did it as a chore. We lived with Daddy and saved most of our $35 weekly pay (this was 1924, remember) for winter. Winters I returned to Mama's housework, my violin practice and school—now the dullest drudgery of all—and attended every concert and vaudeville performance I could. Something began to ferment in my mind as I listened to skilled performers; something I couldn't quite identify. Maybe, with money in the bank, an identity of my own wasn't so urgent. I'd long since surpassed Raymond at bottle piling and barking up customers. Even Mama's demands now seemed almost trivial. Maybe, too, I had exhausted kind Mister Hicks' teaching talent and the Golden Gate was calling. I told myself I would really push the musical career there. At seventeen, having finished my third year at Central High, I abandoned formal education. Had the gambler been born? I'm not sure.

Back in San Francisco and working year-round for Daddy at Chutes-at-the-Beach, I auditioned with a Mister Hoag, a thoroughly fine musician who played in the San Francisco Symphony and conducted the Alcazar Theater orchestra. He accepted me as a pupil and I worked hard. Not nearly so hard, though, as I had with my first hundred-dollar violin in Cleveland. Maybe I was having a recurrence of chronic lack of confidence—it always seems to recur when I'm close to Daddy. At any event, my bottle-stacking fingers didn't seem quite so sure on the violin strings, my ear for notes not so clear. I began to wonder if I really had a talent.

In 1928, with Daddy remarried and his new wife and I not hitting it off, I moved to a rooming house. There I met a woman much older than I, a professional violinist who had led many orchestras in San Francisco. I studied with her too, though she drank excessively and often we could only sit and talk of music. She introduced me to other professionals, the first group of people I had met who really seemed to understand musical ambition. They were drinkers too, I discovered, often in need of a dollar or two to tide them over, and too often ready to fly at each other's throats in vain arguments about nothing. Ever so slowly, I felt the stars in my eyes dim out. Squinting, I could almost smell the same jealousies and hatreds that permeated the old rooming house in Cleveland.

At about this time, too, I needed a bow re-haired and sought out a craftsman on Market Street. Most of his business was with professional musicians. I blithely told him I was planning a career in music. He looked up suddenly and stared at me over the violin in his hands.

"Young man," he blurted, "if you know any other way to make a living, take it. I have them in here all the time. Their credit's no good. They drink too much. Not one of them has a damned thing to his name."

It troubled me. I left the bow to be haired but I took another look around that dreary rooming house and I couldn't shut my eyes to truth. I loved music as a man loves his virgin bride. I had dollars to rattle in my pockets and I didn't ever want to be broke again. I had studied with Mr. Hoag two months now. I went to him for advice.

Mr. Hoag gave it to me straight. Yes, with very hard practice and five years time, he possibly could make a professional violinist of me. A concert violinist? Never! As I had secretly suspected for so long, I just didn't have the talent.

I felt no grief. There is a time, as Daddy had demonstrated when Mama left, when you might as well pass, count up the chips and get out of the game. For me, there was just another decision to make. I closed the case on my violin and locked it. Perhaps I would open it now and then to play *Kiss Me Again* for a lady friend playing the slot machines and yakking, or a state senator friend romancing a 21 game. But the big dream was dead. Not shattered; just dead. At seventeen I didn't have what it takes to be a concert violinist but I seemed to have what it takes to be an amusement park games operator.

Right there the gambler *was* born.

10

♦ ♦ ♦ ♦

The Road To Reno

THERE ARE UP and down times of life, I have found, just as there are winning and losing cycles with dice, swirling in currents of good fortune or bad but all adding inevitably to your total experience and making you what you are. My dad didn't blow up when I announced I was tossing over the five years of lessons on my hundred-dollar violin. Maybe, in his self-contained way, he was pleased his teen-age son had made a decision without help. Maybe the ex-farmer recalled that when one crop doesn't succeed, you try another. Perhaps he'd taken inventory of the healthy young body, the strong will and a mind that wasn't too dull, and saw a likely employee who wouldn't steal too much of the profits. He allowed he could use me in the concessions at Chutes-at-the-Beach. A new current swirled through my life.

It was characteristic of many, many scenes between me and Daddy. I had sought him out that morning at his nail game stand where he was opening crates of china. He heard me out. Then, my immediate future decided, he said: "Get me a hammer."

Now we didn't have a hammer that I knew of at any of our five booths. I wandered through them, looking half-heartedly, knowing I wouldn't find one, and ambled back to tell him I couldn't find a hammer. I since have seen Daddy's sudden anger on many occasions but on this morning it flared like Olympian lightning. "I won't stand any can't-me guys around," he snapped. "When I say get a hammer, get one!"

As I walked away I realized I'd better find a hammer or not come back. For the first time, really, I wondered where indeed there might be a hammer in that big amusement park. Someone in all the booths along that pike, or midway, must have one, they all did a little carpentry now and then. I went down the line asking each concessionaire. At about the third booth, a little Greek named Mike said sure he had a hammer. It was as simple as that. I delivered it to Daddy who took it and began to rip open crates. He didn't say "Thank you," he didn't deem it necessary. I have been getting hammers for Daddy ever since, one way or another. I never again have said I couldn't.

Daddy was to demand more of me always than his other employees. "You stand right there at the center of that counter," he would say, "and sell every person that walks by." Or coming up quietly, he'd command: "Speak up to 'em, son. Speak loud. They ain't goin' to hear your pitch if you're whisperin'. An' smile," he insisted. "Show your teeth. These folks are here for fun and recreation." Another time, sternly: "Don't be a smart alec. Don't josh ladies old enough to be your Mama. *They're* havin' the fun—let *them* be the comics; you're workin'." Or he'd growl: "They're walkin' by you! Get out in the pike and turn 'em. Get thirty feet out front and direct the traffic to your stand." It was root, hog, or starve, with him. I soon lost any shyness I may have had. Shouting to be heard over the merry-go-round calliope, I developed a voice like a teen-age foghorn. Turning customers to my booth gave me the gall of a medicine man. And stamina—well, Daddy never heard of rest breaks. Not even to eat.

I didn't satisfy him, of course; not once in the months I worked there. He never indicated I did, at least, and after a while I quit hoping he might. You can't satisfy a taskmaster who's also a teacher and I was Example A for the other employees, a boy who had to earn his salt, and just incidentally the boss' son. I tried hard. I never tried harder to please anyone in my life. I would see the tall, spare figure ambling up the Midway and I'd practically shove tickets in people's hands and get them playing. Daddy would glance at the cash drawer, see that it was in order, the booth neat and clean—I thanked God for Mama's rooming house training—then he'd mosey on without a word. I may not have satisfied him but I learned the trade. After that year on the beach at San Francisco, I couldn't have run a sloppy, unprofitable or tricky game if I tried. With Daddy you didn't stand still; you had to improve. You built pride and initiative with every hard day's work. And if he didn't pay off in smiles and kind words you learned to take your satisfaction from the day's report, the tabulation of profit or loss. Long ago I'd heard my Jewish friends say the bottom line was what counted. I learned now what they meant. I made money for Daddy.

Life wasn't by any means all a grim series of lessons. Daddy had bounced around carnivals and amusement parks long enough by then to be broad-minded about a boy seventeen-turning-eighteen. He wasn't a baby-sitter. At eighteen, he figured, you were a man. Though I still didn't drink or chase girls too energetically, neither did I have a curfew or sermons on whom I should cultivate. I had, in fact, the kind of liberty a teen-ager dreams of when he thinks about quitting school and I had the money in those boom days of 1928 to satisfy my fancies. Every day out there by the Pacific, with the carnival sights, sounds and smells, was pure exhilaration. As I gained moxie—confidence and know-how—I found it was downright fun to meet the public in its picnic moods, try to gauge human nature and persuade people to buy the game *I* was selling. Before work, if I chose, I could go downtown to the theaters to watch greats like Al Jolson or Eddie Peabody in person; when business was quiet on drippy nights and I wanted to take in the Symphony, Daddy wasn't too tough. Raymond and I had our own apartment—with so many fleas we even spread flea powder in the bread bin—and I could drive Daddy's Studebaker for a rental of 5¢ a mile. I was learning to play professional poker and blackjack and avoiding dice. "Friendly" crap games, I discovered at a very early age, have but one end: trouble. I also was starting to box a little, looking toward my twenty-first birthday and the long-promised duel in which I meant to reduce my athletic brother to size. He had a bank messenger job now that paid $16.25 a week, just about half what Daddy paid him for a reluctant weekend day at the beach. Raymond was never to like concession work or gaming. I found I loved them. The shriek of passengers swooping over the roller coaster dips while my customers plunked down their dimes was almost as delightful to my ears as Strauss waltzes on a violin. I might one day regret having passed up formal education but I could never say it's all bad for teen-agers to get out and start making decisions. The amusement park procedures I learned from Daddy in my late teens were far from a dull education.

◆

In 1929, despite the fact he already had a gold mine going in San Francisco, he took three concessions at Riverview Park in Chicago. I couldn't see how he meant to manage them, 2000 miles away, but I found out soon enough. He sent me to Chicago. I got no briefing or instructions; just a railroad ticket and a cashier's check for $1600. Maybe that was my short course in resourcefulness. Daddy failed to mention that a cashier's check is only a way of carrying money from one place to another; you can't walk into a bank and cash it. Neither did he tell me that Chicago is possibly the hardest city in the world in which to cash any check. He probably figured I'd find that out soon enough too.

I did when I deposited the check. I had only a few dimes in my pocket. The teller informed me I could draw no cash until the check cleared our San Francisco bank. So, at nineteen, I went out in a strange big city to live on my wits. I tried the YMCA first. The room they offered was so tiny you couldn't turn around; you had to back out. The bed was like a board and the bath was down the hall barracks style. It wasn't my concept of how an entrepreneur newly arrived from the Coast should live. I took my credit business to the Dasher Hotel, a small establishment on Belmont Avenue, and did a little better. Then, tightening my belt against my appetite, I hiked off to find Riverview Park. Once there I was perfectly content. An amusement park was home to me.

This was late in March. The season started in April. Our concessions included a dart game in which you tried to puncture balloons, a dish game in which you hurled wooden balls at china dishes, and a goldfish game of which I was to learn more later. At the moment I had to get my booths ready. I was determined, once I got some cash out of that bank, to handle Daddy's money more cautiously even than my own. The little black book in which I recorded expenses soon filled with the costs of carpenters, painters, electricians, materials and prizes. There was nothing to do but hire myself as helper, at no wage, to carry nails, lumber, paint. Those workmen ran me ragged. Then, in my first experience as an employer, I was faced with the task of hiring help. The candidates were from the usual transient labor pool that gravitates to amusement parks.

Somehow we got open. The dart and dish games showed they could make expenses. The goldfish game was a flop. For the first time in my life I was into a loser and it was the hammer incident all over again. Daddy hadn't sent me there to run losers. We had 10,000 goldfish in a small tank, and hoops covered with glazed paper. The player scooped with a hoop and tried to catch a fish. This was all he had to do; a five-year-old could have won at it. The trouble was no one would try. Why? Puzzling that out started analytical processes I was to apply to every gambling game I would ever own. This goldfish game seemed such a natural to me, as it must have to Daddy, because it was so easy for the player. Was I using the wrong pitch then? Was there something in my manner that scared off customers? I invented a dozen spiels. No luck.

Even a nineteen-year-old soon comprehends that the way to go broke is to try selling the American public something it doesn't want. I finally concluded that while there were maybe a million fishermen in Chicago, this was phoney fishing; it was anti-human nature. If I wanted my three square meals a day—and I'd found I did, in a little restaurant where a certain Polish waitress held forth—I must do something drastic. Like jettison Daddy's goldfish.

That wasn't easy to do since it would guarantee no profits for a while. I'd already lost our first batch of fish to poison from the paint and had had to replace them. I would need a substitute attraction pronto. I was tempted to try a nail game, in which you drive a twelve-penny nail in a block of wood. Other concession-aires advised me solemnly that would never go in Chicago; the last nail game operator barely got out ahead of the bill collectors. They seemed most eager to tell a downy-cheeked youth what would and wouldn't work. The former operator came by himself to sing his version of the blues. I saw a slovenly, defeated man in his sixties.

That set me thinking along other lines. I'd noticed in San Francisco when an operator begins to lose ground he either gets hang-dog or carries a chip on his shoulder. He tries to economize by giving cheaper prizes or, in the nail game, uses wood so hard no one can possibly win. With a vision of Daddy roaring in from the Coast for an accounting, and no money to go cabareting anyway, I devoted my evenings to finding the answer. Finally I decided to try the nail game, raise my price from 10¢ to 15¢ and give only the best of prizes. Down I would go if I must, but I'd go down with flags flying. Repeat customers, Daddy preached, are the profit in amusement parks. I needed one gimmick to drag people off the Midway, or pike as it's known, and bring them back over and over again.

I've always been one to act out situations and problems that stump me. Now I restricted myself to quarters with nails, hammer and blocks of wood. I concocted spiels and drove nails until my wrists were swollen and my tonsils ached. I got so good at it, I could drive a twelve-penny nail every time with just two hammer strokes. And suddenly I had my pitch. I would sell this game on the ease of it. Since I was a smallish lad of 143 pounds, I would concentrate on big men, particularly those strolling with girls, and challenge them to surpass my two-stroke performance. I wanted them to win, of course, so I chose medium soft wood and tested every block myself.

The night the nail game went into operation I was almost as excited as I'd once been with a new violin. Parking myself in the middle of the pike, hammer and wood in hand, I barked loud enough to be heard across Lake Michigan. *"If I . . . can drive this nail . . . in the block of wood . . . with two strokes of the hammuh,"* I shouted, *"You ought to do it in three strokes and WIN a PRIZE . . ."*

The first man to stop was a husky. "Let's see you do it," he challenged. I knew I was in.

Grinning to show all my teeth, I drew him slowly to my booth, gesturing for the onlookers to follow and see this contest. There was anything but vibrato in my hand when I set my nail. One-slam, two-slam; it was in to its head. The husky tried. He didn't quite make it. With the crowd watching, he plunked down a second 15¢ and tried again. This time he did it and won a pound-box of Temptation chocolates. I whooped as I handed him his prize. He was to come back nightly and carry home cartons of prizes.

Those prizes represented our margin of profit. I'd found a dish manufacturer in Chicago who let me take "seconds" for a few cents each. I selected those with the least visible defects. The candy I bought wholesale at 16½¢ a pound. Players started by winning chocolates and progressed into sets of china. At 15¢ a try, I could make money so long as they took dishes and I saw to it that they did, in swift progression from the expensive candy. I sold many crates of defective china as the months passed. Most weeks I cleared $1000, some weeks $1400. I paid all bills and dutifully deposited the money to Daddy's account. My wages—about $100 a week based on percentage—were chickenfeed in view of the profits, but money wasn't my god. I was intent on proving myself to the old Yankee in San Francisco.

I made it a point to find out why the nail game did work for me. Obviously it appealed to a man's ego, the key to any type of gaming. He derived a measure of satisfaction from driving a nail publicly and beating me. He carried away a tangible reward. It was *quid pro quo,* something for something; not *caveat emptor* as in so many amusement park games. Years before, Daddy had proved this policy at a country fair in Kansas. He'd set up his jacknife wheel between two dishonest games, he found, and was a little dubious whether he could make a dollar. The moment the farmers discovered, however, that at his wheel they actually won and that Daddy did redeem their prizes for cash, they gladly paid their money and took their chance. The sheriff closed all games before the day was over but Daddy, unlike the others, had money to pay his fine and get out of town. The underlying policy of all our operations, including Harolds Club, was formulated that long ago day in Kansas.

It worked for me that first season in Chicago. It worked so well, in fact, it wasn't long, what with the other concessionaires telling me how clever I was, before my own ego ballooned. I was to learn how costly this can be. One day I attended a concessionaires' meeting and a man buttonholed me. He had a new and untried gaming device involving a board with holes holding pickets of pins, through which you tried to propel marbles. The man offered me the patent for a very few dollars. I glanced at it and declared from my lofty nineteen-year-old wisdom it wouldn't earn the investment. Had I studied it thoughtfully, I might have noticed it involved many of the same elements of skill and dexterity as my nail game. I let my ego speak for me and it cost me about $50,-000,000. The device the man wanted to sell me was the original model of the now fantastically popular pinball machine.

Often enough, and particularly with an impulsive individual like me, I have found, folly breeds on success. You get out too far in front and running too fast. You hear the compliments and are deaf to the criticism. Much later I was to read and apply, as best my nature permitted, the advice Knute Rockne gave his great Notre Dame football teams. "Don't read the newspapers," he told them. "You just ain't as good as they say you are." At nineteen, rolling in profits up to $1400 a week, my ego was big enough to fill a moving van, and no one was there to tell me "You just ain't that good." Cocksure and cash in hand, I sought out some of the big Chicago gaming clubs I was hearing about. They were glad to see me and my money. There I discovered one of my oldest idiosyncrasies—I do not enjoy losing. Better men than I, of course, were rollicking along in the same spirit that summer of 1929.

The following October was to take the ego, if not the heart, out of a lot of us. Daddy, the original puritan on most forms of gambling, lost a bundle in the stock market crash. The next summer was grim for the concession business. There weren't enough people at Riverview Park, had I sold every one of them, to earn a living. You just can't sell fun and recreation to people who are scratching for eating money. I had to stick it out; it was all I knew. I played the horses all summer on my own money and came out about even. That is, as broke as when I started. Daddy couldn't criticize, though, having lost his Wall Street game. Actually, having worked stony ground all his life, he was already looking ahead to where the next crop of dollars might be.

♠

Back home in San Francisco for the winter, we were at his house one night playing cards when I happened to glance at the calendar. It was September. "Raymond," I said, pointing to the date, "you'd better start training. I'll turn twenty-one on February 23. We have a date with the boxing gloves." I don't recall his exact reply. Something offhand, I'm sure. Raymond still didn't take me too seriously.

He didn't know why I had to fight him. I suspect he doesn't really understand it to this day. Raymond has never felt a need to prove anything to anyone while something in me has cried out from childhood for recognition. A part of it naturally centered on him. He bullied me, as older brothers will, way back on the Vermont farm when he and his buddy tried to make me eat chicken manure. He always excelled in athletics while I contended with glasses and adenoids. He successfully avoided housework in Cleveland and accepted Mama's babying. I had promised myself, and Raymond, I would lick him on my twenty-first birthday. Like trying to please Daddy, it was something I had to do. Raymond never dreamed I would do it. It never occurred to me that I wouldn't.

I'd worked on my timing and footwork for two years. Now for four months I trained as rigidly as Jack Dempsey ever did for a title fight. I skipped rope, punched the heavy and light bags morning and evening and ran every mile of the way through Golden Gate Park to my work at the beach. With every step and every punch I chanted: "*I've got to win . . . I've got to win.*" I wasn't angry with my brother. I didn't hate him. He was a symbol. I couldn't lose. I had to defeat him with my hands or somehow know I would never be up to the challenges of adult life which would begin February 23, 1931. Something of my fever spread through the Smith household and among the concessionaires. We both had our supporters.

Raymond still wasn't taking it too seriously when we met that day in the old YMI gym off Market Street. He admitted later he expected to knock me out early and that would be that. Approximately thirty of our friends showed up. Only one who counted was absent. Daddy refused to watch the fight. Perhaps he sensed the desperation in me and knew Raymond had the advantage. Perhaps he was fearful. The doctor who had operated on Raymond's mastoid years before had said he must never be hit on or about his left ear. One solid blow, the doctor warned, would kill my brother. I, too, was aware of that. We agreed to six three-minute rounds. Herman Schweitzer, a professional acrobat, was to referee. My whole life seemed to hang right there in my hands as they laced on the gloves.

At the bell, Raymond came out coolly and efficiently. I sidestepped his first hammering right. I slipped another and knew a bursting jubilation. He was not going to get his quick knockout. My months of boxing had brought just a little more skill than he anticipated. I was just a little faster than he expected. I hooked him hard and felt the same confidence you know when you've doubled down your bet on a six-five and the ten falls for a perfect twenty-one. I looked for my opening. It was there, but dangerously close to his vulnerable left ear. I held my punch. He gave it to me again in the third round. It was only an instant when his arms were up; this time I needn't worry about his ear, I dug my left to his belly. When his hands came down I jarred my right to his jaw. As perfect a one-two as Dempsey ever threw in his prime. Raymond went down, and on his face I saw a look of utter disillusionment. He weathered the round and came out for the fourth to get me with one punch. He couldn't land it. I failed to knock him out but the decision was mine. After the fight, he congratulated me and demanded a rematch. "Any day!" I whooped gleefully. At that moment I felt invincible. There wasn't any rematch. Daddy said no. Maybe in his inscrutable way he knew the greatest good now had been accomplished and that a rematch might end in permanent defeat for me. He said only that we had work to do.

♣

Daddy had found a soft spot in the stony economic ground of

the Great Depression. Up at Rio Nido, fifty miles north of San Francisco on the Russian River, a Bingo game had folded. This is a resort area for Northern California where families for a century have gathered during summer. Bingo had done well there before the disastrous '30 season. Daddy thought it could be resurrected and took over the operation. He sent me up to run it. Bingo is, of course, a variation on the child's game of lotto. You buy a numbered card and a handful of markers. As numbers are drawn and called, you cover the corresponding number on your card. The first card to be filled wins the money. The game has had tremendous popularity in California from time to time. It was very good during the depression years.

The game we took over at Rio Nido, however, could hardly be called a golden opportunity. There was only a two-month season, for one thing. Families gathered there in about mid-June, when school let out, and stayed on through the middle of August, when school resumed. After Labor Day only the birds were left. Our game wouldn't, in fact, have provided full-time work for a healthy young man in ordinary times. There was a campfire gathering, community sing and entertainment by San Francisco radio stars each evening, then people drifted off to rest from a day of sun and swimming. You had maybe two hours for Bingo on week nights; on Friday and Saturday nights, with an influx of weekenders, you might get three hours. The depressed times, however, contributed several saving conditions. All we needed for our game was a frame lumber booth on bare earth with stools around a counter for the players, a board to light up the numbers as they were drawn, a lighted glass showcase for prizes. I wired that myself, though I'm an atrocious mechanic, and built a bedroom behind the booth. I found I could get by comfortably for about $2.50 a day.

One thing more I required. I knew I was cut from the same emotional cloth as my mother and clinging to the hard rock of Daddy's reality. Resent I might his domineering, but I couldn't escape his logic. "These people are here for fun," he had preached in San Francisco. "You're here to work." I knew I could blow it all at a summer resort in those self-indulgent Prohibition days. I faced the fact and agreed with myself to tend to business and not be swayed by impulse or skirts. That formula for self-discipline later—except for a period in which I went wild—was to preserve my equilibrium there and subsequently in the never-never land of Reno. I wasn't a genius at twenty-one, you must understand, and I wasn't a celibate monk. Daddy was just a little closer to my operations than God.

I had, of course, absorbed some traces of his craft. Bingo, I knew, is not a game for high-flying rounders. It's a mild gambling pastime for women and children. And while I don't like to refer to any lady of fifty as old—let's just say middle-aged—I knew I must sell my game to females in the fifty-upwards bracket. Young people understandably would have other fish to fry on summer nights. Fortunately I've always liked older ladies. I knew that you had to cater to them and walk a path of personal rectitude. Though the dance hall was only twenty feet from my Bingo booth, I resolved not to be seen there every night with pretty young girls. I would avoid the "whippersnapper" label.

Each morning I'd go down to the beach for a swim and exercise in the sun. Each afternoon I cleaned up my booth as if Mama herself were looking over my shoulder. Ladies don't like to sit on dusty stools or lay their arms on a dusty counter and it could get mighty hot on the Russian River on summer days. I scrubbed, raked, and wet down the dirt to kill dust. In the cool of the evening, when fresh breezes from the river stirred the redwoods, I would set up the game.

I still had to sell the people back on Bingo after the previous year's flop so I asked orchestra leader Jackie Souter to let me make an announcement the first night. In its way, that was important to my future too. It was my maiden appearance as a speaker before an audience of 2000 persons. I was fearful of vibrato in my voice which in turn could lead to a lack of confidence in my game. I rehearsed it and decided I must get it over fast. "My name is Harold Smith," I said. "I am running a new Bingo game and would appreciate it if you will come and look, whether you play or not." (Years later, I wasn't to take many more words to introduce Lily Pons to her premiere audience in Reno town.) But at Rio Nido that night people nodded and murmured with interest. The ham, or incipient carnie, in me couldn't resist. "The first game winner," I bellowed in my barker voice, "gets a Beacon blanket." That did it. Beacon blankets were popular in those days. They cost us $3 wholesale, and since my Bingo cards sold for 10¢ I obviously was offering a bargain. The ladies almost tripped over themselves getting to my booth.

From that night on my Bingo game was the ladies' nightly meeting place. I was attentive and courteous. I offered a nice, clean and accurate game. I treated every lady as if she were a queen and even worked on my speech to avoid slang and mild cusswords. The ladies appreciated it and I prospered.

There were temptations to be sure. A lovely group of young people gathered at Rio Nido that summer of 1931 and I got out occasionally with them to roast hot dogs and sing a song or two. But I danced only two dances during the entire season. I tried to remind myself I was waiting for the one girl whose image I had held so long. To strengthen my will, I observed bad examples. Next door a man a little older than me had opened a lunch counter and did nicely for a few weeks. Nights, however, he was out drinking and cowboying around the camp. In a month the lunch counter was under new management.

One evening, looking up to call the numbers, I spotted a new face at my counter. A young and lovely face. I felt my voice falter. She glanced up from between two old ladies, where she was following three cards, and smiled. Something happened in that instant. Nothing like it has ever happened to me since. When all the tense dice games are forgotten, when I can't remember the god-awful agony of a big-stake 21 game I have beat, I will still remember the electric shock I felt when I saw that girl. I see her smiling up from the Bingo cards, in short green leather jacket and white skirt with big red polka dots, red sparks glinting from the brunette hair beneath a perky white hat. The smile lingered and I forgot about loyal old ladies. I wanted this girl to win. I wanted to give it all to her.

Her name, I learned, was Dorothy McPherson. She was just eighteen and worked for a lawyer's family at Willows, a farming town in the upper Sacramento Valley. The family was at Rio Nido for vacation. The lawyer was giving full time to the three children. She had plenty of time for Bingo and, as it turned out, for me. We understood from that first smile that we liked each other. Romance blossoms swiftly at a summer resort. She would come each morning to wake me with pebbles tossed at my window and we'd go down to the river to talk and swim and talk. No love ever can match that first real infatuation between the one girl and her boy. As the glorious summer came to an end, we were married, August 24, 1931, in the little Methodist Church at Santa Rosa. It would have been the most glorious season I ever had if I hadn't made a penny. Actually, in that dire depression year, it paid off a net of $4500.

Later, when love's bloom got off the ledger, I would analyze that summer's success with a game that had failed for another man. The answer was clear enough. The previous owner had been a conceited old rascal who thought he could give junk for prizes and make his customers take potluck. Though the booth was built over a creek which sent up cold breezes at night, he didn't even think to enclose it with plank walls. He didn't treat his customers as if they were real ladies trying to buy enjoyment with their money. I did and prospered.

♥

A few months later found Dorothy and I on our way to Miami, Florida, where Daddy had acquired a Fascination game in the South Beach arcade. I remember the trip well, and not because it was my honeymoon. We had to cross Texas at twenty-five miles per hour to save Daddy's tires from blowing on the unpaved roads. We took an apartment over a garage and I spent the rest of the honeymoon working harder than I ever had before. Daddy suddenly was dangerously sick. His first doctor diagnosed it as diabetes and put him on such a limited diet he soon was suffering from acute malnutrition. Daddy never carried much spare weight. When he got down to bones, that was it. He almost died. I had to work the concessions alone.

Fascination is a form of electric Bingo in which the player shoots balls into numbered slots to fill his card. We had twelve units, which meant only twelve could play at a time. I charged 5¢ a game. Out of the 60¢ total, I gave a 25¢ prize. I had to keep all those games filled and playing or the new Mrs. Smith and I would be hungrier than Daddy. I would start each evening at six and keep going until midnight. A game took two and a half minutes to play. I would collect the money, run off the game, pay the winners, and rush immediately into the next go-round. I had no relief to eat. When nature called, I had to answer fast. I would start the game, dash to the back room, and return before the game ended. After work I had a three-mile drive home, where I slept as fast as I could, then returned to the park early to service my machines. I was never a good mechanic. Sometimes it took four hours to make minor repairs. Then it was time to clean up the booth, rush home and eat and get back for the evening's play. I did this every day for months and broke even on the season. When I thought of the big gambling casinos raking in bundles of currency in Miami, I could have cried.

The next summer, 1932, I went back to the Russian River alone. Mama had turned up in San Francisco that winter with a new husband, a steel worker sent out to help build a hangar for dirigibles. It was a one-shot job, like jumping off the Brooklyn Bridge, and soon he was looking for work and joined me at the river. Thereafter, Mama was never to be far from the rest of the Smiths. Dorothy was in Willows awaiting the birth of our first child. When he came, on August 5, 1932, he was an absolute jackpot of 10 pounds 3 ounces. I named him proudly Raymond I. Smith for Daddy. Strange are the swirling currents, though. Years later my first born would go into court and ask that his name be changed legally to mine, Harold S. Smith, thereby forcing me to add "Sr." to mine and to accentuate it in all my dealings in order to keep our escapades separate.

We were back at the Russian River with Bingo each summer from 1931 to 1937. Winters, with men selling apples on city street corners and bread lines across the land, we did the best we could where we could. *Brother Can You Spare A Dime?* was, I remember, one song hit of the winter of 1932. With a wife and baby to support, I recall that a dime was big money. I couldn't find a job and neither could Daddy, though he was feeling whole again. We decided to try a whist game in an old hall on Fillmore Street. Every day I got up bright and early to dust 300 chairs, clean toilets and spittoons, and scrub the old linoleum; every night I went down to start the game knowing we were going to lose money. We lasted thirty days.

More experience, more grist for the mill, more of the inevitable currents flowing into my life. During the winter of '33-34 we had Bingo in Modesto, a small San Joaquin Valley town, and Daddy sent me to Portland, Oregon, to try to resurrect a game that had failed. It was one of the only two thievery stands I ever heard of in Bingo and I couldn't do a thing for it. I gladly told Daddy to try getting this hammer for himself. At least I was gaining self-confidence. In '34 we added penny roulette to the Modesto operation. I knew so little about the game, in which "O" and "OO" are known as house numbers, I thought customers couldn't play them. More experience, more grist in my mill. We banked a dollar or two out of that embryo casino on Skid Road before the police closed us out. Reform was in the land, it seemed, and a dead end waited everywhere we turned.

The little town of Reno, across the Sierras in Nevada, hardly looked more promising except that gambling was legal there. I decided to look it over. It was not an auspicious first look. I broke out with a fierce case of poison oak just after I boarded the train in California. The conductor brought me some medicine at Sacramento that eased it until I got off at Reno. I eased it a little more with a drink of whiskey every thirty or forty minutes while I looked over the town. There weren't any neons in the biggest little city then. A high-rolling player would have got pretty sleepy action. I strolled into one club and tried a $25 bet on the crap table. I threw a 7 and when the dealer paid me I let the $50 ride.

"You can't do that," the dealer said huffily. "The house limit's $25."

A tinhorn town, I thought. *And this is legal gambling! I saw better action than this in Chicago in 1929 and Miami in 1931. This is child's play.* I couldn't at that moment have conceived of a glittering casino only a poker chip's throw away which one day could give back half a million dollars in refunds to its patrons before it filled its own vaults. I was seeking an end to dead ends and I couldn't think very big just then.

It was September 7, 1935.

11

♥ ♥ ♥ ♥

A Giant Born

THE INFANT THAT was to become the world's largest gaming club was born of hope and frustration and weaned on chicanery and violence. It should not even have survived its first days when it clung to life by a tattered shoestring and the ignorant innocence of its sires. It started for me with a cracking headache.

One hour before the doors were to open, I stood alone at the corner of Second and Virginia Streets debating whether to blow town. Reno's 4500-feet-elevation had brought an attack of altitude sickness. I could hardly talk. My ears were clogged; every membrane in my head and chest screamed for relief. Some people, I knew, died from these attacks.

Why not take the train down to Sacramento? urged a fearful voice inside me. *You're in no condition to start a new venture. Why not open next week?*

I must have stood there several minutes debating with myself, only vaguely conscious of foot traffic moving along Virginia Street toward our new shop. I remember distinctly pondering that term *shop*, or store. It's Daddy's word. Never in his long life has he spoken of his concessions as anything else. Never, never as a "joint". Nor could anyone else, no matter how second rate the carnival or amusement park in which he operated. Somehow over the years, through illness, divorces and other disappointments, he kept his pride in his word and his work. In the end, too, the trouper spirit got the best of my miseries. The store must open.

I was riding a hunch. Harassed by the law in California, plus the depressed times. I had studied Nevada's legal gambling setup and decided there was a spot for us. I'd located a tiny shop on South Virginia and brought Daddy up for a look. The man who owned it was stuck. He'd run Bingo three months and still owed for his lumber, rent and prizes. I sized him up as a nickel and dime incompetent, reflected in his person, his old car messy with Pekinese hair, and his personality. "I know this lousy racket," he protested to me. "There's nothing to it. The town's what's sour." What a pity, I thought. Attorney John Davidson was trying to collect bills totaling $500 for this expert's creditors.

Call it a hunch, extrasensory perception or what you will, Daddy and I were in that dingy Bingo parlor only five minutes when I felt the electric tingle. "This is it," I declared. "We must have this place." Daddy stared thoughtfully at the ten lonely customers, half of them shills. He was learning to give my hunches more than passing thought. We took the place.

Daddy and I pooled our money. It was only $2000. We paid $500 to Attorney Davidson to settle the creditors' claims. The remaining $1500 was our capital, very thin and destined to get thinner. We drew up no contract with each other and conferred no titles. Daddy was boss as always. We took the train back to California to clean up the Modesto wreckage.

It was Modesto and the law that had driven us to Nevada. Earl Warren, then State's Attorney General, was sweeping over California with a big broom. He was sweeping up Bingo, which long had operated in a shadow land of legality, and all other forms of gambling. Our penny roulette on Skid Row, though marked with shamrocks and horseshoes instead of numbered squares, Double- and Single-O, brought us into the dust pan. We were fined $500 for running a gambling game and given a ninety-day suspended sentence. We were weary of building up businesses only to lose them. We didn't want to go to jail.

Pondering a name for our Reno store, I remembered a happy occasion when we set up a Bingo game in the streets of San Francisco's Chinatown for a Pagoda celebration. The moment I started calling the game, hundreds of Chinese tykes crowded around crying: "Har-wold Lloyd! Har-wold Lloyd!" I did resemble the famous silent movie comic with my round eyes and horn-rimmed glasses. It seemed most auspicious recognition. Later I named my Bingo game at the Russian River "Harold's." Now, with no intent of sounding grandiloquent, we simply added the word "Club" and took the apostrophe out to read Harolds.

Digressing momentarily, I should point out how Daddy had lost his concessions at the beach in San Francisco. It is part of the Harolds Club saga. George Whitney, who owned Chutes-at-the-Beach, was a man obsessed by money. Slowly but steadily he squeezed concessionaires until they got out one by one and left him the businesses they'd built. Much as I loved the beach and that park, I would not spend a dime there again so long as he lived. That's another of my idiosyncrasies—I don't forget, whether it be a slight or a kindness. A few years ago, for instance, when Mr. Whitney's son, whom I have reason to consider a sweet guy, finally took over the Beach (now Playland) on his father's death, I was delighted to return. Recently, in fact, I made a sentimental pilgrimage to the games that made me a gambler. The word quickly got around that the man whooping and hollering from bottle game to basketball to flat wheel was Harold Smith of Harolds Club. We drew a throng. "Plunging" with dimes and quarters, I came away with 45,000 merchandise coupons to trade for toasters, lamps and blankets. I've never had a better time gambling in Vegas for hundred-dollar bills.

◆

All this, however, is a far cry from the Harolds Club we opened February 23, 1936, my twenty-sixth birthday. We didn't get much for our $500 investment; one long room 25 by 125 feet in a block close enough to the railroad tracks to be almost Skid Road. Our cubbyhole was jammed in between two Bingo parlors under a walkup hotel. There was a cut-rate restaurant at the corner of Douglas Alley, then a cleaners and loan office. We looked out to the usual hodge-podge of a small western town's lower main street. At the moment, the Bingo parlors on each side of us were having a "war" to stimulate business, offering multiple cards for 25¢ and better prizes.

We weren't going to compete with them. We installed only the penny roulette that had killed us in California. The Modesto police had apologized when they arrested us, acknowledging we were a family operation and ran a clean game. They didn't lock us up and they didn't impound our equipment. I paid Willie Trinkle $1 to unload it when the trucks rolled in over the Sierras (Twenty-five years later, at age 85, Willie has a permanent home on my ranch). The game we set up used one eight-foot wheel suspended from the ceiling with a gigantic mirror and 43 layouts for players. This way, the player could sit down before a layout of four narrow columns of numbers, place his bets and watch results as the wheel lit up the numbers. This "flasher" wheel, as they are known, was the first introduced in Nevada.

Our "grand opening" wasn't really very grand. We had no funds for newspaper ads or radio plugs. After settling my debate whether to open the store or flee to Sacramento, I simply opened the doors at 7 PM. Any elation I might have felt was tempered by the fact my first daughter, Joan, was born just nineteen days before. I had not gotten drunk or passed out cigars—just as Daddy didn't when I was born twenty-six years before. I now had another mouth to feed and I had to let the opening of the new shop be my celebration. It was, too. Reno has always been beautiful that way. It turns out to give a new place a grand opening and a courtesy play even though it may let it die the next day. Harolds Club was loaded its first night.

In the weeks that followed we didn't quite die but neither did we make money. We were open from noon until midnight seven days a week, the whole family working like prairie dogs in a sandpile, and lost $2000 on the year. My brother Raymond, still unmarried and out of banking due to the depression, had come on to help. Mama followed with Harry Duffitt, her steel worker husband, a Newfoundland Irishman with a temper to start forest fires, though he worked compatibly with Daddy. Dorothy, of course, was home with baby Joan, and I lived at the club from dawn to dawn.

We were, obviously, the most innocent operators in the land and every crossroading son-of-a-bitch in Nevada wanted to work for us. We hired most of them too, I think, as time went on and we added games. We also learned from them. The first slot machines in the place, for example, were put there on concession by a gentleman here in town. They weren't quite as old as the printing press from which the Gutenberg Bible was struck, but they were close. They dropped exactly one jackpot in a year when the "bug" that controls jackpots fell out. It embarrassed me more than if they had *never* paid. I resolved to get my own machines as soon as possible.

I had to go back to the Russian River to run Bingo during the summer of '36. When I returned to Reno that fall we put in our first 21 table and I hired a gentleman at $5 a day to teach me to deal. One afternoon I ran around the corner to get a sandwich. I returned to find my tutor dealing to a man known as Russian Louis. Mr. Louis earlier had taken $250 from me by crimping, or marking, cards. I stopped that by changing decks with every deal. Now I found my teacher "sluffing off"—throwing the bankroll, we call it, by deliberately letting Russian Louis win—and he had $300 more of my money stacked in front of him. I fired the dealer on the spot.

There I learned something of international gaming. Crooks there are in the business, but they have a code. An employee who steals for himself sometimes can live it down and work again; an employee who sluffs off the boss's money is through everywhere, permanently. It doesn't matter whether he stole from the good guys or the bad. So it was with my tutor.

In the face of such experience, Daddy was most reluctant to add new games. Once in Troy, N.Y., when I was still a tyke, he'd had a crap game backed by only a $50 bankroll. He ran so scared, knowing one good loss could clean him out, he never quite got over it. There would be no dice in Harolds Club that first year. When we did add craps in '37, I took no chances on professional tutors. I simply stepped in and dealt. The mechanics of the game I knew. Protection was another thing.

Daddy, incidentally, has never felt secure in this business and has resorted at times to rather drastic protective methods. Once in the early days, for instance, a young man came and asked for a job watching out for crooks. He had been reared by two professional cheaters, he explained, and had learned all they knew. He was quite proud of his ability, and with reason. He could take a deck of cards, shuffle them, let you cut, then shift the cut right back and deal four hands: four aces, four kings, four queens and four jacks. Daddy was fascinated. The young man said he'd gotten a little discouraged with his play when, in Mexico City, he got caught cheating and was stabbed. He showed Daddy the wound. Now, he said, he was going straight. He knew cheaters and their tricks. Daddy hired him. He lasted just three days. The trouble was that he thought everyone was crooked. He would grab a deck of cards from a dealer—who could hardly deal off the top, let alone the bottom—on the assumption she was cheating. One of our local judges came in one day to watch the roulette game—Nevada judges do this frequently to familiarize themselves with games and conditions that may be involved in court trials—and our boy ordered him out. He thought the judge was a suspicious character. The place was in turmoil. We had to let our "protector" go.

We weren't any luckier with the first bouncer we hired. He stole the currency box from our first crap game and a sum of money I well remember. It was $96. Through him, however, we learned something. His girl friend shilled for his game. We noticed that she would get up from the table periodically and go to the ladies room, always with a handkerchief to her nose. It was the first I'd seen of this nose trouble bit. The table was losing money, so I looked closer. I found that each time she got up, hand to nose, the handkerchief contained silver. Out of that we devised a habit all employees must acquire. When a dealer, for instance, leaves her game for lunch or a break, she automatically pats her hands above the table as if dusting her palms. It's a quick little gesture to say *I'm through for now* and looks most tidy. It shows us she isn't palming the profits.

Today I think of those early problems as "good troubles" because we learned from them how to survive and even earn a little money. We also had Mother Providence looking over our shoulders. There was a time in the first year, for example, when we tried to trade our location for a movie theater building on Center

Street. That seemed a desirable location then because it was just across the street from the Bank Club. We offered our Virginia Street cubbyhole for the theater and $2500 cash. (It makes me nervous now even to think of it.) The little man who owned the show, had he taken our deal, would have relegated us to a back street just before the Reno boom began. Instead, he insultingly refused the deal and stormed out. What a favor he did us!

♠

Other currents were swirling in my life again which, though they seemed tragic at the time, were to contribute to the future. I went to the Russian River for the summer of 1937 as usual. Before my nice old ladies could even get seated, the law arrived. The sheriff took me down the road to a justice of the peace. I paid a $25 fine and closed my Bingo stand forever. It was June. I returned to Reno to concentrate on Harolds Club. Bingo, I might add, was open at the River the next year and operating on the self-same basis of merchandise prizes redeemable for cash. Again, all for the best.

In Reno, the crazy Smith family operation was the ridicule of shills. People spoke of us as "those carnival men" and predicted we'd break shortly. We didn't realize there was more to the talk than idle gossip. Daddy and I had heard pessimism before. We weren't about to quit, though in truth it was Labor Day of our second year before we handled $1000 gross in one day. We knew we didn't have a golden goose laying big fat eggs. We hoped we had at least a nesting hen. Enemies were something that didn't even occur to us.

There were, as we were to discover, certain gaming interests in Reno that had their sinister eye on us and were not beyond using "the weight," as gamblers call it. I shan't mention true names—having no desire to collect a bullet—but I suddenly commenced to hear things about this clique. I would like to believe, and I do believe, the eventual success of Harolds Club, Harrah's and several others was all that saved legal gaming from the clutching talons of those racketeers.

They were not a Syndicate operation as the term is used today.

Let us say they were a local mob with options on outside talent. They had a club—we'll call it the Gibraltar—and it did a good business. Who owned it in fact, I cannot, or will not, say. However, a very prominent Nevada citizen whom we shall call Mr. Senior was sufficiently regarded at the Gibraltar for every employee to snap to attention at sight of him. Baby Face Nelson, the Chicago gangster then on the lam, had made the Gibraltar his local headquarters and might be seen playing Pan there any day. Rumor had it the Cribs and their fifty-odd prostitutes down by the river were Gibraltar-owned. So was at least one Reno city councilman. Against them, we Smiths were the most innocent babes in the woods.

They never sent any word of warning to us. That wasn't the protocol; they were more discreet than that. When, for instance, the Monte Carlo Club opened just before our time in the section of the block now occupied by Harrah's, no warning went to its owners. Nor was there any rough stuff. The clique simply infiltrated its thieves among the employees and stole the bankroll. The Monte Carlo Club was broke in three months.

We, however, were luckier and were even beginning to branch out a little by 1937. Then it was that Mr. Senior's Third Ward councilman made his move. The moment I saw him arrive with other members of the council, I knew they weren't there to play penny roulette. They were there to examine our big roulette wheel hanging from the ceiling. The city's ordinance imposed a tax on each gaming wheel. The Third Ward councilman was trying to persuade his colleagues to collect the tax instead on each of our 43 roulette layouts since they were played from a single wheel. Fortunately he wasn't able to sell his plan. Forty-three licenses would have put us out of business. I had, however, felt a little nudge of the weight.

The real showdown came just before 10 AM a few days later when Raymond and I were alone in the place. Seven men sauntered in, all big, all sashaying from side to side to knock over whatever, or whoever, got in their way. I had heard through the grapevine our place was going to be wrecked. I was ready, though I would have liked to have had more witnesses. The men headed straight for Raymond, standing behind the crap table, when I reached under the roulette counter for my loaded .38. "You're not going to shoot any dice," I declared, "so just turn around and walk out that door." Not a tremor of vibrato was in my voice. I simply couldn't stand there, aware of Raymond's vulnerable mastoidal ear, and let them tear my brother apart or wreck the store. Had any of them taken another step I'd have put a bullet near his feet and the next one into him.

They halted and turned to face me. Anyone, I believe, knows when an armed man means to use his gun. They could see by the line of my lips I would use mine. They knew, furthermore, as I knew, that unless I faced them down Harolds Club was through in Reno. Every hoodlum in the area would take his turn at clobbering us. We would be their mirth, out in the street dodging our furniture. If, on the other hand, they retreated before a gun, the psychological advantage was ours. We would have made our stand and the word would be all over town by noon. Public opinion might save us from further rough stuff. The seven men put their heads together in solemn pow-wow, turned stiffly and marched out the door. I took my clammy hand off the pistol grip and murmured a silent prayer.

We were in Reno to stay though I continued to carry the gun and watch every shadow as I drove home nights. Daddy agreed to add to our games. He brought the first top-of-the-table roulette wheel to Nevada. We added more 21 tables, put a poker game in the back, tried Ace-Away, lo-ball, crapless craps, even Chinese Fan Tan to woo customers. In 1938 I gave Raymond a one-third interest in Harolds Club and, though I couldn't have guessed it then, set him up as a future millionaire. In 1939 a young giant named Jim Hunter, who had never dealt a gambling game in his life, came to work for us at $3 a day. One day he would be our assistant general manager.

Mother Providence seemed so fond of her babes in the gaming woods she almost laughed aloud at times. There was, for example, the incident of the mouse game. My Dad has always been a pushover for strangers with exotic schemes. This one arrived one day when I was out of town on business. I returned to discover Daddy had hired the man and his game for $100 a week, which was just about double what the rest of us earned. That wasn't what aggravated me though.

The mouse game is actually a form of roulette using a live

mouse as the ball. The creature is placed in a box on a table top in which are numbered holes large enough for him to crawl into. Usually there is a drawer under the table to recapture the mouse when he drops through a hole. Each hole is numbered—ours ran from 1 to 50—and the player places his bet on the number he thinks the mouse will choose. The box is lifted and Brother Mouse makes his run. Winners were to be paid off at the same odds as roulette.

I had spotted a version of the mouse game when I first worked concessions in Florida. I smelled "clip" all over it and made a point of studying the gimmick. No one was winning. I soon saw why. When the box was lifted the mouse would edge out, sniffing nervously at holes; any noise or quick motion sent him scurrying down the nearest hole. The operator watched closely. He kept very quiet while the animal approached holes on which players had bets. When the mouse sniffed a hole on which no money was riding the operator would wave an arm and shout: "Anybody for a Coke?" Zip! Mr. Mouse was down that hole. After the winless players departed, the operator invited me to play. I declined pointing out I had no chance to win. He smiled and acknowledged I'd figured it right. Now I return to Reno to find this clip game in my own club!

Daddy was only mildly appalled. The game intrigued him even after I demonstrated it couldn't be protected for the house or customer. He insisted on letting the man work out his week. That was the fantastic thing. Someone took photos of the game. News picture services carried them across the United States with stories of the roulette played at Harolds Club with white mice. Even that was a laugh since we used common ordinary gray mice we caught in the attic. The publicity, which cost us not a cent, brought curious crowds from far and near. Harolds Club suddenly had an international reputation as the casino that "started from a mouse-roulette game." Twenty-five years later, people still ask to see the game and won't believe it was here only a week. (Or that no one won on it.) I would have prevented it from showing at all if I hadn't been on my business trip. Yet to save my soul I can't remember where I went or what the business was.

♣

Until 1941 we were to draw our trade from local residents and a few venturesome tourists who tackled the games skeptically. Then in the early months of '41, suddenly, we began to boom. California seemed suddenly to awaken to Reno's legal gaming (Vegas was nothing) and people came pouring over the mountains with their money. We added games and machines and expanded upwards, downwards and sideways through the old buildings in that block of Virginia Street. Dorothy came in to help because we couldn't train employees fast enough. One of our best 21 dealers then, and for years afterwards, was Daddy's brother Harry Smith, an avid Jehovahs Witness who dealt cards all day, sold *Watchtowers* at Second and Virginia nights, and preached on Sundays. Finally I saw my own name in lights; an illuminated HAROLDS CLUB sign soared three stories straight above the sidewalk.

The advertising campaign we started that year was to make our name known on every continent of the world. Now that we'd got our feet wet, we weren't happy with Nevada's reluctance to promote its legal gaming. We started building roadside billboards extolling the FUN of playing at our club. The 25 signs we put up within 500 miles were to grow in the years ahead to more than 2000 scattered over much of the civilized world. (I understand one even was raised inside the Antarctic Circle.) As the crowds poured in, we would have had to be geniuses not to make money. We made it and expanded the club more. It was still a pretty rough gem, however, to sightseers expecting a deluxe casino. As Daddy admitted: "It took us five years to catch up with our advertising."

Daddy was somewhat faster catching onto the fact we must have drinks for sale if we wanted to hold customers. An absolute teetotaller himself, he'd once prevented me from taking over a bar at the Russian River and held out for several years against liquor in Harolds Club. When he saw the dollars walking away from our club to casinos that had bars, he capitulated. We ex-

panded backward to absorb one bar which we let out as a concession. We also established hard and fast rules on drinking with
gambling. I won't interrupt the chronological account here to detail them but will devote a chapter later to all our gaming house
policies and how they developed. Harolds Club would have closed
before people heard of it if we hadn't set such policies.

I personally drank very little in the early days of the club and
held my gambling to a frightful, crying minimum. I didn't have
extra money, for one thing, or the time. I was working twelve
hours a day at the club and giving every extra minute to my
family. Dorothy was a wonderful mother with Junior, Joan, and,
later, June, but I was almost as good. Those were the happiest
home years of my life. I gladly changed diapers, mixed Pablum
and baby-sat. No man ever enjoyed his children when they were
little more than I. No man ever believed his cup had been so
filled to overflowing.

One other thing obsessed me in those early Nevada years. It
was something again that went back to the Cleveland boarding
house days when I dreamed of guns and horses with silver saddle
mountings. I wanted to be a Westerner accepted by the real cowboys who frequented the club and I would have walked barefoot
through cactus to achieve that status. Instead I entered the "green-
horn calf-tying" event at the 1941 Fourth of July rodeo.

It is not an easy feat, if you please, to run down a rope to a
healthy young bull calf, flip it over and bind its legs with pigging
strings. I weighed only 145 pounds; a good calf could give me
quite a tussle. As I had for my birthday duel with brother Raymond, I trained hard for weeks. The trouble was I trained on
sluggish white-faced Herefords and the cowboys threw me in with
a black Aberdeen-Angus which could snap the arms off an octo-
pus. I still was nervous when I had to perform before a crowd
and every seat in the stands was filled when I arrived. Wanting
that silver buckle as badly as I'd once wanted a violin, I did a
foolish thing. I had a cab driver bring me a bottle of rye whiskey
and gulped several stiff belts before I mounted. It was 95 degrees
out there in the sun. My head was wobbling the moment we
pounded after the calf. My roper got him. I dismounted, stumbled down the rope, flipped the calf and sprawled on him,
suddenly aware I was dead drunk. The Angus was only furious.
He couldn't get up with me flopped over him and the crowd was

whooping. Somehow I got the pigging strings on his legs and tottered to my feet, only to hear my roper drawl: "Better tie him again, kid. He's getting up on you." Desperate now, I twisted and knotted the strings. The calf bawled and shook them off. My silver buckle was long gone. It had cost $100 I couldn't spare for calves to train on. I was the mirth of Reno and whiskey had done it. I could have bawled. Instead, I slammed my hat on the ground and staggered off the field. Again Mother Providence was watching. In the West, sometimes, trying is as good as winning. The cowboys remembered. They would always give Harolds Club their action but spare it their horseplay.

Only five years had passed since we entered the business knowing nothing of gaming and playing for peanuts. Roulette at one cent. A $5 limit on 21. Dice 10¢ to $5. I didn't even know what a man meant when he walked up to my 21 table and asked: "Hey kid, how about me bellying up to one of these snaps for a couple of shifts to get eating money?" (A 21 game, I learned later, is known as a "snap" and he wanted to shill for me.) Now, if you please, we hired the Thomas C. Wilson advertising agency to circulate our fame throughout the land. They did a job, too, including the development of our covered wagon symbol with its "Harolds Club or Bust" slogan, before they went over to the competition at Harrah's.

We were discovering, however, that the very best advertising we could have was free. We had raised our betting limits swiftly as volume increased and discovered that a big win by a player amounts only to a "temporary loan." He'll come back for more and return our money. Despite the fact we'd set a policy early never to announce big winners, the word spread faster than wildfire. People would rush into the club saying they'd been sunning themselves on the beach at Miami, Florida, yesterday when they heard someone, probably Eddie Sahati, had just won a quarter of a million dollars at Harolds Club. The truth might be that it was only $25,000, but those players wanted in while the dice still were "hot." That word of mouth advertising was as effective, I believe, as all our billboards.

The times were with us too. As the great depression eased off, the factories that supplied World War II began to hum. Many of them were in Northern California, two hours by plane from the Reno gaming boards. The war years were fantastic ones for casino operators. I had registered for the draft, of course, along with other men in their thirties and was just as eager as any angry American to haul out my guns the day of Pearl Harbor and shoot Japs. But I was a family man—June was born July 22, 1942— and it would be some time before I was needed. As a matter of fact, from a purely business standpoint, there was never a time when I wasn't needed more at the club. I recall, for instance, the day Uncle Harry went to Daddy and said: "That girl counting money with me is just too quick. I can't follow her hands but she's just bought a new home and automobile. Maybe you'd better get her out of the counting room." We did, naturally, but that gives you some idea of the cash we had to work with. Later, Daddy was to be faced with running the whole business himself.

As he has done from time to time while avoiding outright gambling himself, he sank a bundle in some mines. I might point out that Daddy knows about as much about mining as I do about skin diving. Nevertheless, he acquired the Redbird cinnabar mine, out of Lovelock, once one of the world's greatest producers of quicksilver; a tungsten mine out of Golconda, and a zinc mine with no zinc in the desert out of Imlay. After a while he sent me out to get the properties on their feet so we could dispose of them before they broke us.

I was off in the boondocks when the draft board finally called. They granted me six months to finish the mine cleanup, and refused a further extension. The lady at Carson City acknowledged that the government needed quicksilver more than it did one foot soldier family man with bifocals. She glibly informed me, though, that I would be deferred as in necessary industry if I would go to work in someone else's mine.

"Put me in the Army," I said. "I'm not trying to avoid a fight." I was thirty-four and married, with three children. They really needed draftees from Nevada. After me they could only call priests and convicts from the state prison. "Your going in will be good for the morale of the community," one of my neighbors pointed out. He was right. I've been thankful ever since. A gambler I was, to be sure, but now I was not just a gambler. In khaki I could be the same as any other soldier. Or so I thought.

♦

I entered the Army on January 16, 1945, went to Fort Douglas, Utah, for two weeks and was furloughed home. Next I went to Camp Lee, Va., for basic training while the Army tried to decide what to do with me. Their classification book had listings of every occupation there is, including strip teasers, but not one for a civilian life gambler. They finally asked if I thought I could handle post office work. I said I could try and was assigned to postal school, thence to the San Francisco Port of Embarkation with the understanding we would ship out within six weeks.

I never went anywhere except to Reno on weekend passes. Raymond was training pilots for the Air Force. Daddy was doing all manner of things, hiring women even as floor bosses as men were turned to essential work, dolling up the club to resemble a Western museum, and, incidentally, filling the banks with dollars. I, on the other hand, was compiling a war record to equal Phil Silvers' Sergeant Bilko. My comrades, knowing I was a professional gambler, insisted I get in their dice games. They couldn't beat me. When I won—$700 on one payday—I had to take them all out on the town, including steaks at John's Rendezvous. Major Robert E. Sharpe, a taskmaster Tennesseean who was my commanding officer the final nine months, used me as general handyman-driver. One day, not knowing that my carpentry was no better than my mechanics, he ordered me to build a doghouse for his Samoyed. I studied the problem and did the best I could, draping chicken wire across the ends of two barracks buildings, enclosing the space between them, and herding his dog in there. There being ample space, I then brought my own three Dalmations down from Nevada and was a complete gentleman soldier.

Only once was I able to excel above and beyond the call of duty. Our mess hall was in a playground at Seventh and Harrison Streets, near downtown San Francisco, and one day the cook accidentally got a handful of lye in his eyes. I didn't stop to consider regulations. The Army hospital was clear across town at Fort Mason and the man was in agony. I rolled out the major's car, pushed the cook in the back seat and set sail for Letterman Hospital. Across Van Ness Avenue we went, screeching in and out of noonday traffic at eighty miles an hour. I had no siren. I was praying for a police officer. None appeared. All I could think was: *He's got lye in his eyes! I've got to get him there!* Ten times we had near misses with other cars and accidents that might have killed us both. Finally we wheeled up to the sentry post at the fort. "He's got lye in his eyes!" I shouted, and roared on through. At the hospital, the doctors said my fast trip may have saved the man's sight. Later, I learned, I was subject to court martial. According to the book, I should have called an ambulance for the injured man. Had I wrecked that staff car and injured myself or the cook, I might still be in Leavenworth Prison. So I got no medal.

Another current, a sad one, was swirling under the hijinks of my Army life. Back home in Reno, men and women were caught up in the hysteria of the war years, meeting and dancing and romancing to the champagne and throbbing saxophones of officers' clubs. There was a fine officers' club at Reno Air Base and Dorothy was one of the local ladies who helped entertain the lonesome, handsome officers. Pfc. Smith, the unhandsome husband, was several hundred miles away at the unglamorous service of an Army post office. I heard disquieting things.

Many and many an hour, after whooping with forced jocularity over a dice game, I lay on my bunk and brooded. Time and again my mind went back to Mama and the handsome man with the Star car. Could my own angel also have feet of clay? I tried to reject the thought. I tried to think it out. What might I do? How might I study it through to win in the end, to keep my wife and my little family intact? Many another serviceman was to suffer similar anxious hours. And always I remembered Daddy's advice: *When a woman looks at another man, you might as well pass. Count up your chips. You're out of the game.*

I was mustered out of the service on December 3, 1946, and flew home. My children were happy and well but my bread wasn't all jam-up. Dorothy wasn't quite the same angel who had smiled and caught my eye over three Bingo cards by the Russian

River. Life wasn't the same at all. I hiked into Harolds Club, booming noisily along, and it wasn't the same either. Eventually I found my way to the vault where money was stacked in piles of $100, $500 and $1000 bills. Never had I seen so much money and two-thirds of it legally mine. (Daddy had never taken more than a salary.)

To a man who has been poor, money can seem to offer its own solace.

12

♠ ♠ ♠ ♠

Dealing With

Tears In My Eyes

WE HAVE NOW reached the point where I must reveal more of the personal ruler of my life than anyone ever has seen. All the seething tides of my restless, sensitive nature were to swirl to the surface in those hectic post-war years. Though my gaming house was making money faster than the United States Mint, I, the chief beneficiary, was about to become spiritually bankrupt. Even my sanity was to crack. And no one, not even the others involved, knew how bad it was.

From the day I returned from the Army, December 3, 1946, I had one agonizing concern. How to save my marriage? How to hold together the home I cherished, the woman I had worshiped, the three lovely children? June was just three, Joan ten, and Junior fourteen. It was the time of the criterion hand, as we say in gaming, when you must make or break.

More than anything in life, I ached to recapture, if I could, the bliss of my first year of marriage. No man, I will insist to my dying day, was happier than I. Now, after fifteen and a half years, no man could have been more miserable. I had received no Dear John letter, as many soldiers did. I knew nothing factual, really, and yet I knew it all. Dorothy had met and been charmed by handsome young officers while her husband was away in the service. I could understand this. I knew about loneliness and war hysteria. I'd seen it affect ladies from far Virginia to the Top of the Mark. We're all human. I didn't blame Dorothy. I don't now. I resolved to ask her nothing, accuse her of nothing. It was a time, I told myself desperately, for reconciliation and honest forgiveness.

Unquestionably I indulged self-pity. I am a jealous man and a sensitive one. I believed I had been a model of husbandly virtue. Until the war separated us, I never looked at other women except as wonderful, decorative creatures. Even during the summers at Russian River, a summer resort filled with delectable females, and particularly the summer of 1932, when Dorothy was in Willows to have Junior, I played the game honestly. That isn't always easy, if you please, when a man is young and vigorous. It hadn't always been easy either after we came to Reno to start Harolds Club and circumstances made me a target for temptation. Lying on my hard Army bunks, mindful of rumor and certain intuitions that make me a gambler, I'd given it all a lot of thought. My one objective then, and when I returned to Reno, was a program that might offset the failure of our marriage. I didn't want it to fail.

It wasn't easy to be philosophical. It isn't now. I must weigh my words carefully as I attempt to describe events which led to the terrible scenes that followed. I wish to say nothing that might tarnish the name or image of Dorothy, my partner through so many good years. After the war, all I wanted was to take up where we'd left off, to understand that what happened during the war had happened, to play them as they lay. But there had been episodes.

There was the time my outfit moved from Camp Lee to San Francisco and the troop train stopped at Reno. I had friends among the officers at Reno Air Base. They came down to try to get me off the train for a party, bringing armloads of good whiskey to grease the way. Dorothy turned up with them, laughing and chattering and, oh, so attractive to me. She was only having fun, as I knew. But she was getting involved and I knew that too. I decided to stay with the train. My captain, after all, was under orders to report in at San Francisco with all his men. I took a good, long think, and a long, long drink as the train crawled over the Sierras.

Other incidents were almost too trivial to count, yet they added to my state of mind. While I was stationed at San Francisco, I could come home on weekend passes to help Daddy and keep an eye on things. It wasn't an easy trip over the mountains in the kind of cars available in those years but I was trying to act like a man and keep my family together. I heard rumors. Dorothy was going out with officers from the air base. I said nothing. It would only aggravate the situation and make her want to go out more; it wouldn't get the job done. One night a captain—a real nice guy among a lot of nice guys at the base—invited us to a party. I was, of course, only a private first class, which they overlooked. When the car pulled up, Dorothy jumped out laughing. "You can't come in here, Harold," she taunted. "This is the officers' club." Now I knew that Max Baer, the former heavyweight champion stationed there, had the run of the club; no one would have thought to remind big, ebullient Max he was only a private. But suddenly I couldn't go in. Dorothy had made the distinction too clear. I excused myself and went back to Harolds Club.

I would remember that episode in a different light when I returned from the Army as a civilian. Once more Dorothy and I were invited to a party, this time at the Sierra Ordnance Depot. As a civilian I could dance with the captain's wife, drink with the colonel and enjoy myself thoroughly, which I did. When the Italian prisoners of war, who served as bartenders, had to be returned to their compound, I took over the bartending. Dorothy, I noticed, was not having a gay time at all. The young lieutenant of whom she was fond was there with another lady; with me on the premises, he kept a noticeable distance from Dorothy. Nevertheless, I happened to bump into a major I knew in the washroom. He'd had a few drinks and his inhibitions were freed. "Harold," he demanded, "what kind of a Goddamned fool are you? Why don't you tell your wife to stay away from that Goddamned lieutenant?" I said nothing. There was nothing to say. I played it the same way next morning, when Dorothy berated me for singing too loud at the party and making a fool of myself, "Oh did I?" I inquired. "I'm sorry."

One thing I was determined to do. I would control my temper. Once at my nail game in Chicago I had come within a hair of killing a man. He aggravated me until I had a hammer raised to bash his skull. I knew in that instant how close a sane man can come to homicide and I've never wanted that sin on my conscience. Away back there I started to discipline my passions and resolved never, never to start a murder unless I meant to complete it. Why anyway, may I ask, should a civilized man dignify a woman by hitting a man she has encouraged?

♠

Not all the pertinent episodes involved Dorothy, I must confess. There was a night in San Francisco when I dropped into a bar to substitute bright lights and gaiety for my brooding. There I met a merchant seaman, a big, fun-loving man with the most wonderful black eye you ever saw. A few moments later we were joined by a Navy sailor. We had a few drinks and I suggested we adjourn to John's Rendezvous where we could dance and live it up a little. They wanted dates. I thought that could be arranged. I turned up a blonde, who paired off with the Navy man, and a little brunette who seemed to like the merchant mariner. For myself, married fourteen and a half years, I was content to have a dance or two and let it go at that. I can be a very quiet kibitzer under such circumstances and I was.

After a while, though, the little brunette engineered a switch in partners. We found we danced well together and could talk with each other. I told her I was married. She said she was engaged to a Navy officer overseas. We seemed to share a mutual loneliness. Maybe, I thought, maybe this girl can help me understand that Reno situation better.

Night clubs closed for servicemen at midnight in those war years. We left in my little car and the merchantman soon saw his date had changed her affections to me. He dropped off after a few blocks. So did the sailor and the blonde. The little brunette and I had a bite to eat and went to her apartment. She was nothing of a bad girl; she was just a lonely girl. Neither of us was sailing under false pretenses when we lay down on the Chesterfield. *If it was a fact* that my wife was untrue to me, I did understand it better. Understanding, however, isn't quite enough for a man who has been true blue over fourteen and a half years of marriage. The next day, a Sunday, I was conscious-stricken and miserable. I walked down Market Street feeling as though I'd committed a terrible crime.

I have said it helped. There are those, I know, who will wonder just how. If nothing else, it deterred me from asking too many questions at home in those fading weeks of 1946.

♣

Fortunately, too, other matters came up to claim at least a part of my mind. Harolds Club up to that time had operated as a simple partnership between Raymond and me. Now it was too big and too profitable for such an arrangement; we had too much at stake every time a high-rolling bettor stepped through the doors. Returning service men, jubilant and self-confident at surviving the war and jumping at us with accumulated pay and severance pay, were registering some of the biggest wins ever seen at the club. We had to be ready for all contingencies. On December 27, 1946, we incorporated. Daddy was general manager.

Nice things happened to me too. There was the night, for instance, when General of the Armies Hap Arnold, who had commanded the Air Forces in World War II, came to Reno to make an address. Everyone in town turned out for the cocktail party and reception at the Riverside Hotel and Arnold, a wonderful, gracious man, charmed us all. They wanted a gambler to show him through the city's casinos and explain games he might not know. I was privileged to draw the assignment. Privileged, I say, because I had only just set aside my Army suit with its private-first-class stripes and now I was host to a five-star general. I took particular delight when our cabs rolled up before the club I have called the Gibraltar and there, glaring, were the men who once had controlled gaming here and had tried to drive me out of town. It was in their club that General Arnold took me by the arm and asked me to explain Faro Bank. I didn't hesitate to tell him how it can afflict one with the dreadest of gaming diseases. Nor did I forget for a moment that not too long before I didn't have the rank, in some people's eyes, to visit an officers' club.

It was at this time, too, I met a strange man who was to have a profound effect on me. It started innocently enough with a baseball game between our night and day shifts. Brother Raymond pitched for the day side and I played third base for the nights. The losers were to buy beer for the winners. This led to some high spirits—I didn't drink too often in those days—and it wasn't long before Skip Vincent, one of my buddies, and I saddled my Palominos, Yankee Doodle and Speedy, and went galloping up and down Airport Road like a couple of Paul Reveres. I was in a wildly exhilarated mood. Once I let Yank go at top speed for sixty yards and then stood him up short, a spectacular, foolish stunt, and probably the closest I ever came to getting killed by a horse. I only whooped louder. I hadn't felt such release since I came home to my problems.

Inevitably we came to the Normandie, a night club near the airport, and inevitably we stopped in for a drink. The club was owned by Eddie Sahati, a one-time San Francisco bookie and drug addict who also owned the Stateline Club at Lake Tahoe. I had never met Sahati although I was well aware of his reputation as a gambler's gambler, a real gambolier. He wasn't in the Normandie when Skip and I came in. Had he been, he might have taken one look at my khaki shirt and dusty clothes and told us to leave. In the mood I was in, that might have meant trouble.

My exhilaration sent me straight to the dice table. I bet as I felt, wildly, and was a galloping winner from the first throw. With $5000 to $6000 in cash spinning through my hands and suddenly not a trouble in the world, I made Diamond Jim Brady look like a stiff. I champagned the house, sent $500 to the orchestra, toked the girl crap dealer $1400 (as I learned later) and generally made my presence known. When I ran out of cash, I simply stormed the crap table again. They changed dealers on me and they changed dice. I continued to take their money and spend it. Finally they telephoned Sahati at Tahoe to tell him a high roller was disintegrating the house. I didn't know it, of course, until he stepped through the door with his bodyguard and a couple of very rough playmates showing their teeth like barracudas.

That was my first glimpse of a man who had but one passion. Gambling. He was big, six feet and 215 pounds, with cool brown eyes and long, dark straight hair sleeked straight back. He dressed immaculately and spoke as softly as a librarian until he got angry; then he might scream in the shrillest of falsettos. A Syrian, he took in money matters at a glance; he got them dead accurate. I saw him come in. I was, at the moment, spent out again. "Your dealers not only changed dice on me," I shouted to him, "they also changed the size of the dice. Now I need $300." He looked me over and his eyes seemed to say sadly: *You have taken my money and spent it all over the place and now you want to borrow $300 from me. What kind of man are you?* But he gave me the $300. In time he was to learn pretty well what kind of man I was.

♥

It was at his Normandie Club on New Year's Eve of 1947 that the final public incident of my marriage to Dorothy occurred. The entire Smith family gathered there with friends to celebrate. I was afraid of an incident. I pleaded it was a busy night in the club and I should work. Before the evening was far along, however, I had a telephone call. Dorothy had arrived for the party alone. At the club, however, she met a young man she knew, and we knew, but who was not of Reno's socially elite. She had insisted he join the party. The family felt I should make an appearance. I did, steeling myself to be on my best manners. I have never been more miserable in my life than I was with that man sitting at our table. I managed to keep my self control but this, I knew, was as far as I could go. Somehow we welcomed in the new year 1947.

I have always had a policy with anyone who's been drinking not to discuss the situation until two days have passed. Dorothy had been drinking that night. I waited until January 3. "Dorothy," I said then, "I want to talk to you. Do you have any idea what you did in front of our family and friends?"

That was when she gave it to me. "Maybe we ought to get a divorce."

I recognized it as the natural, defensive reaction of an angry woman. But I also recognized that we could go no further. "That is a good idea," I said softly. My fifteen and a half years of marriage were done.

There were mechanics to be performed, of course, and they have a bearing on the over-all story of Harolds Club and me. I saw our attorney, Mr. Diskin, next morning. He, wise man that he was, did not attempt to dissuade me. Dorothy, who, above all, was never a fool, left the details in my hands. She wasn't vicious and she didn't want to hurt me. We agreed there would be no contest and that we would create no new problems. She readily accepted the attorney Mr. Diskin recommended for her. We were, after all, going to cut up a bundle—my two-thirds interest in Harolds Club, among other things—and we needed men of integrity.

While the lawyers worked out the business details, I, the lifelong sentimentalist, had some personal details to handle. I telephoned Dorothy. "Honey," I said, "we came into marriage first class. We had a lot of wonderful years together. Let's go out first class." She, God bless her, had the courage to accept.

So, on January 8, halfway between our last argument and the divorce court appearance, we had our breaking-up party. We held it at a night club that since has burned and it was a very good party. Twenty of our closest friends were there. There was no quarreling or needling on her part or mine. We danced together for the sheer love of dancing. We put aside our differences, if you please, and celebrated the years that had been good in our marriage. Once during the evening—in the powder room—I heard Dorothy wavered toward calling off the divorce. I knew that could not have been. The show was over for me. I was prepared to tell her: "This is the condition—you say you're through and I believe that you mean it—so we are through." Fortunately I didn't have to say it.

On January 20, 1947, Dorothy appeared at the Washoe County Courthouse here and got the decree. The formal charge was cruelty. I did not appear. I wanted her to have the divorce against me. She was the mother of my three children. She was a lady then, she is now, and in my heart always will be. Under the terms drawn up by our lawyers, I relinquished 50% of my Harolds Club holdings—one-third of its ownership—to her. She, who had come into our marriage with $9 in cash, was now a millionaire in her own right.

I readily gave her custody of the children for I wanted them to stay together as a family. I particularly wanted Junior to be with his sisters and help to look after them. I took only my house trailer, saddle, a desk and chair, my rifle and shotgun. Dorothy retained the big family home I had loved so much. Still there was no great sadness until I was packing my suitcase. Then it was little June came to me and said: "You build a house, Daddy, and I'll come live with you."

Despite all of my planning, thinking and philosophizing, I walked out of my marriage with tears in my eyes.

13

♣ ♣ ♣ ♣

Cowboying Through

The Trees

THE DAY AFTER my divorce I started out for Arizona to buy a quarter-horse named Barbara B. She was a great horse, later to win a $50,000 side bet at Santa Anita, but I didn't buy her. She was sold by the time I got to Arizona. I didn't get there right away. My cowboying era had started.

As an old rancher friend of mine says: "It's pretty hard to keep a squirrel on the ground in treed-up country." Between Reno and Las Vegas, Los Angeles and New York, being a freshly divorced sentimentalist and a newly consecrated drinking man, with money to burn, I was in treed-up country and I was a squirrel.

It showed in my drinking. The minute I was divorced, liquor hit me differently. That Arizona junket was the tip-off. I had as bodyguard then Jim Simpson, an old-time deputy sheriff from Elko County, and Jim had his pistol. Going down the highway between Tonopah and Goldfield, him driving and me drinking, I suddenly had an impulse to shoot his gun. It was a wild and reckless feeling that went right along with roaring over the flat desert country. He gave me the pistol and I started shooting at mile posts. I was hitting them, too, at seventy, eighty and ninety miles an hour.

That was part of the change in my drinking. I was launching into a bout of weeks-long boozing in which I would put away as much as four quarts of whiskey a day. Yet I didn't collapse, didn't stagger or permit myself to get bleary or sloppy. I stayed fastidious in my person and discovered I could be mentally alert and physically capable of things like shooting bullseyes at ninety miles an hour.

It was strange to discover this wild potentiality in myself. I'd been a rather incompetent drinker until then and could count my few alcoholic experiences on my fingers. One was when I was eighteen in San Francisco and went with Raymond to visit his Italian girl friend's family. They served wine with dinner and I got terribly sick. I blamed it on my not being used to wine and drinking too much too fast. Then in Chicago, in 1929, when I was running the Riverview Park concessions, I woke up one morning to find myself in bed with my clothes scattered over the floor. This was during Prohibition, of course, and I blamed bad beer. At Rio Nido in 1931, after I'd closed the Bingo game one night, a friend offered me a social drink. I had no intent whatsoever of getting drunk and took it without a qualm. The bootleg hit like an earthquake. I came to later wedged under a shelf in my booth, absolutely unable to extricate myself. Lady, my police dog, sat there kissing my face until daylight while I vowed never to touch bootleg again. I was appalled with myself.

Now all the bars seemed to be knocked down. My marriage was gone and nothing else mattered much. I didn't want to marry again. I didn't want to be around nice girls. I just wanted to raise hell—to get off the ground in this treed-up country. When Jim Simpson and I reached Vegas, I forgot Arizona and started on the prowl. It wasn't long before a gentleman I know (he's since gone straight) introduced me to a girl. She was young, she had all the proper equipment and she was crummy—just right for me in the mood I was in—but I couldn't have touched

her with gloves on. *What would she look like clean?* I wondered.
I had another drink and thought about it some more. Suddenly it
became necessary to me to clean up this crummy little whore. I
doubt that she has ever had such an experience before or since.
We went to my hotel room and I put her in the bathtub. There I
scrubbed her as I would have a child. When I was satisfied the
skin was clean, I handed her $500. "Go get your hair done and
buy some clothes," I ordered. Then I gulped some sleeping pills
and some more whiskey and fell into bed. The next few hours are
a sort of montage in my memory. The tune *Open The Door,
Richard* was currently popular. I remember my hotel door swing-
ing open and my girl friend singing—she had a voice like a
cracked bell—*Open The Door, Richard*. She was togged out in
a blue suit and a white waist. I gave her some more money and
told her to buy a hat. I went back to sleep. The door opened to
Open The Door, Richard and she needed more money. She had
a hat with more feathers on it than an ostrich. More sleep.
More improvements. If she thought she was ever going to earn
her money, I guess she realized she was dealing with a pretty
sleepy square. I never touched her. I couldn't. Something inside
me, after fifteen and a half married years, just wasn't ready.
Open The Door, Richard. I will never forget the song. It was the
theme music that opened my Pandora's box.

◆

I drank for weeks, gambled around Vegas and went to Arizona
to learn my horse was sold, gamboled back to Vegas and returned
eventually to Reno. I realized my thinking was all wrong. I
knew that I was no good to anyone the way I felt.
Still there was a girl—
Lois Morris, a tall and utterly feminine girl with big blue eyes
and shoulder length light brunette hair, dealt chuck-a-luck and 21
at the club. I had noticed her when I first came back from the
Army and deliberately stayed away from her. I knew she had
been married before and had two children, David, five, and Diane,
a year and a half, and that she lived with her mother in nearby

Sparks. I still was convinced I wanted nothing to do with nice girls. I knew Lois was one girl who would tolerate none of my cowboying. And somehow I knew that she knew she was the only woman in the world I could have married right then.

One night Jack Filtzer and I finished shift and went across the street for a drink. We'd just sat down at the bar when Lois came in with a girl friend from Harolds Club. The only seat open happened to be next to me. Lois sat there.

The bartender assumed we were together when he took our orders. I ignored that, but paid for the drinks. I was very conscious of the young lady beside me. I was most conscious of my own feelings. It was no good.

"Bright eyes," I said to her, "why don't you take a walk before you get hurt?"

She moved a little closer as if to hear me better. Lois Morris knew me quite well. To this day I call that bartender Cupid. He asked for our orders again at just that moment and I drove Lois home. The next day, February 20, 1947—exactly one month after my divorce—we were married. The ceremony was performed in the selfsame courthouse by District Judge A. J. Maestretti.

There are those, I know, who will question how I, a professed Catholic, could twice go to the altar without once doing it in my own church. I will explain that while I'm revealing so much of my personal ruler. I had married Dorothy because I loved her more than any woman on earth. She was very much a good Methodist and I knew that in the eyes of God she was a good girl. I assumed I was excommunicating myself, but I didn't let religion become a point of issue. When I married Lois the second time around I simply figured I was already out of my church's good graces. I would have to play it as it lays. I was most serious in this second marriage, I assure you. I adopted Diane and David as my own and have helped to raise them with all the love and attention I gave my own.

I continued to drink and gamble as the mood struck but my life wasn't all horseplay. Harolds Club still was booming. I worked the night shift, some 90 hours a week, in the vault, on the floor, counting money in and out, keeping an eye on things generally. I didn't permit drinking on shift and I didn't do it myself. One of the most dramatic moments the club ever had, as a matter of fact, occurred one night when, thank God, I was cold sober.

There was in Reno at that time a "turtle" named Mickey. "Turtle" is our name for a professional rodeo cowboy and Mickey was a spectacular one. He was over 6 feet tall and weighed 220. At that, he was the baby of his family. His eldest brother was 6 feet 4 or 5 and weighed between 260 and 270 pounds, all of it concentrated muscle. These two men were so powerful they could grab an 800-pound Black Angus cow and hold it by the horns while another cowboy milked it into a Coca-Cola bottle. Sober, they weren't too bad; drunk, they were trouble. "When that Howard and Mickey tell you to git," the other cowboys used to say, "you'd better git."

We'd had to bar Mickey from gambling in our club for trying to take advantage of the 21 tables. He would try to slip in tens on us to make blackjack. If the dealer caught it, Mick would start a fight. The fight, in fact, was more pleasurable to him than our money. One night after he'd been barred he came in and motioned to Bill Everhart, a bouncer, that he wanted to speak to him. Bill went over and Mick swung. Now Bill, an Air Force colonel and topnotch trap shooter, was plenty tough himself. He was not, however, any match for Mickey when the cowboy was sober. This night he was drunk. Bill ducked the punch, dug a left to Mick's stomach and dropped him with a right to the jaw. Then he dragged him out of the club.

I got the report when I came to work and summoned Bill. "This isn't the end of this incident," I warned him. "I know this man and his brother. There will be repercussions."

It couldn't be any other way with these turtles. Their friends would needle them into further action on the basis of masculine pride. Once again my club threatened to become a battleground for hoodlums. I could picture the scene out of a Western movie when the good guys and the bad guys tear up the saloon as they go at each other. One week later I came out of the vault and spotted big brother Howard casually strolling through the back of the club. He was too casual as he gave Bill Everhart a quick, appraising glance. This was a man he meant to take apart and he was in no hurry. I looked at the size of him, the easy swing of his shoulders, and knew we were in for a real go. Then I spotted the others.

There were six of them in addition to Howard and they were coldly, calculatingly sober. One sidled up to the back bar and ordered a beer. He didn't drink it, but stood caressing the neck. A beer bottle can be a horrible weapon when smashed on a bar and the shattered neck is used for a slasher. I recognized the other men as renegades, particularly dangerous when the action is going for them and you're on the floor.

Jim Simpson drifted up. "Get your friend," I muttered. He nodded and went after his gun. I saw our head floor man kibitzing the situation; he had just recovered from an operation. "Stay out of this," I told him. "All the way out." I walked over to Bill Everhart. "They're here," I said. "Get ready." He stepped into the checkroom for his blackjack and dropped it in his pocket. I ducked into the vault for my snubby .38.

The issues were very clear. Bill Everhart had bested Howard's baby brother in a man-to-man tussle when Micky was drunk. Howard wanted to hurt Bill; really hurt him. He was sizing Bill up now, solemnly, watchfully, before he moved on him. Either it would be settled here in the club or he would get Bill outside. One way or another, in his mind, the job had to be done. From our standpoint, the peace of the club was at stake. We had to stop this or be prepared for a running war with the roughneck element.

I knew Bill Everhart well enough to know he wouldn't run even though he had no chance against the gigantic cowboy. He was a loyal employee. He'd only been doing his job when he bounced Mickey. I had to back his play. If the tough guys got the idea they could move in on Harolds Club the word would travel faster than wireless. Out of the tail of my eye I saw Bill Reder, a Reno patrolman, looking on. Bill was a very fat man who always stood with his hands in his belt; he was so fat, in fact, when a holdup man shot him once the bullet never reached a vital organ. He could be helpful to us. He had practiced shooting from the hip and had killed at least one man with a hip shot. More important, we had the law present if I had to use my gun. I meant to use it. I'm not the fastest draw in the West so I had it in my side coat pocket, finger on the trigger, ready to shoot through the pocket. People still were playing quietly at the tables but you sense it when deadly serious business is being done. A tomblike silence was settling on the club.

I backed up to a big pillar to guard against attack from the rear. Jim Simpson was to my right, between Number 6 and 7 21 tables. I caught a glimpse of him from the corner of my eye, big Western hat pulled down on his forehead, deadpan, hands at his sides, covering the whole thing through squinted eyes. I heard his false teeth gritting; he was ready. Bill Everhart was poised near the end of the bar. Four of the renegades were within reach of him. He wasn't concerned with them. The key man was big Howard, now silently walking to a 21 table in front of the bar.

At that moment, when a spark could have touched off the dynamite, one of our lady customers stopped in front of me. "Harold," she demanded, "what's going on here? It's too quiet." I never took my eyes off Howard. "I'm very sorry, Mrs. Gootch," I said. "I don't know of anything wrong." She sniffed and walked on.

Howard had sat down to the 21 table, still watching Bill, stalling, playing $1 bets mechanically, thinking. He was weighing the scene, considering what he could lose and what he could win. The young man with the beer bottle eyed me. I had him covered; he knew it. He wasn't afraid. The small smile on his face seemed to say: *You probably would shoot, you son-of-a-bitch.*

The tension was terrific. For fifteen long minutes Howard played his mechanical game of 21, waiting for Bill Everhart to crack, to make the mistake that would give him justification to attack. It seemed a week to me. Howard, I could see, was not a dull man. He recognized in Bill a man who might get hurt badly but wouldn't walk away from a brawl to save himself. The wrong word or action was not going to come from him. Howard finally got up. Quietly, leisurely, with his coyotes following, he walked out the back door.

It was the end of the feud and I think I know why. Howard knew his brother was a troublemaker when he drank. Now he had tested Bill Everhart in his own crucible and hadn't cracked him. He would never love the Harolds Club bouncer, but he had to respect him. Never again would he or Mickey come into our club. He had ignored me throughout the tense watch. For me he had no feeling whatsoever. He concluded I wasn't a murderer. Quite frankly, I would have shot him.

♣

There are other unforgettable scenes from those years. They are part of my life and they've had undeniable influence on me, Harolds Club and my relations with Daddy and other members of my family. These were my bad years, remember, when I was to wander close to the borderland of insanity.

Once, I recall, I had been drinking heavily for about a month and gambling in every club in the state. I was leaving some pretty good markers behind me, all of which would have to be paid when I got sober again. This evening I was in the Bank Club playing Faro when I felt Daddy's presence behind me. He had come to get me out of the game.

"Harold," he drawled finally, when I let him get my attention, "how would you like to play a game of Red Dog?"

He didn't fool me for an instant. I knew he was appalled by my drinking and gambling and meant to teach me a lesson. Years before, when he wasn't quite a teetotaller in all things, he had played Red Dog quite extensively. He had, in fact, quit it only when he found it interfered with his business. He knew the game well.

All this I understood. But I wanted my dad to know me a little better too. I wanted him to see that what I contended was true—that it didn't matter how much I drank if the cards or dice were running right. My brain still functioned. I said: "Yes."

We crossed the alley to Harolds Club and found a table. In twenty minutes or so, $200-300 passed back and forth. Nothing consequential. By now, however, Reno people were aware of Daddy's concern over my antics and a crowd was gathering to watch us. That might have been okay with Daddy had he been trouncing me, but he wasn't. Then he overheard someone remark: "Isn't that a shame? A father trying to take money from his own son when he's drunk!" That got under his tough Vermont hide. "Let's go out to your house and finish this action," he snapped.

"Okay," I replied. It made no difference to me. We drove out to Whispering Winds, the big house south of town where I still live. On the way I did some thinking. When we sat down, I suggested: "Let's play $5000, win or lose, with a $50 ante."

He snapped up the suggestion. I don't say I detected a smug look on his face but he did reveal he meant this to be a real costly lesson for me.

Here I should explain Red Dog, which is a hard, fast game requiring special concentration. You each ante up a set amount of money, in our case $50. You are dealt five cards. The object of the game is to beat, with one card from your hand, the top card turned on the deck. If, for instance, a 10 of clubs is turned, you must have Jack or Queen, King or ace of clubs to win. If a 4 of hearts turns, you must have a higher heart. Always, you must have the higher card in the same suit as the top card turned on the deck. Four aces obviously would be a cinch hand, but how many times do you see four aces in five cards? It's rare when you get high cards in all four suits at once. You simply can't go against such obvious percentages when you play Red Dog; you must count the points. You will never take the pot, for instance, with an extreme hand, say five cards in one suit, even though you have ace high. With that hand, in fact, you wouldn't bet. You'd ante up again.

That's the method of play and we had agreed on conditions. We would each ante $50. When the cards were dealt, and before the deck card was turned, we either had to bet $100 or "go for the works"—which means bet an amount equal to everything in the pot—or pass. If we passed, we anted again. At least once an hour in Red Dog the cards seem to go crazy, no one can win a bet, and the pot builds. It went as high as $3000 sometimes in our game. Daddy was good, no doubt of it, and he was cold sober. I'd had two drinks while we played in the club. I had another when I got home, straight whiskey backed by plenty of water, but I wasn't dull. Our playing skill was about even. I had mild hunches, bet them and won the criterion bets. In two hours I took him for the $5000. The lesson, as it turned out, was a good one for Daddy. He wasn't so sure now I couldn't use my head when I drank.

He wasn't, to be sure, convinced I shouldn't drink. But that would be settled later.

♥

I have told you that Harolds Club got where it is by fantastic good luck and timing. Clearly Mother Providence had her eye on us in the years when I was floundering about in the wake of my shattered marriage. I am thinking now of the night I peeweed the dice in the biggest crap game ever seen in Nevada.

Until that night we weren't the big club in the state though we did the volume business. We were considered a tourist club, a slot machine house with incidental 21 and dice. Real high rollers wanting action went to the club I've called the Gibraltar. This was the night that would change all that.

It started about midnight when I learned two big players were in the house. Robert Carnahan was a casino operator from the Midwest. Marion Hicks owns the Thunderbird in Las Vegas. They were playing 21. Bessie Hoyt, a quiet, dark-haired, motherly little lady who has dealt for Harolds Club twenty years and earned more than a million dollars for us, was clobbering them. When I stopped at her table Hicks owed $15,000.

"I can't get even here," Carnahan was saying. "I've got to shoot craps."

He was a dapper little man whom I knew by reputation to have a mile of guts when gaming. I saw a man about 5 feet 8 and 145 pounds in a sharply pressed brown suit and a brown fedora hat that wasn't to come off once in the next thirty-odd hours. He was having a few drinks, I noticed, but he had the eyes of a real gambler whose judgment isn't going to be swayed by alcohol. Now he wanted to shoot craps and he wanted higher limits than we offered. My decision could cost Harolds Club a tremendous bundle or it could put us in the big leagues.

I didn't send for Daddy and I didn't ponder the matter more than a second. I okayed the higher limit, $500 a hand and double odds. Carnahan immediately showed his intent to break us fast. He beckoned to two companions lurking in the background and started the play as though the $500 flat limit automatically included them. Together, they were betting $1500 a hand and going for double odds, which is pretty fast action. On the first hand Carnahan threw a winning seven. Of itself, that didn't bother me, but I didn't like the subterfuge. The higher limit was for him alone. Chuck Webster was dealing and I'd stepped behind the table to assist, or box for him. Now I stopped the play.

"Bob," I said, "let's knock off this rubbish. You don't need these two gentlemen. If it's the money you're after, I'll up your own limit to $1500 a hand, double odds. You can play it yourself."

Maybe it sounded like a challenge. Maybe it was only what he wanted in the first place. He nodded without comment. The two men stood back. Now, and for the next 33½ hours, it was to be me and Bob Carnahan, for big money, over a green felt surface on which two dice could make or eat up a fortune.

The game started fast and went faster. All action at other tables and other floors slowed as the players came to stare. As it always does, and though it was 2 AM, word flashed through Reno that a terrific play was in progress at Harolds. People even got out of bed to come watch. Within an hour we needed two bouncers to keep spectators from crushing the table. People climbed onto stools and other tables to follow the action. I was aware of a great, pressing surge of suppressed excitement.

I couldn't take my eyes off the play even to see who was watching. Casual players came into the game and got out. One man shot an $86,000 hand for Bob Carnahan. But that was about the size of his luck in those first hours. He couldn't win consistently and he wouldn't get out. We were grinding him down at $1500 a hand.

I was aware when daylight came outside. Occasionally I glimpsed faces of our day shift. The hours ground on and the dice bounced harder. I sent for a sandwich. Carnahan declined food. Occasionally he accepted a drink. He did not leave the table even to go to the men's room. Twelve hours went into fourteen, sixteen, and it was evening. The night shift came on. Carnahan was stuck $150,000 but was still intent on beating the game.

I caught a glimpse of Daddy's tall figure pushing away from the crowd. He had come and looked but said nothing. Perhaps he stayed just long enough to determine I was having nothing to drink. I glanced at the solemn faces around the table and saw people in awe. Some of them I realized, had been there more than twelve hours. They simply stood and stared, saying nothing, caught up in the deadly seriousness of the game.

Once during that first day two drunken women had crowded in and tried to make a play for Carnahan. He didn't even look up. "Look honey," he said quietly, "I'm stuck." I knew how he felt and nodded to Jack Filtzer, one of the bouncers. He tried to ease them away. "I'm gonna stay right here," one of them shrieked. She had a creepy-looking boy friend a few feet away. I prayed we wouldn't have a real scene. Carnahan was shooting the dice.

I heard Filtzer say: "I'm going to have to throw you out."

"Who's gonna throw *who* out?" she retorted.

"*I'm* going to throw you out!" Filtzer growled.

I heard the temper rising in his voice and glanced up. He was pushing her toward the door and he did throw her out. He even kicked her in the seat of the pants. But I couldn't reprimand him for that just then.

My big player from the Midwest quite clearly was having one of those days I've spoken of when Mother Providence turns naturals to craps. He couldn't win. It was after midnight and going on 4 AM when I finally got the time straightened out in my mind. We'd been playing 28 hours and I was exhausted.

I tried to project the situation a few hours ahead should he continue. At $1500 a hand—up to $4500 at times with his odds —one good run would get him out of the hole fast. Several good hands on top of that would put him out in front and from what I'd seen of Carnahan, once ahead he'd work us over good. I would need to be sharp if his luck turned. I realized I was very tired. I slipped off to my hideaway bedroom for a quick nap.

Fifty minutes later, gulping hot coffee, I crowded back to the table. Carnahan and I had agreed he would lose no more than $250,000. From the look on his face, I guessed he was in much deeper than that. He was. The boxman reported he now owed us over $300,000.

There had to be an end to it and just before noon of that second day, when he'd played continuously for 33½ hours, I stopped the game again. "Bob," I said, "we've got to end this crap game. When the dice seven out we're through. A quarter million was your limit. You're over that now."

"Let me go half a million," he pleaded.

"No," I said, though I understood how he felt. Suddenly I was hit by one of my impetuous notions. "Do you want it real fast?" I asked.

He said he did.

"All right," I said. "You now owe us $348,000 according to the markers. I will shoot you once for the difference between that and half a million. We'll peewee the dice to make it quick. Then we can both get some sleep."

I wasn't trying to be dramatic but there was a gasp from the onlookers. Peeweeing dice is sudden death. Each player gets one die and one roll. The higher die wins it all. If Carnahan accepted the condition, he would be rolling to reduce his debt by $152,000. If he won he owed us $196,000; if he lost he owed us an even half million.

He accepted the condition without a change of expression. Carnahan was the ultimate gambler. Neither fatigue nor hunger nor the magnitude of his debt shook him.

For my part, I was as serious as I have ever been in my life. A half million dollar deal is important to any company. It was very important to Harolds Club in those days. Tired though I was, I had not lost any sense of the value of money. I understood precisely what I was proposing. "Do you want me to go first?" I asked. He nodded that he did.

I picked up my die. It was red with white spots and it glistened under the lights. I picked it up with the ends of the fingers of my right hand and I didn't palm it or shake it. I knew pepper from salt in that moment. I was throwing one dice for $152,000 or $500,000. The onlookers held their breath.

The die bounced off the far end of the table. An ace.

There is no number lower on the die than the ace. Carnahan had five chances in his one throw to beat me. Someone let out his breath explosively. I was ready to turn away. Carnahan was picking up his die.

A man would have to be terribly unlucky not to win in that situation. Carnahan didn't permit a smile to cross his weary lips. He'd watched dice hop before.

There was absolute silence as he threw and his celluloid cube bounded across the green. Then an outcry. He had an ace.

"That's how my luck is tonight," he said quietly. He had just failed to reduce his debt.

I picked up my die again and threw quickly. A deuce.

Now there was a slight relaxing in Carnahan. It was inconceivable he would miss again. To win, he needed only a 3, 4, 5, or 6. He cast the die. A three. It was enough. Instead of one half million, he now owed Harolds Club only $196,000.

The long strain told though. Carnahan strode straight to the men's room and vomited. I was waiting when he came to the bar. "You know, Bob," I said, "that will happen when your nerves let down."

He nodded.

It was almost noon. Our game had gone through half of one night, through an entire day and an entire night and halfway through the second day. In those final throws it became the biggest game ever played in the history of Nevada's legalized gaming. Harolds Club was now established internationally as a big gaming house, a serious casino, yet I had no feeling of exhilaration. I was dead tired. Without further talk Bob Carnahan and I went our ways.

Pappy's signs say it all.

Not very elegant here. Jim Hunter
(left) and me at our quicksilver mine.

Real elegant at last, with
Lois at the Waldorf-Astoria.

ond A., whom I helped make a millionaire, signs checks.

We like our publicity stunts BIG. That's me in glasses.

Son Junior cuts up with our Gay 90s girls.

As you see, I'm pretty fond of my Fun Room show.

I still like to tog out western style and play at emceeing.

Yankee Doodle (with me up) is my idea of real horse flesh.

A happy trap shooter am I.

Wife Lois with Fifi and Simon, the blue-ribbon poodles.

I asked my neighbors' help in picking a title for this book and paid off $2,000 in prize money but liked my own idea best—*I Want to Quit Winners.*

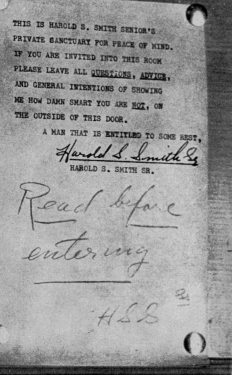

The note on my sanctuary door speaks my mind.

Locked in my hideaway, I pursue knowledge.

14

♦ ♦ ♦ ♦

To The Doors

Of Madness

I MUST SPEAK here now of the carousing that contributed to my nightmare years of the late 1940s and early 1950s. I mention it with no sense of braggadocio, or of shame either, though I did more boozing in those ten years than some men may do in a lifetime.

I believe I was not, nor am I now, an alcoholic. I was a squirrel in treed-up country and nothing, but nothing, was going to keep me on the ground. I did, to be sure, take antabuse to curb my drinking at one point, underwent psychiatric guidance at another, doctored extensively, was hospitalized, and, in the end, wound up in the psycho ward of St. Mary's Hospital. However, Dr. Floyd O. Due, an eminent psychiatrist in Oakland, California, assured me I was not alcoholic.

His assurance is important to me now that my sobriety hangs on the thread of an oath to the Big Gent Upstairs. The true alcoholic

I can't quite explain except that he seems to have a disease as a tubercular or polio victim has a disease. I should like to believe I suffer only from the afflictions of self. Apparently I was a periodical whose periods crowded so closely on each other at times as to find me drinking daily and for weeks at a crack.

It was bad in all ways and this I knew. I carried a load of guilt as heavy as my grief at the turns my life was taking. But I didn't drink for oblivion. I did not try to escape into a bottle. Even after twelve and thirteen days of steady drinking I knew salt from pepper. I was trying to have fun and it was natural in my environment this should include heavy gaming.

For me, the excitement of gambling well may stem straight from years of poverty, insecurity and domination followed by marital happiness, then disappointment and frustration. I don't really know. I just remember I'd been a grounded squirrel until unlimited funds and domestic freedom turned me loose in the treed-up never-never land of Nevada.

My friends and associates, furthermore, were such as Eddie Sahati a gambolier with no time for dull people. Eddie showed me how to bet money quickly and heavily. He showed me, in spite of his unfortunate narcotics habit, that you must remain alert at all times, searching out weaknesses in every player with whom you contest. Eddie would dig, dig, dig until he found that one weakness, then proceed to take fullest advantage. I learned from him that most people are afraid to bet their money; I learned how to raise in a poker game and scare them out, how when it "gets too rich for your blood," you can be raised out of every pot. All this I learned while drinking heavily.

There was one game, for instance, involving a foursome of us, all gamblers with an interest in casinos, all known to each other. In this game we considered ourselves as in business against each other, each trying to win as large a bundle as possible. We played what is known as a "$40 condition." This meant the first man must ante $40 or pass; the second man must then ante $80 or drop out. When the first two stay, the third antes $160 or quits and the fourth man, the dealer, must come up with $320. If he does, the first man makes up the difference between his $40 and the $320. Then the players in turn, making up the difference between their antes and $320, have met the condition before the draw of cards. Now the raises begin. We agreed to "table stakes." In other words, you could, if you wished, bet all the money you had in front of you, but no more than that. You couldn't dig. Each of us was there to make a killing, as I say. We were not playing for peanuts, as is done in "friendly" games where a limit is set on the number and amount of raises.

Eddie Sahati bet his thousands as if the United States Mint were working just for him. He bet so flamboyantly on every round it would appear he must have a "cinch hand." Knowing Sahati and his current finances didn't help you guess his hand. It would have been the same if the money he used was borrowed, was the last few thousands he had, or some of the million or more he had made gaming. Eddie bet the same poor as rich. His raises in our game would chase you out of any pot unless you had a great deal of courage and the bankroll to back it. Sometimes, obviously, you were going to have more courage and bankroll than luck and you would lose. You couldn't afford to play that kind of game drunk. You had to know that salt was salt and pepper was pepper.

I was in a lo-ball game one day, for instance, in which Eddie had chased out everyone but me with his huge raises. Lo-ball, of course, is a game in which the lowest, or worst, poker hand wins. There was one pot finally with about $8000 in it. Eddie abruptly raised me $3000 and I had a hunch he was bluffing. I called and caught him with two pairs, which is about as bad a hand as you can have in lo-ball. Actually I had a pair of threes and was bluffing too.

Another day, though drinking, I knew enough to drop out of a lo-ball game. This is a point, too. It was a table stakes game and each man had about $150,000 on the table before him. Eddie was dealing. A player I shall call George opened the first hand, betting $5000. Eddie met and raised $10,000, at which point George pushed in all the money in front of him, his table stakes, approximately $145,000. Eddie hesitated only a moment. The amount remaining before him was about $135,000; he pushed it in. George then admitted he'd been bluffing. He asked if he could forfeit $15,000 and take back the rest.

"No," Eddie said. "It was a legitimate bet. I believed you had 'the nuts' (the advantage) when you made your bet. You almost bluffed me out of my $15,000. Play it as you called it."

George, however, had a bad hand to play. He'd really been bluffing. He had to draw four cards. Now he had a hunch that the cards on the other side of the deck would be better than the ones on his side. He asked for a cut before his four cards were dealt. Eddie didn't expect that. It upset him.

It was rare for a turn of a gambling game to upset Eddie Sahati. He must have sensed he had the winning hand and resented the interruption. More than a quarter of a million dollars in one hand can warm the ice water in the coolest gambler's veins. It can prod his ego.

Eddie made the cut and dealt George his four cards. He now had a strong hunch to deal himself the next card. He was drawing one card to replace a picture card in his hand, which was otherwise a good lo-ball hand, Ace, deuce, three and six. Here, however, is where emotions can hamper a man's gaming. Eddie somehow came to the conclusion he must ask for a cut of the deck too. He got it and dealt his card. It was a 3, pairing the 3 in his hand. George, though drawing four cards, had no pairs. He won the big pot.

How does this apply to my heavy drinking while gaming? I am convinced Eddie asked that unnecessary cut as a sop to his ego. He ignored his original hunch to take the next card. It cost him a fantastic pot. I have enough ego without expanding it with liquor. If I was to drink and gamble I had to control the effects of that drinking and I did.

I have said my drinking changed radically from the day of my divorce. It did. I wasn't defeated, as so many alcoholics are, and I wasn't beaten down. Far from it. I was kicking up my heels, trying to show I didn't give a damn. I did, of course, though I couldn't quite pinpoint what I gave a damn about. Actually I was confused about myself. Something inside of me which never quite got as drunk as the rest of me sat in disapproving judgment and complained unceasingly that I was doing wrong and hurting myself.

This held me to three pre-set rules of conduct:
1. Never to drink alone in my bedroom.
2. Never to drink in or about automobiles if I had to drive.
3. Never to have a bottle in my room for morning (although I might repair to the nearest bar quite early).

I developed other little disciplines. I would always keep myself as neat and clean as if I had an important appointment. Cleanliness became a phobia. I picked up bars of soap from every hotel so I would have them with me in saloons or service station restrooms that might be out. I shaved frequently and changed shirts the moment they wilted. I collected skin lotions and deodorants and used them liberally. I knew better than to drink wine. In fact I carefully observed the advice a heavy-drinking doctor once gave me: "If you're going to drink," he said, "drink good bourbon or good Scotch with plenty of plain water. No soda or fizzy mixes and pass the beer."

Controls there were on my drinking. There was also a certain defiance. I didn't want anyone "mothering" or "fathering" me. I didn't want advice. I didn't want anyone invading my privacy. I was handling my whiskey, I figured, and it wasn't anyone else's damn business so long as I wasn't annoying him, borrowing money, insulting him or interfering with his life. I could get most abrupt with those who tried to take advantage, and plenty did. Many a rival club operator in Reno and Vegas hoped to get me into a big game when my wits might appear to be addled and at least one Hollywood card sharp did his best to inveigle me into a gin rummy game I could never have won. I vaguely remember seeing Nick the Greek on the edge of that play.

There was a morale problem at Harolds Club whenever I came in to drink, no doubt of it. Employees seeing me at the bar took liberties they never would have otherwise. Some came to borrow pocket money, some to make a sex pitch, some to wheedle for advancement. Decorum went out the window and horseplay started. Daddy was only too soberly aware of this and consistently disapproving. I didn't like it myself. I upbraided them severely and got the name of a "mean" drunk in some quarters.

Basically, though, I still was out to have fun. I loved to ride horseback, shoot my guns, laugh uproariously and dance. Married I was, but I still liked the ladies. Some I liked very much. But no tramps, no chipping just for the chipping's sake. Let's just say I may have been an easier target for feminine wiles than I was to be in a later, soberer time.

There was talk, lots of it. Reno is quite a small town and the Smiths by then were a big family. Daddy was married for the fifth time and starting a new family of two girls and a boy. Mama was around. Raymond was married and had a family. Dorothy was remarried and sat in on our board meetings as third owner. In 1950 my son Junior was eighteen years of age and a witness to my cowboying. I had two daughters with Dorothy and an adopted son and daughter with Lois. I was somewhat of a local celebrity.

Still and all, I wasn't unique. I remember sitting one day at a trap-shoot at our gun club talking with a doctor and a cattleman's wife. One word led to another and I was recounting for the doctor my experience of going overboard for one woman, of losing her and kicking over the traces, drinking, gambling and defying convention. The doctor, an old friend, listened intently.

The cattleman's wife, however, had to "get human." "I just can't understand you, Harold," she said. "If it had been me, I would have—" She "would have" done a lot of things differently.

The doctor shook his head slowly. "What has happened to Harold," he told her soberly, "could happen to anyone. Even you. Tomorrow could change your entire outlook."

It was like a prediction. Not long afterward her husband fell in with a chorus girl at the Mapes Hotel who played up to his ego and had him doing juvenile handsprings. The strait-laced wife, overcome by bitterness and disappointment, did everything she had criticized me for doing, with possibly a few exceptions. She drank heavily and gambled heavily. Worse, she gambled in desperation, not caring if she won. In time her husband had a heart attack and they went back together. But she was never the same person who looked down her nose at me.

None of us are the same after walking through that morass.

◆

I hadn't run out of troubles by any means. My family co-owners of Harolds Club obviously spent some sleepless nights while I cowboyed around the town and obviously had to do something about it. They did, in 1949. I could give it to you in all the gory detail but I think it's told about as well as it can be in a statement Daddy's lawyers prepared later when some of his property purchases got him into an involved case with Internal

Revenue. The pertinent section is headed: *"Option to buy Harold's stock in Harolds Club"* and this is what it says:

"Raymond I. Smith (Daddy) became greatly distressed and worried when his son Harold, upset by his divorce, took to drinking and gambling excessively. He was able to persuade Harold on four occasions to stop gambling in other clubs, but Harold returned each time to his heavy drinking and gambling. He gambled for very high stakes and in unwise fashion. He was encouraged to do this by rival gambling establishments which gave him unlimited credit. He thus lost practically everything he had saved in prior years. His father feared that rival gambling establishments might be able to acquire from Harold some or all of Harold's stock in Harolds Club.

"The father and the other directors . . . felt that it would be necessary that the petitioner (Daddy) control that stock for its own protection so that if Harold had to sell it for some reason in connection with his wild gambling it would not get into unfriendly hands. Harold's gambling was mostly with competitors either in Reno or Las Vegas, and the directors felt that if any of the stock of Harolds Club got into the hands of such persons they would interfere with the petitioner's operation of the bars in Harolds Club. . . .

"The petitioner (Daddy) acquired on September 6, 1949, a first refusal option on the stock in Harolds Club owned by Harold S. Smith, entitling the petitioner (Daddy) to buy the stock for $500,000 if Harold S. Smith should offer it for sale during the next five years. The directors of the petitioner felt that there was real danger, that the option was necessary and that it might have to be exercised. . . ."

The option was never exercised, I should point out, and expired in 1954. I would have been a fool, though, if I thought I was to be treated in the future as anything but a little boy. Daddy even set a limit on my gambling in my own club of $50,000 a day.

♠

That wasn't all the bad news of 1949 either. One day I struck a match to light my cigarette. A bolt of lightning hit my right eye.

I had iritis, an ailment so agonizing I would not wish it on my worst enemy. It is, technically, an inflammation of the iris and results, I understand, from an infection elsewhere in the body. A Reno doctor diagnosed it correctly. He did not, unfortunately, have an effective cure.

I gobbled Anacin and gulped whiskey. The eye felt like a red hot coal sitting squarely in the nerves leading to my brain. I went off with my bodyguard to Spokane, Washington, to present a trophy at the races. I thought I would disintegrate in flight.

Finally, in an agony I can't even begin to describe, my bodyguard led me, a tottering, pain-wracked man, to the San Francisco offices of Dr. Roy Parkinson, who had treated my father's eye troubles since shortly after World War I. To some patients he is one of the greatest eye men on the Coast. To me he was, and is, an angel.

Dr. Roy had known and treated iritis over many, many years. He had tried to interest other medical men in his treatment, which consists of an injection under the skin of the eyeball. He had not, unfortunately, convinced very many. Our Reno doctor didn't even know of it. Having that needle stuck in your eye is, as I said, much earlier, no mirthful thing. It is an ordeal to be compared with no other in this mortal life. But it gets the job done.

Three times since, at intervals of two years each, that lightning has flashed in my eye and I have had to go running to Dr. Roy. It has never been anything but an excruciating experience. Yet out of it has come an association with a wonderful, understanding and wise man. A philosopher, if you please, with extraordinary patience.

If in the end I do quit this game of life winners, it will be in great part because I have had from time to time to climb down off my high horse and go crawling in anguish to my friend and physician.

♣

The months galloped by, the tides swirled and the squirrel skittered from tree to tree. In 1951, with my forty-first birthday, however, things appeared to be leveling off some. Mother Providence gave me a glance again, at least.

One fall night in the Riverside Hotel I began to turn some pretty hot dice hands. I was drinking, of course, but the tingling electric hunches came clearly and I bet them as Eddie Sahati had demonstrated. Heavy. The hands followed me around the circuit of clubs next day. It was the hottest winning streak I had ever had. By the end of the week I had a pretty bundle of cash and the streak wasn't ended.

For the first time since I accepted Dorothy's challenge to divorce her, five years before, I felt like a winner again. In life as well as at the gaming table.

The National League baseball race of that year, you'll recall, came breathlessly down to the wire with a tie between the Giants and Dodgers. The Giants won the first of the best-of-three playoff games, lost the second and were trailing 1-4 in the ninth inning of the final clash. Then it was that Bobby Thomson hit the dramatic home run that won it, and the league title, for the Giants. It was one of the most exciting moments in baseball history and a profitable one for me. I picked nine straight games correctly, including that key one, bet them confidently and added to my bulging bankroll.

It was interesting to note that no one, not even Daddy, had a word of complaint about my gambling in those winning days. I was bursting to climb the tallest tree in the world.

Long before, I'd adopted a habit, when winning, of sinking a chunk of the money in something concrete, something I could keep when the spree ended. It's the only system I know to keep from blowing your winnings after a heady triumph at the tables and I still practice it. Now the Cinderella Giant team was going to bump head-on into Casey Stengel's bold Yankees in one of the most talked-about Series of the century. I was a life-long Yankee rooter. I had never seen a World Series. Why not blow some of my roll on a rollicking trip to New York?

There was sentiment mixed all through the idea. I had dreamed of seeing a World Series from the time I was a poor boy doing housework in Cleveland. Even before that I'd heard of the Big Town, New York, and the fact that the greatest mark of affluence you could have was to go there and stay at the Waldorf. Suddenly, with thousands of dollars in winnings in my pockets, I could afford it. I could make a pilgrimage of it, pretending I was taking that long-ago poor boy to the Big Town at last and treating him to the best of everything.

Reno's high-rolling rounders were making up a party to see the Series. An operator colleague, Ray Ryan, who owns the El Mirador Hotel in Palm Springs and may well be the top gambolier in the world today, provided us with the best of box seats. It was colorful and exciting and fun but somehow my long-awaited first World Series didn't quite turn out as I, the lifelong sentimentalist, expected. I had anticipated it all those years through the eyes of a boy, getting to the Stadium early to watch the stars warm up, rooting right down to the wire with hot dogs in both hands, hanging around at the players' gate to watch the heroes leave. My rounder friends didn't play it that way. We left our hotel late in chartered limousines, straggled into our boxes at the first pitch, filled the innings with tremendous bets and were up and out to meet our limousines before the last batter took his cuts. The Yankees won it four games to two and I added to my bankroll. I felt a sadness as I did. Not even my dreams could be the same any more. I wasn't a wide-eyed little boy. I was a bigtime professional gambler.

That fact was demonstrated one afternoon at the Polo Grounds when another gambler approached me. "Harold," he said quietly, "we're going to have a big game starting at 8 PM. There will be no kibitzers. I guarantee the men and the dice. Let me know if you want to join us."

"Who'll be there?" I asked. I was aware every gambler in the country knew I was on a hot streak and carrying a bundle. He named several of the most famous men in the fraternity. One of them was a notorious "Don't Side" player and I'd always had a feeling anyone who got hot and made a series of passes could devastate Don't Side playing and end up with a fortune. My man had vouched for the dice and the players. That meant no "weight" or "nuts" or chicanery. His word was better than a lawyer's contract. So I accepted.

We met that evening in one of the most luxuriant suites in one of the world's most famous hotels. There were five or six of us. Each of us knew the rules and knew they were ironclad. It was to be a big game but a quiet game; no foolish mistakes. The conditions were established quickly and accepted quietly as real gamboliers' always are. There would be no arguments, no unnecessary discussion and no drinking of consequence. Each of us was there to win as big a bundle as possible. Any foolishness would only endanger our health or our lives.

Our host took a pillow from one of the chairs and leaned it against the wall at a 45-degree angle. The rules and conditions were simply this: Slam those dice against the pillow, don't try to manipulate them or curve them. Hit the dice hard against the pillow and it's a good roll. "No dice" would be called if one or both dice failed to hit the pillow squarely. This was to be a "blood game" so just rattle the dice, kick them out and slam the pillow. Whatever comes face up is good enough for everyone.

The courtesy bet was $500 on the line, to be bet for the "house," or our friend who had organized the game. When a point appeared—4, 5, 6, 8, 9 or 10—we took $500 odds and the real wagering was in the side bets with either the banker or one of his associates recording each bet in a little black book. If a given man had the dice, for instance, and his point was 9, there would be betting on the side as to whether he would make the 9. An associate of the house had a deck of playing cards; he would lay the 9 card out to indicate the point. That way there could be no question or argument.

On a 9, as all operators know, the odds are 3 to 2. So someone on the Don't Side would say quietly: "$6000 to $4000 he doesn't make it." We could take as much or as little of that $4000 as we wanted. Generally the maximum bet on any one point was around $16,000. We had, then, from $4000 to $16,000 in side money riding on every roll of the dice.

We needed very little cash and no chips because of the running record being kept in the black book. Each of us was good for whatever that black book said we owed, whether it be $5000 or $500,000. When a man won, say $25,000, the house man simply paid him off. I have never in my life seen $1000 bills handled so quickly and casually. It was faster even than your bank teller counts out ones. And it was accurate. He had one envelope containing only $1000 bills, another full of $500 bills and another simply stuffed with $100s for change. Even some of us operators, discussing it later, remarked: "He handled those bills as though they weren't money."

We drank only orange juice or black coffee during the progress of the game and there was no unnecessary talk. You heard the low-voiced "Lay you $12,000 to $8000 on 9" or "I'll take $8000 to $12,000 he doesn't make the nine" . . . "Lay you 16 to 8 he doesn't make 4" . . . "$8000 to $16,000 he does make the 10." No bosh, no loud talk, a gathering as quiet as a board meeting in Mister J. P. Morgan's bank. Every man present was hep, a gambler concentrating on trying to win money. It would have startled every eagle-eyed player there if any one had been so foolish as to try a "shot," controlling one dice to prevent a crap. It would also have been most foolish on his part.

It was not a long game as time goes, about two hours, and none of the players ever asked another how he did. Just by keeping your mouth shut and watching closely, though, you saw that some picked up as much as $100,000 in winnings. The house man paid off all winnings; the losers made arrangements to reimburse him. Those in the habit of carrying large amounts of cash settled right there. Others gave checks, others their marker. He operated like a department store in that connection, permitting 30-day credit, although, unlike the department store, he had methods of collection. You paid or you wouldn't live long.

I wasn't lucky that night. I dropped $8000 which I paid off in cash. Then some of us did some heavy drinking to relax from the mental strain of concentrating.

The evening was only an interruption of my winning streak, which resumed the moment I returned to Reno. Before that streak ended, I had won $150,000. I have never had one so good since.

♥

Many, many times during the ten bad years of my life I thought of God—the Big Gent, as I have chosen to call Him—and Jesus Christ, the perfect man. Even drunk, I made it a point to say my prayers, looking at my crucifix warmly and concentrating upon it. I declare this not in a spirit of sanctimonious penitence or rehabilitated righteousness. I mention it only because it has been a condition of my life.

Because it has been a condition, I had to carry a solemn burden all through my troubled years. Though I do not consider myself a religious man even now, I know I have always been spiritually oriented.

Often, so very often in those days and ones to follow, I would slip into the Cathedral here and sit in a specific pew where I could lift my eyes to a particular stained glass window portraying Christ on His cross. I vowed there again and again to be good to other people in spite of myself and never to expect their appreciation. Many times, finding true peace as I gazed up to that glass picture, I have found myself listening far more to it than the priest in the pulpit.

I recall so clearly the day a beautiful six-year-old person took his First Communion in a church in Buffalo, N.Y. Forty-five years later I remember every detail of the interior of that church and the sacred ceremony. It is one of my beautiful memories.

That boy had a right to the Sacraments of his church. He was right in himself, in all ways, to receive them. He was a trusting boy. He admired his father, loved his mother and clung to beauty. He saw The Passion there for the first time and witnessed his Christ's suffering. He accepted Christ with no reservations.

That boy is not the person sitting behind this desk telling of a life in which most of the Commandments have been broken not once but many times. The boy and the man are not even close to each other.

Yet, through scenes of self-imposed suffering, I see them somehow draw closer to one another. At least I see a kinship.

◆

Even a squirrel must weary of running through the trees and come down for rest. A clock that is wound too tight too often will break. And so must a man. By 1956, though I didn't recognize the signs immediately, my great vitality was cracking. I had to come down from my cowboying through never-never land whether I wanted to or not.

My aggravations of family, gambling, money and a club with divided ownership I still had. Drinking somehow didn't put the necessary walls between us any longer. I was terribly nervous at times, often emotionally upset at others, irascible, discouraged, weary and frustrated. That was the time, you'll remember, when tranquilizers circulated so freely. My doctor prescribed Miltowns.

Being me, I ate them by the handful. Yet I didn't relax. Riding horseback didn't calm me. Gambling didn't get the job done. Pretty girls held my attention only momentarily. I lived day and night with the feeling I was going to fly out of my skin; yet that doesn't describe it either. Try as I have, I find no terms to describe it accurately. I simply felt that I was disintegrating and couldn't understand why. I had never felt myself in such a situation before. So I took more pills.

By June I was thoroughly perplexed. I couldn't seem to make decisions even on such minor matters as selecting a suit of clothes. I found myself weighing each word I spoke. My speech and comprehension slowed to a crawl. More pills. With David, my stepson, I flew to Helena, Montana, for a trap shoot. There, clearly, I began to comprehend that something ominous was happening to me. And I couldn't guess what.

We were to fly to Eugene, Oregon, to meet Junior and Lois, then to drive to the little town of Drain to visit two wonderful friends, Harold Woolley and Harry "Cub" Lupher. Woodsmen and practical men, they would, I knew, offer a safe haven. I seemed to be apprehensive now, to have some vague dread of something I knew not what, that was bound to happen soon. In Seattle, en route from Helena, I found it impossible to remember what I must do next. As a result, David and I missed our plane and had to charter one to fly us to Eugene. Lois and my friends recognized immediately that something was wrong. When we got to Woolley's house, I asked him and Cub to step down the corridor a moment. "If you please," I pleaded, "I am not at my best. Something is terribly wrong with me. If I do or say anything wrong, please consider this."

They couldn't understand it. I wasn't drinking. I took some more Miltowns. We stayed at a motel there a few days and went salmon fishing on the ocean out of Winchester Bay. There I ran out of pills and was feeling a little better. Had we stayed on there, I might even have fended off the inevitable. But Reno is home to me and I had to hurry back.

My mental confusion increased. I started to shoot craps at the Riverside Hotel one night, won $9000, and couldn't even count the chips. I saw Ruby Mathis, the boxman, frown as I fumbled with them. I simply couldn't coordinate. Then I felt impelled to make an announcement to the crowd at the table. "Please consider, ladies and gentlemen," I said. "I'm not at my best. Please consider." They glanced at each other in amazement. I repeated the little speech three times as if the needle had stuck.

Have you ever found yourself in a position where you simply don't know what you are going to say or do next? It is monstrous. It makes your confusion even more horrible. I was to stumble around Reno for several weeks in that condition, head bowed and shoulders stooped like an old, old man, fumbling, stumbling, hesitant even to step off the curb of familiar old Virginia Street. It was like being a child again, only worse. I took to hiding out in my bedroom at the club.

I was there on the afternoon of August 9, 1956, bemused by the antics of a moth. It had fluttered up from somewhere and kept flying around and around the room without going near the light. That caught my attention as though it were supernatural. A moth that wouldn't go near a light? There was a rap on the door and my dad came in. I told him about the moth. I started to talk about God.

Daddy listened to that for about two seconds. "I can't stand you guys always talking about God!" he exclaimed. It was the same tone of voice he'd once used to say he couldn't stand "can't-me" guys around him.

"You can't!" I shrieked. "You're mad!" I got up from the bed and walked to the washroom door, where I stood with my hand on the jamb, seething at my father for getting mad when I was only speaking of the Big Gent. I knew that he understood nothing of illness—when you were walking and talking you must be all right —and that, if the chips were down, he was mightily concerned for me. Yet he seemed to infuriate me.

"Make up your mind," I shouted at him, "all your cunning and guile isn't going to fool God!"

At that moment, fortunately, the door opened and Dr. Francis Kernan came in. I had, I remembered, telephoned him to come. "Dr. Kernan," I shouted, "we're having a terrible argument. I want you to referee. In this bedroom, I contend, I am the boss. Second to no man. This is mine—my privacy!"

"That's no way to talk to the doctor," Daddy interrupted.

He infuriated me further. My voice, I am sure, could be heard over in the club above slot machines, dice players and PA announcements. Doctor Kernan was studying me carefully. He didn't argue when I said I was going home. But he made it a point to be there that night. He listened graciously and with understanding when I explained how Daddy's refusal to talk about God had angered me.

One way or another, without really stating what he suspected was wrong, Dr. Kernan persuaded me to go to the hospital. He drove me himself with Lois riding in the back seat. Suddenly I was hilarious as I cruised through Reno in pajamas and robe, joshing him about the little window on my side of the car which wouldn't work.

We were shown to a second floor room at St. Mary's Hospital. A young orderly stood by there to help. "And what's your name?" I asked of him.

"David Daniels," he replied.

"Of all things!" I exclaimed. "Here I am sick in a hospital, thinking and talking about the Big Gent, and the first person I meet has two good Biblical names like David and Daniels." I was truly impressed with what seemed a coincidence.

Daddy turned up in the room and flopped on the other bed. He was saying what I ought to do was go to a good cold climate and take long hikes that would wear me out. I strolled around looking at my room. It seemed very quiet. "What the hell is this?" I demanded suddenly. "A mausoleum?" Daddy told me to be still. As I passed near the window, three nurses jumped and grabbed me. I laughed uproariously. They thought I was going to jump. I wasn't. I had no thought of it.

Someone apparently was worried, though. Dr. Kernan came in with a wheelchair and made me sit in it. They'd decided they couldn't have my loud mouth among sick patients. They wheeled me downstairs to another ward and that's where the show really started. Immediately after they put me to bed I demanded to know where the crucifix was. There was none on the wall though it was a Catholic hospital. Someone got one and placed it on a stand facing me. Dr. Kernan noticed that. Upset and nervous I might be, but the mind was working.

I was lying there quietly awaiting the next move when a big young orderly stopped beside my bed. I reached out and belted him on the chin. Why? Because he looked big and strong to me and I suddenly resented someone who was young, big and strong. It didn't hurt him, but the nurse holding my left hand suddenly gripped it very hard. Another orderly came in. I knew him well. I punched him in the stomach. Then I was relaxing under their medication.

The next day the nurse came with a thermometer. I looked at it and recognized it. A metal thermometer. I knew now where I was. "The psycho ward," I muttered. "I made it at last." It did not occur to me that I might be insane. I knew I was not. I knew exactly what happened after too many Miltowns, too much intrigue, too many aggravations. I was having a nervous breakdown.

There had been a man in the room in a bright plaid lumberjack shirt. I had thought him the janitor the night before. The next day he was back, still in the bright shirt, to ask me a lot of questions. "Just a moment," I interrupted. "To whom am I talking?" He told me then he was Dr. Raymond Brown, a psychiatrist, that he was going to take care of me and would have me out of that ward as soon as he possibly could.

As it worked out, I was there under lock and key for three solid months. I knew why I was there and I wasn't worried. I planned, rather, how I would defeat this crippling thing that had caught me and of course I turned toward God, believing that if I were truly penitent He would help. "This is my lot," I prayed. "I accept it. So be it. I will get better." It was His judgment that put me there, I believed. It was part of my life.

Those three months gave me time to think and to meditate as I never had on eternal things. Though I was locked up physically, my mind was free. Getting back my mind was something I wanted very badly. To get it back, I found I had to turn more and more to spiritual thinking. In the process I was to return to my religion.

Not everything was shut out, of course. Though I was too nervous to watch television, even passing the World Series of that year, I listened to radio, read the newspapers and had visitors. I caught up on all the gossip, including things that were happening in my club; among them the fact it was being run now by my father, my son and my ex-wife. Strangely, I had anticipated such a state of affairs. Daddy had made Junior his protégé and it had gone to the young man's head. He was just 24 and found himself something of a squirrel in treed-up country too. One of the things he did was to extend $10,000 credit to a real louse and learn a quick lesson about people. Daddy was real rough on Junior.

Dr. Brown would come in each day and ask: "Percentage-wise, Harold, how do you think you are today? Compared with what you should be capable of." I would answer honestly: "Today about 85%. I know I'm not right yet." He would continue his psycho-analysis and treatment. I itched to be out in my old haunts but I tried to cooperate. During the last six weeks I was even keeper of the keys and helped the nurses with errands.

One night, however, I got so lonely I decided to sneak out. I knew they had gotten careless with me, knowing I wasn't violent; though I had only pajamas and bathrobe to wear, I determined to walk home. The nurse was talking on the telephone as I slipped past her station. She didn't see me. I was just eight feet from the door and reaching for the knob when she called: "Where are you going?" It infuriated me. I blew my top. "What is this, any-way?" I shouted. "A jail?" It did no good. A big orderly was there in an instant and I surrendered. You lose all fights in the psycho ward, as I had observed, so there's no use starting any. When they tell you what to do, do it, or they'll restrain you. That, too, was a revelation to me with my nature. It was part of my general submission.

One more scene from the ward. On October 5, when I had been confined nearly eight weeks and was close to being discharged. Lois came to see me. We were alone in the room and my wife was speaking of the drinking which she believed had helped lodge me there. She was worried as to what would happen when I got out. I sat listening, giving full consideration to her worry about me. I had done a good deal of thinking about drinking myself. I knew it wasn't good.

"All right," I said, and it was not an impetuous decision, "we will get this over with right now."

I crossed the room to the wall beneath the crucifix and kneeled. There I took an oath not to drink one drop of alcoholic beverage for four full years, or until January 1, 1960. That oath I kept. And you now have seen more of the ruler of my life than I ever showed before.

15

♥ ♥ ♥ ♥

One Gambler's Word

THERE ARE THOSE to this day who look down their long noses at the close friendship I once had with Eddie Sahati. He was, as everyone knew, a narcotics user. It's a matter of public record that Eddie was convicted and sent to prison hospitals as a result of his addiction to this vicious, cruel and illegal habit.

Still I found things to like in him, deliberately cultivated his companionship, traveled openly with him, gambled extensively with him, and made no bones of the fact I admired a lot of things about him. No doubt but that this open association has helped to keep me on the other side of the tracks socially in Reno. So be it. I learned valuable lessons from Eddie Sahati. He was part of my life.

Let's make no mistake here, if you please. I did not, and could not, condone Eddie's nasty habit. One of the precepts of a real friendship, however, is: I overlook your failings and you must overlook mine. That is an absolute condition of friendship.

I didn't know then, nor do I know now, what narcotic Eddie used. In all our travels it was never mentioned. I never saw it or the paraphernalia for using it. I never saw or heard him make a purchase. I never asked how or when he did it or how he acquired the habit. We did not, at any time, discuss his addiction. Except once.

The day came when my son was eighteen and beginning to gaze about at the wonders of never-never land. I felt a tinge of worry. Eddie Sahati was a fantastically flamboyant and successful gambler, perhaps the luckiest in all Nevada at that time. Junior was inclined to pick heroes and emulate them. I wanted no tragedies of this kind in my family.

I was sure my concern was unnecessary. Long before I went about so openly with Eddie Sahati I had established to my own satisfaction that his habit was a private and personal matter and that he never attempted to infect anyone else. He never "pushed." I wasn't a policeman. I was resolved to mind my own business, which is gambling, as was his. I did, however, want his reassurance.

"Eddie," I said that day, "if you or any of your friends should ever do anything to spoil my son, I will get to you. I will kill you."

He didn't even dignify me with an answer. He glanced at me just momentarily and saw I was deadly serious. A look of infinite sadness came into his solemn brown eyes. The look said it all. I had hurt him.

It hurt him because Eddie liked me. I was one of the few men in this world he did like and respect and with whom he shared his time. Possibly this stemmed from that first play I gave his Normandie Club back in 1946, when I stormed his tables, champagned the house and ended up borrowing $300 from him. I did it with a gusto he liked. He also was impressed with the fact that while I was very drunk at the time I observed his arrival with his barracudas and could tell him accurately afterward just which door he had entered, how he was dressed and who was with him. Clarity of mind impressed Sahati.

From that day until his untimely death in 1951 at the age of 43 Eddie Sahati and I were as rollicking a gambling team as Nevada may ever see. Eddie was the absolute, ultimate gamester. Nothing else, not even beautiful women, could stir such a passion in him. He had a fantastically keen mind which he trained and controlled to one end. Never have I seen a human so utterly devoted to gambling.

♠

He simply had no equal for getting hunches, recognizing them accurately and putting his money on them. Let me give you an example. One night Eddie came into Harolds Club to use the men's room. He had nothing else in mind until a dice table caught his eye. He felt a hunch. One hour later I cashed in his chips for $25,000. He strolled back out of the club without realizing he never had gotten to the men's room.

Eddie's perception and reception of mental telepathy were so great, seemingly, he knew what the dice would do before the roll even began. (He also had absolute concentration in a game, yet seemed to know what was occurring behind his back.) Waves of information seemed to strike his subconscious like a clamoring bell. He might be up at Lake Tahoe when such a wave would strike and advise him it was just the right time to drive into Reno, about an hour away, and get into a crap game. He might believe consciously he was driving to town for some business reason or to meet a friend or relative but subconsciously he knew the dice were going to "romance" him. It was uncanny.

I know because he won half a million dollars from Harolds Club during that incredible period of lucky gambling. He won that much again from other casinos, all in a period of two or three years. Needless to say, he was a most expensive customer. Eddie used to say that a good hunch was far better than money in the bank because with a hunch you added to any bankroll. He made every cent of his million-plus from hunches and this I had to admire.

There were other things. Eddie wasn't lily white, obviously, but I never saw him hurt anyone. I saw him help plenty. Many a show girl down on her luck found she could touch Eddie for a $200 or $500 bill to tide her over; he made no demands, not even for repayment, and died with many hundreds of thousands of this money still outstanding. To the best of my knowledge, he absolutely refused to inflict his company on nice girls. If you were talking with him and your wife came up he quietly disappeared. Eddie knew what he was and what the mores of society expected. He wasn't all bad. He considered it a waste of time and mental energy to decide who to be nice to and who not to be nice to so he was as nice to everyone as he could be. He never wanted or expected appreciation. For this I esteemed him.

One scene I remember well. Eddie and I had been gambling around for several days and nights. We stopped in a coffee shop before going on to bed. Eddie, as always, was as clean as a violinist's fingernails though his expensive suit was a little rumpled and the long, dark hair was falling over his temples, as it did when he'd been shooting craps for several sleepless days. Something jogged my memory.

"Eddie," I said, "this is Easter Sunday. Would you go to church with me?"

He nodded. We got in my car and drove over to the Cathedral; my church, though Eddie, who was Syrian, probably was of the Orthodox faith. During the beautiful ritual I suddenly realized my friend was on his knees beside me. The hair still fell over his forehead but the look in his brown eyes was soft as he looked upward in prayer, genuinely, sincerely, earnestly. Say what you will, I know you can't kneel in prayer with a man and misjudge him completely. Eddie Sahati had his bad habit, to be sure, but he was real.

He was so real to Daddy and my brother Raymond when he was taking the club for half a million, they wanted to bar him. "Nobody can be that lucky," Daddy complained. "He must be cheating. I bristled at that, believing I knew Eddie completely, convinced he was a man of basic integrity and incredible gambling instinct. His reputation as an operator, for one thing, was far more precious to him than money. With the right reputation an operator can always raise money; more than a million dollars if necessary. Found cheating in any way, he's liable to be out in the alley, devoid of associates, customers and credit. My father and brother hadn't studied Eddie in action as closely as I had; they wouldn't recognize real cheating if it went on under their noses. When they raised the question I would argue: "What's his 'weight'? What's he trying to 'push' on us? Loaded dice? Is he changing dice on us?" They couldn't tell me that, of course. I wasn't about to let other people do my thinking for me. I was convinced I was right about Eddie. The accusations came up daily so long as he won from us, but Eddie continued to play in Harolds Club.

Oh, he wasn't perfect. I don't mean to imply that. I saw him lose that controlled soft-voiced patience and scream like a hyena when a shill let the dice hit her hand and ruined his play. Once in Harolds Club when he had all the numbers loaded with bets and crapped out, a boor of a dealer laughed. "What are you laughing at that for?" Eddie shrilled. "Is this so funny? What the hell are you laughing at?" It was a bad scene. Eddie Sahati, the narcotics addict, was attracting attention to himself. I heard people sniff. But I couldn't have answered what that dealer *was* laughing about. It wasn't funny to me either.

Eddie found it hard to accept any loss. One evening, for instance, he was entertaining two girls when one of them mentioned something about a new Easter bonnet. Being the gracious gentleman he was, Eddie volunteered to put up money for their hats. Better, he decided, he would win it for them at the dice table. They marched into one of our casinos and Eddie lost his first $100 bet. Two hats would have cost far less than that. But Eddie, having dropped that bet, was obsessed with a need to get it back. He stayed at the dice table all evening and lost more than $129,-000. I don't know what ever happened to the girls or their Easter hats. Eddie had lost enough money to keep them in mink coats the rest of their lives. That didn't bother him at all. What troubled him, until he figured it out, was why he lost.

He had the answer by the time he told me of the incident. Eddie had decided there were two reasons for his losing. One, he was playing for money to buy something specific and therefore the cash he risked was the same as "needed" money; big lucky streaks almost always go to players with surplus money. Two, he had involved the feminine sex in his game; he knew as well as anyone that you can't gamble successfully when women in whom you have an interest are watching. Having reached these conclusions, he didn't mind the $129,000 loss at all. Mistakes he didn't mind making once; we all make them. He just didn't want to repeat his. He considered the $129,000 a part of his education.

That was his reasoning and it seems strange in retrospect, considering the whopping mistake he was to make with me later.

♣

Don't get the idea Eddie Sahati had no respect for money.
I remember another incident quite clearly. We'd started off together on a gambling spree we hoped would last, through good
luck, into maybe a week. Eddie, who was all but indefatigable
in those days—he stood 6 feet and weighed 215—bet me 40¢
that he could stay awake longest without going to bed. I took the
bet and all but forgot it. Three days later, having romanced a
score of games up and down Nevada, we found ourselves in the
lobby of the Riverside Hotel. We flopped to rest in two big chairs
and suddenly I realized Eddie had fallen asleep. I shook him
awake to advise him he had lost our bet on staying awake. Eddie
smiled very slyly. "I'm not in bed yet," he pointed out. "The bet
was who would stay awake the longest *without going to bed.*" I
paid him the 40¢. He took it, too.

Eddie Sahati then was a millionaire and only in his late thirties.
He had made it all with his own wits, starting with illegal racehorse books in the San Francisco area. Later he bought the State
Line Club at the south end of Lake Tahoe, which straddles the
California-Nevada state line and is now the site of Mr. Harrah's
big resort casino. With that purchase, Eddie branched into night
club and casino operations and acquired the Normandie Club in
Reno. He also launched into the fantastic lucky streak that for two
or three years made him the scourge of Nevada.

I have said he won around $500,000 from Harolds Club in
those years. He took more than that from other casinos because
he moved his play around and gave us all a chance. He showed
no partiality at all, considering our money all the same shade of
green. He took it readily. One large club had, in fact, barred
him and asked that he take his action elsewhere. They had their
reasons, I presume, though I suspect it was only that they couldn't
stand his pressure. I know I wouldn't bar him or any other big
winner from my club. For one thing, the big winner always returns. You'll get your chance to take the money back. Eddie,
among others, was to prove this to me.

He never exaggerated so I knew it must have been a terrific stand that caused the other club to bar him. Afterward, when he would win a good hand somewhere and I would congratulate him, he always answered: "Harold, if you thought this was good, you should have seen the one I had at ————." (The club that barred him). I never learned how much he did win in that stand. You never ask a gambler a question like that. You look and listen but you don't even ask what time it is. He would have told me if he wanted me to know.

It would be foolish to say Eddie won every time he played. He didn't. But he won so much more often than he lost, and the amounts were so much greater, we operators all felt the bite on our bankrolls. No one, it seems, could sense better than he the exact time to get into our crap games. He would be the first, however, to admit that gambling involves risks and that no one should expect to win all the time. He had one unusual habit tied to his persistance and aggressiveness: if he got in a game and lost his first bet he might remain at that table for three days until he won back that first bet. I wouldn't recommend this system for most people and must point out that, in the end, it was part of Eddie's undoing.

In his heyday, however, I wanted to be around Eddie as much as possible. I knew he could teach me a great deal about gaming. I wanted to know what made him tick. Why was he such a consistent winner? What were his techniques? Why was he head and shoulders above the rest of us in ability? The "tuition" for playing alongside Eddie was terrific but I always learned and some of these things I have never forgotten. Whatever his faults, being with Eddie sandpapered away whatever rust spots were accumulating on my brain cells. With Eddie, there were no squabbles, no nagging, problems or irritation of any kind. He was a gentleman at all times, as good a loser as winner. I beg to give you a case in point. Eddie and I frequently pooled money to form a gaming partnership or "corporation." One evening we each put up $10,000 to play at the Mapes where Bernie Einstoss, a mutual friend, was casino manager. The sevens chopped me off immediately and I lost my share of the partnership in less than 25 minutes. I was betting $200 on the line and $400 odds, or $400 on each point. Taking all the "Come" bets, I might have as much as $2400 ($400 on six numbers) on the table at a time. The shooter would roll three or four numbers, then seven out. It doesn't take long to lose $10,000 at that rate.

I still had an urge to gamble so I asked Bernie for $10,000 credit. Eddie, I should point out, had about $5000-$6000 of the corporation bankroll left. The credit I got from Bernie had nothing to do with our original joint venture; it was my own obligation.

It was now the middle of the night. We weren't clock watching, though; we were out to beat a crap game and time was of no consequence. If Lady Luck smiled, we might stay there for days or weeks. At some moment in the early hours of the morning Eddie was called to the telephone. I asked to play his high limit while he was gone. Bernie okayed the request. So I now could play $400 and $800 odds, or $1200 as against the original $600 Bernie allowed me.

I did no talking or loud pleading with the dice as many players do. I believe it better to concentrate on the cubes especially if someone else in the game might throw hot hands for you. Talking could affect the confidence of the shooter. At the moment, I found we had a real dice game hustler—a woman who makes her living by getting into games in the hope winning players will toke her for rolling good hands—in our game. She proceeded to shoot a very good hand and followed it with 15 or 20 numbers for me. In the few minutes she had the dice she never shot a seven and I won $15,000.

Eddie returned from the phone call, which I learned later was of no importance, and saw the pile of chips before me. With his mind, he immediately took in what had happened. "And I had to get a phone call," he muttered. "I had to get a call." She still had the dice. I had all the numbers covered with Come bets. Soon I had $30,000 in winnings. Eddie was all for me and glad to see me win but he couldn't overlook facts. That might have been his bankroll. When at last the dice hustler finished her roll I had a feeling Lady Luck was turning away. I cashed in $35,000 in chips and quit, throwing her a $100 chip to "buy a pair of stockings." I paid off my two markers of $10,000 each with Bernie and still had $15,000 winners. Eddie, who'd decided the phone call interrupted his chances, now split the $6000 remaining from the corporation fund. Our partnership had lost $14,000, or about $7000 each. He was out that much for the evening while I was ahead $18,000. I didn't offer Eddie any of my winnings. That isn't the way things are done between professional gamblers. He understood and took his loss without a moan.

Perhaps another Eddie anecdote will illustrate how this can be. One day he lost several thousand dollars and was down to his last $5 chip. He put this last one on 11 on the crap table. On the very next roll 11 came up and paid 15-1. Now Eddie had $80 (15x$5 plus his $5 bet). He let it ride on 11 and 11 repeated. Now he had $1200 and that is gambling money. Twenty minutes later he cashed in over $10,000. Eddie Sahati the consummate gambolier.

But we can't win all the time, as he well knew. To Eddie Sahati, as it must to all of us, came a losing streak to equal the great winning streak he had enjoyed. The curious thing is how his came about.

♥

One evening after taking more than half a million from Harolds Club, Eddie came in and beat us again for another $75,000 in two or three hours time. I personally dealt the dice to him. When he quit I got a loaded .38 to escort him to his hotel room down the street, as I do for any big winner. (A big winner is usually pretty noticeable while winning and if he were to be held up someone might start a rumor that it's "no use winning at Harolds Club"). Eddie suggested a cup of coffee when we got to the hotel and there resumed a theme he'd been strumming for two weeks. "Let's go away. Let's take a vacation."

Eddie talked with a slow drawl. I was thinking of problems while I listened, of Daddy's constant yakking at me, of things at home, the fact I hadn't had a real vacation in my life. Eddie was offering to make this a fantastic odyssey on his gambling winnings.

"Eddie," I finally said. "You're asking and I'm going to take you up. But I want you to know I'm an expensive guest. If you're serious and want to take me, consider my conditions. I've never had a real vacation. Let's make this one we'll remember. No crap games. That leaves out Saratoga Springs, New York, Miami, Cincinnati."

He nodded agreement, seemingly most serious.

"We'll get a plane to Honolulu," I suggested, "charter a yacht loaded with liquor and go fish among the South Sea Islands, then do some big game hunting in Australia."

Eddie seemed eager for that. I began to get enthusiastic.

"We'll have plenty of liquor and shipmates who are charming and beautiful. I never did like strictly stag affairs."

I remember distinctly what I said next. It is the key to the whole incident and Eddie's downfall, I believe.

"Don't give me any bosh," I said. "If you're serious about going, we go right now. I'm married and Lois will blow up a storm when she hears I'm off for three or four months. You don't have that worry because you're single."

He acknowledged the validity of my position. A contract between two gambling men was being sealed. Such promises, as I have said, are not given lightly.

"I'll get our tickets, have a carpenter pack my rifles and ammunition, get trunks ready," I suggested. "Remember, we're not coming back for at least three months."

Eddie still appeared to be most serious.

"You're fat now with Harolds Club money," I said, "so take $40,000 or $50,000 and we'll live like kings."

"Yes!" Eddie responded. "We go!"

That, so far as I was concerned, was as good as a lawyer's contract. An operator's word is oath.

I was so excited I couldn't go home to sleep. Though it was 6 AM and I hadn't slept in two days, the thought of that wonderful trip refreshed me more than ten hours sleep. I rushed to the club and told everyone I was going. The word spread fast. It was even in the Reno newspaper that day. By evening I had everything packed. Daddy, though surprised, raised no objections. I decided to notify Lois after I was on my way. We were to leave Reno by plane next morning.

Morning came but no Eddie. I ate a nervous breakfast, fearful he might have gotten in a crap game. He didn't appear all day.

It was twenty-four hours before I saw him and his expression spelled trouble. "What the hell's wrong?" I demanded.

"Where's Woody?" he asked evasively. Woody was his valet.

I didn't know. "What difference does it make?" I demanded. "We're going on the trip, aren't we?"

"I wanna find Woody," he said. I sensed some hesitance.

"We made a contract!" I protested. "You asked me to go on a trip. Now let's go."

Eddie, I suddenly feared, was sniffing a crap game. I have never heard an operator before or since plead with a customer not to get into a game, but I pleaded. I went looking for the valet and when I got back my chin dropped. There was Eddie at our Number 1 dice table. What I feared most was happening. If ever he started losing, our trip was killed. I actually found myself hoping, if he must play, he would win my house's money.

Eddie lost $2000 and moved to Table 2. He dropped $2000 there and went to the second floor, where he lost $5000 in the Covered Wagon Room. He was stuck $9000. Now he asked me for $5000 credit. He lost it and requested another $5000.

"All right, Eddie," I said, "just $5000 more and let's go."

"All right," he replied. Another contract.

But he didn't keep it. Eddie had started on a losing streak and couldn't admit defeat. He stood at the table sending Woody down the street for more money. He was stuck $30,000 and I was sitting getting drunk in my disappointment. That day he lost $96,000.

It was the turning point in Eddie's fantastic lucky streak. After winning more than $1,000,000, he was started that day on the biggest, longest and unluckiest streak I have ever witnessed. I was never to hear of Eddie Sahati having one lucky day again. I was never to hear of him winning again. From that day until he died a few years later, he was to lose every time he played. He lost almost all the million to Harolds Club and now, ironically, there was no question in Daddy's or Raymond's mind about cheating. We all but bankrupted Eddie.

I went to his hotel suite the morning after his first bad day. I tried to get from his own lips why, when he had dropped the first $2000, he had felt stuck. He wouldn't answer. He wouldn't, or couldn't explain anything.

"Eddie," I finally said, "I'm going to tell you something real good and only once. You made a contract with me. You were going to take me on a trip. I had my clothes and everything packed. Your word was good with me. Now I won't depend on you to take me. I'm going myself some day, alone. I'll go first class and without you."

"Aw, don't say that," he pleaded.

It could never be the same. We both knew it. Here was a man I had respected and admired and he'd broken his word to me. "You didn't intend to go at all," I accused. "You were just making with the words. I didn't expect that kind of talk from you."

I got over my peeve after a few days and made a point of expressing my forgiveness to Eddie. But the deed was done. He came to my club to gamble and there was a difference. He lost every time he played. It wasn't temporary. He became as consistent a loser as he had been a winner. There were no times that he won. Something subtle happened after he broke his word. He no longer radiated brilliance or flamboyance. His confidence was cracked. Probably, every time he saw me, he had feelings of guilt, subconscious though they may have been. They interfered with his play. His hunches no longer came through clearly. Eddie Sahati had broken his word and he was dead as a gambler. It is a strange fact, but true. I saw it happen.

Not too many months later Eddie lay in agony on a hospital bed, his great body as wasted as his once-great fortune. It was cancer and he was down from a robust 215 pounds to a pitiful 75. I can only love the great broken spirit still trying to get well. Late one day as the shadows were falling, he motioned his brother Nick to come closer. As Nick leaned close, Eddie raised his wasted arm, shook his clenched fist and whispered hoarsely: "Nick, we are going to make it!" A gambler's wishful thinking, but no hunch. He was dead two hours later.

We gamblers came down in a silent group from Reno to San Francisco to bury the man who had beaten us all and then succumbed as every mortal must, a victim of his own words and deeds and frailties. It was November of 1951.

In my heart I still feel a love for this big, soft Syrian boy who, in spite of his terrible habit, was as gallant a competitor as I have ever known. In my desk I have his marker for $40,000, a reminder that even the greatest gambolier of them all quit a loser.

It has given me increasing food for thought.

16

♠ ♠ ♠ ♠

Dice Have Ears

DICE ARE MADE of celluloid and playing cards are made of pasteboard. They have no brain, no soul, no sensitivity, nerve center or memory. They know nothing about you or me or our feelings. They are, as I say, inanimate cubes and rectangles of paper. Yet, and I say this with utmost gravity, the key to the entire engrossing mystery of games of chance—why we win and why we lose—lies directly in the state of mind we establish between ourselves and those cards or dice.

Insensitive they may be, yet surely they respond. I do not say this lightly. I've been watching gambling games from a closer-than-ringside seat for a quarter of a century. I have seen many thousands of people gamble their money. I have lost over $1,000,000 of my own money. I have won just as much. My winning, however, commenced to exceed my losing only in recent years when I began to heed the eerie and recondite facts I observed.

I'll say it flatly. The key to whether we win or lose at games of chance is the state of our minds when we sit down to play. We

241

can prepare our minds to win. Too often they are prepared to lose. We will win or lose as they are conditioned.

Let me tell you a story. One night, with nothing in particular to do, I strolled across the street to the Horseshoe Club to chat with my friends Bernie Einstoss and Ruby Mathis. I had no personal problems whatsoever. I felt good, clear-headed, at peace with the world. Suddenly I had a hunch: *Play the dice table!*

I did and lost a few hundred dollars. *That's all right,* said this inner feeling. *Keep going.* Then I got a very hot hand. *Here it comes,* said my hunch center. And it did, one hand after another. In a very few minutes I won $37,000. Now, abruptly, I knew: *That's all of it.* It is hard to describe how I knew; my exultation simply flattened out. My conscious mind interjected: *You've had your pitch at the table. Take your money and walk away.* I obeyed. As I picked up my chips, though, I watched the next hand to the remaining players. I would have lost badly on it. Strolling back to Harolds Club, I had a bite to eat and sat down to watch the floor show.

Now came the inner debate with which every gambler is familiar. *Maybe this is your real lucky day, Harold. You're out in front of the play. Maybe you ought to go back.* Another part of my senses recalled the flattening of exultation. *Down, boy, down,* it seemed to protest. *You've had it for today. Control yourself, Harold. Don't go back.* A friend of mine who once drank heavily swears that throughout his wildest drunks there was a part of him that never got drunk but tried to send messages up to the runaway mind that was. This is the way it was with me in that debate.

I was letting my runaway mind suggest that I could still knock Hell out of the crap game. It wasn't a hunch or anything approaching one. It was wishful thinking, impetuous, willful, angry. I wanted their money. Where I'd been cool and serenely clear-headed on my first trip to the Horseshoe, I now was tensely excited. The blood pounded in my temples. I lost the $37,000 in ten minutes.

Dropping $37,000 you have won is no pleasanter than losing $37,000 from your bank account. I don't hate money but I do hate to lose. I want to quit winners, whatever I do. It was a weak and meek man then who trudged back to Harolds Club. My tail was between my legs.

Remember, if you will, what I said at the start of this book. I'm a professional, total and unrequited gambler. I've gotten thrills from gaming that some men derive only from the ultimate love act. Taking the cubes in hand and making them bounce to my bidding produces pure passion in me. I know all the risks inherent in games of chance and that nothing I do can remove those risks. Yet I go for big money, often so big it's more than I can afford to lose. And I hope to win. I expect to win. I must and do give complete credence to seemingly nebulous things like hunches, luck and extrasensory perception. And I do win more often than I lose. Rather, I win more money than I lose.

Some of the facts behind this I shall attempt to describe for you now. A little later I will tell you in detail how I play each game. I'm not, frankly, afraid you'll use this knowledge to break my club. You still will be hobbled by your human nature—your mind—the cornerstone of winning and losing despite the absolute, material nature of cards and dice.

◆

I speak of hunches and I know them well. I cannot, however, give a pinpoint definition of one as, say, a mathematician can cite an equation. I say only that they exist and the true gambling mind recognizes them instantly and intuitively, just as a man and woman sighting each other across a crowded room know *this is it*. It's a feeling, uncanny, intangible, inexplicable.

For want of words, we speak of it as wooing Lady Luck. I believe she visits everyone—well, *almost* everyone, for there are a few ill-starred souls who never see her and I can't explain them— at some time and place. She can't be everywhere at once, like Santa Claus on Christmas Eve. We must be ready for her calls. Some folks are. They seem to sense it when she approaches their neighborhood; we call them "lucky." Too many, however, can't even recognize her tap on the shoulder. That is a pity. I have heard it said that when Fortune knocks and gets no answer, the next time around she sends her daughter, Misfortune.

Perhaps this sounds like airy-fairy stuff to you and not the coldly logical talk of a gambler whose rule is Play It As It Lays For The Action. But remember, if you please, a gambler always goes for the dough. If believing in Mohammed would help him get it, he would turn toward Mecca ten times daily. I know it's foolish and stupid to worship money. I contend it's just as foolish to hate money. Doubters who scoff at Lady Luck, calling her superstition, imagination or dream stuff, are the ones, I notice, who never win. They don't admit to a dislike for the minted green but I suspect they have one; hidden, deep-rooted or subconscious though the hate may be.

The tipoff very often is the manner in which a player handles his money. I watched one just the other day. He got twenty silver dollars for a bill, stacked them neatly and laid his bet precisely in the right square. There was a deftness in the way he pushed the silver over the green felt. The wheel stopped and he had won. He actually looked surprised. He hesitated, glanced up at the dealer as though he didn't quite believe it, and fumbled the silver when he dragged in his winnings. Why? He didn't expect to win. He was prepared, subconsciously, to lose. Soon enough he *was* losing. There wasn't any fumbling or surprise then. He pushed out his bets once more as skillfully as a bank teller. I recognize a man like that for a consistent loser. He has come to the game in a losing frame of mind. Lady Luck will accommodate him as long as he cares to play.

Negatively conditioned minds invariably reject her. You have seen them, I'm sure. They pick up the dice and say almost cheerfully: "Watch me crap out." If they would only turn that negative confidence to action, they would lay their bet with the odds that pay 7-1 for such foresight. But they don't. They're prepared to lose.

♠

The work of the mind in determining the outcome of games is demonstrated nowhere so clearly as in the old adage: *No one should gamble with "needed money."* This, of course, is money that should go for the rent, grocery or doctor bills. I understand why people do play with needed money; their needs exceed their bankroll, they're trying to get more money quickly. Deep down, could they only bring themselves to consider facts, they would remember the house odds grinding against them and the skill-plus-luck it takes to win at a given moment. They'd be wiser to go pay the bills. The bitter truth is, as all gamblers know, needed money never wins.

How do the cards and dice know this is needed money? You communicate it to them. You're distracted by fear and guilt and worry. You don't play your cards confidently. You bet fearfully. A few losing hands undermine whatever hope you may have had. Anger, greed, resentment interfere. Instead of wooing Lady Luck, you're cursing her. Invariably it communicates itself to the cards and dice. (Even to slot machines.) They begin to fall horribly for you.

Your best chance of winning is when you have no problems at all. No marital upset, job worries, concern for the rent, or passion for the lady next to you. Oh, I know we're never completely free of problems. There are, however, days when we feel adequate to our problems and will tackle them in their time and place. The excitement of gambling will help to shut them out. You must help a little more. If you hope to win, you must actually do some mental setting-up exercises before you board the bus for Reno or step through our doors.

Examine yourself most carefully. Can you gamble today with a free conscience? If not, turn around and go home. Save your money. If you can, tell yourself so, just as a good football coach tells his team it *can* go out and win. Give yourself that winning pep talk. Be positive that no nagging worry is going to confuse you, consciously or otherwise. Your mind must be focused clearly on the game. Assure yourself the money you're wagering is free of encumbrance and isn't needed for pressing things. Then go to it, Mister, in a winner's frame of mind. Remember, too, it's just as easy to win a $1000 bet as a $1 bet. Make your mind see an image of you as a big, successful winner. Lady Luck likes that. The cards and dice will get the message.

♣

I don't know why the good lady is so kind to drunks. Some, of course, she simply passes over. Others can't make a wrong move. They bet like idiots and win like geniuses; they can't count their cards or see the dice but Lady Luck does. This happens night after night in the gaming houses; too frequently, in fact, to be just coincidence. I am convinced that the drinks, in slowing down many of the drunk's mental processes, also free his inhibitions against winning. It's not an admirable state of mind, perhaps, but it is a winning one for some.

My studied conclusion is that people who can control their drinking play better if they have one or two. They must know their capacity, of course. I don't advocate gaming for souses. In fact, since I've taken myself off liquor, I have had to develop sober pep talks to prepare myself. Once—and this I do recommend for the moderate drinker—I would have a drink about thirty minutes before I got into the game, another about thirty minutes after I was playing, then nothing for an hour. An hour after that, have one drink. Such drinking, I found, did not dull me or make me giddy. It did stimulate me, stopped my tendency toward doubting myself, and gave me the fraction of extra courage to seize the betting advantage when the dice got hot. If, however, there is any question in a player's mind as to his taking one drink and starting a chain, leave it alone. That man won't win. He simply won't escape his subconscious mind.

If you still have doubts as to the mind's part in winning or losing, watch a shill sometime. We don't employ these men and women to encourage the play in Harolds Club but most other Nevada casinos do. You can spot them in a dice game by the way their silver dollars are stacked neatly in the slot before them; alternately, some on their edges, some face up, and the rest on edge. (This is so the house and dealers will recognize them as shills.) In a card game you recognize shills by their desultory play. They're earning a dollar an hour for pretending to play. They play mechanically, scarcely glancing at the cards, always betting the same amount, usually one dollar, taking the best and worst of hits with no emotion. Since it is the house's money, they have no fear of losing. Like the baseball player who is already a .400 hitter, they can stand up there unconcerned, knowing they'll get a hit. I have seen girl shills make twelve or thirteen straight passes and pile up $300 or $400. Watching the money go back to the vault later, I never fail to think: *What a waste of good luck!*

Actually, most shills are bored with the play. I have experienced a similar feeling after playing too long. Say the dice have been comme çi, comme ça; not good, not bad, just grinding away. It's not that I get bored exactly. I simply lose interest in the game. This should be a significant moment to the player. If you play after you reach that point, your money's a gift to the house. Silly? Especially when you know the dice and cards have no feelings? Maybe so, but you lose. That's the time to back off and walk away.

I quit cold when I realize I've reached this point. It isn't a hunch that tells me to quit. There's nothing of the hunch in it. It's more like a stalemate. You've become so disinterested as to be almost bored. Eddie Sahati was always amazed when, after dropping $10,000 at a dice table, I could quit cold. He couldn't understand the lethargy that came over me. All I knew was my money was going down the drain and the game seemed pointless.

Every gaming situation presents its own conditions, of course. One night I "formed a corporation" with Eddie Sahati, as I described to you, to shoot craps at the Mapes Hotel. These "corporations," incidentally, are rather common among gamblers and deserve an explanation here. Two men, for instance, may decide to form one for $10,000, both of them to play and the proceeds, or losses, to be split. There is an obvious advantage if one of the partners is very lucky; he can more than make up the losses of the other and both can go home with money. Each man puts up $5000 —it may be done on the spur of the moment and there's no such thing as a contract. Both understand the terms. If the $10,000 is lost, then it's gone. If one partner loses and the other wins, the original investment of $5000 each is paid, then the profits are split 50-50. As often happens, one partner may be most unlucky and get out of the game fast. He is completely free to start playing again on his own money and, on his own money, he may win.

None of that winning is owed to the corporation fund he just lost. On the night I speak of, Eddie and I each put in $10,000 for a $20,000 corporation and I lost mine. I hadn't reached the bored or stagnant stage at all. I didn't have any particular hunch to keep playing. I was alert, eager, in a contesting mood. So I bought chips with my own money, while Eddie continued with his half of the corporation funds, and I won.

Bridge players, I'm sure, understand what I mean by boredom. The cards run consistently bad for them at times. It's not easy to understand, what with 52 cards in a deck, each player receiving 13 cards, many shuffles and reshuffles, and two decks in and out of the game, but it happened to me just the other night. I started off bidding a big slam and making it. I was alert as a fox, discovering where the Queen of clubs was and deciding which of two ways to finesse it. I almost felt that Queen sending brain waves to me. Then I went flat. For four and a half hours I sat there and looked at nothing but bad hands. I wanted to quit, and would have quit if the stakes had been big, but for a penny a point you sometimes have to stay in like a gentleman and let others enjoy their hands. You just can't do that when you've got your own good money on the line. When the cards go dead and your interest flags, quit.

♥

There's another time, while I think of it, when you'd better get out of the game. That's when you feel anger. Once more you're losing control of those all-important mental processes that do influence the flow of cards and dice. Oh, I guarantee you can get angry in a crap game. When you're playing big money and the dice seven out, you feel the fury explode. One quick-tempered man I know never wins for that very reason. He has all the courage in the world when it comes to a fist fight. When it comes to a dice game, though, he loses his courage and his temper. As sure as night follows day, then, he loses his money. He simply isn't a real contestant when he contests with anything but fists.

Keeping mind over matter is, I hasten to assure you, a very difficult thing to do. I have walked up to a table at the highest pitch of elation, knowing I was going to make the cards fall or the dice bounce, only to have an incident flatten me out in three minutes. It may only be a glimpse of my son close by or my Daddy glaring at me or a lady laying her bet down late. Or, though I have searched my mind and believe I have problems under control, something may suggest one. I feel a little duress. I know then that I'm at a disadvantage against the house and its odds. I will be giving my money away if I continue. So I practice what I'm preaching. I quit. I won't bet so much as a quarter on a crap game unless I have a very happy mind.

This, of necessity, means that my father, under whom I have worked so long, must not be anywhere near the game in which I play. The censureship parents exercise over their children, I am convinced, dogs them to their dying days and affects their success in life, where boldness and courage is needed, just as much as it does their winning or losing at games. Much as I love my father, I am convinced that he, or the thought of him, was responsible for some of my biggest losses. I know that when I lose, or fall into a disastrous losing streak, the thought of him reaches straight from my subconscious mind. I remember, for example, one night twenty years ago when I was playing Faro at the Bank Club. Daddy heard I was losing and came to get me out of the place. He stood just behind me for a few moments. I lost every bet. Every single bet! When he approaches my table you'd think the house suddenly had loaded the dice against me. I am aware that he doesn't gamble and has always preached to me against it— while ventilating the earth with speculative mines and oil wells— that he is disturbed and angry because I do play the games. When he comes near, even the cards and dice seem to know the story of our life. I might as well throw my money down the gutter. Only occasionally, when Daddy and I were getting along real well, have I been relaxed enough to be able to see him and still win.

Many a man loses money because he carries such personal censureship to the tables. It might be his wife or his boss who has chided him for gambling. He worries about that, he can't feel hunches, he's too upset to do anything right. I honestly believe there was a certain amount of this in Eddie Sahati's final losing streak after he broke his word to me. I know I exercise a certain negative influence on my son's luck when we're playing near each other. There's a competitive handicap in our mental processes then. We both try too hard. Junior and I realize this. We have an agreement. When either of us is playing, the other goes into the next room or even the next building.

I check this finding constantly when making refunds. A man has lost badly and needs his money back. "Does your wife want you to play?" I ask. "No," he answers invariably. And there you have it. You are playing against others' wishes, fighting them as well as the odds. You don't have a chance. On the other hand, man and wife come in together, both rooting for each other, both hoping to take home a bundle, and they win. This is true particularly of the Chinese and Jewish people of whom I have spoken. Both certainly know the value of money; neither puts a tabu on gaming. I recall a woman, encouraged by her husband, who made thirty straight passes with the dice, one of the hottest rolls I ever witnessed. Fortunately she was playing for small stakes. Had a real gambler had that luck he'd have taken $50,000 of my money in a twinkling.

♦

I spoke of greed. You'd best rid your mind of it before you try the gaming tables or you'll surely go home empty-handed. Greed is what gives the house its hidden percentage—the fact people will stand a shorter time winning than losing. They are greedy to get out with the loot. They're afraid to bet when the tide is with them. The great bulk of players who visit Reno have not, I am sure, even given this a thought. Yet it is responsible for a common occurrence at our tables. A player comes to town for a few days and wins every time he plays. Then, just before he starts home, he decides to play for half an hour more. He may be $1000 or $2000 ahead. All he can think of is the money in his pocket. He's excited. He doesn't analyze the game carefully as he did when he started. He simply slaps down his money, betting at the highest rate he had built to in his winning streaks. His luck has changed now. He can't see it. He doubles his bets. He trebles them. His winnings go down the drain in fifteen to twenty minutes.

This club has survived, frankly, because certain players in their most incredible lucky streaks were so eager to hang onto the money won they wouldn't double and redouble bets when the wave was cresting. They would bet a dollar, for instance, and drag the dollar won. They might win ten passes and have ten dollars stacked in front of them. On the eleventh hand the cycle changes; they lose and now have only nine dollars. The grinding-away begins. All because they were so eager to pick up one dollar they refused to let it accumulate. A good gambler, on the other hand, knows he must make five to ten times his original stakes to make up for expected losses which must occur. He understands that he can't win all the time and thinks it through. Personally, I never drag a winning bet. I make the house's money work against the house. I know that if I can get two wins in a row when my luck is running and I triple my bets I will come out ahead even though my average is five losses to four wins.

I contend that the courage necessary to win at a crap game is the selfsame type of courage needed to win in the game of life. Most of us have to work on ourselves to build such courage. It stems from ego, I suspect, and ego is directly involved in gaming. You lead with your ego when you place a bet, you put it on the line each time and risk it on every play. You think not? Watch anyone walk away from a slot machine after his last coin is gone. That hurts the ego just as surely as the pocketbook. Aren't other people watching? Haven't they seen you fail to succeed? By the same token it lubricates the ego when we win. As a matter of fact, if we continue to win and carry off a large sum we can find our egos inflated beyond all reasonable proportion. It takes a certain kind of courage to limit and control this ego. Some call it common sense. That, however, is a term I dislike because the common sense we talk about so much never will be common among most of us. Given the chance, our egos run rampant at the crap table or card table and I've seen great financial losses as a direct result. Still another reason why we must condition our minds before we start to gamble.

Occult things still will happen to change the game on us. You hear of them daily in the gaming business, little protests or comments that spring spontaneously from people of all walks of life and all types of minds. One you hear most frequently is: "Every time I increase my bet I lose the bet." I don't know how many times a night dealers hear this. A player, for instance, has been betting $2 each hand and winning. Now, certain that his luck is running, he increases the bet to $4, $6 or $8. That bet he loses. It happens so often you come to expect it. Why? I have no explanation. I just know that it does happen again and again and again.

It takes a positive and confident attitude, as I have tried to show, to win money. The fact remains, though, that you must also have luck running with you. No matter how positive your mental preparation, you simply cannot win if the dice are rolling against you or the cards are bad. Usually you discern this after a few minutes. That's why I play conservatively until the run starts in my favor. Remember, I have thought this through before I started gambling and my mind is prepared as best I can get it to control emotions the game will produce.

If I do have some of that luck, say three or four wins in a row, I will be playing $120, $240 or more on each bet. It will now be the house's money, winnings, I am using. If I don't find my luck running—if I can't make at least two winning bets in a row—then I know it is time to quit. There's a time for living as the Good Book says, and a time for dying. It doesn't say anything about a time for committing suicide or bucking a losing game. *You must make up your mind in advance that you will quit if the cards or dice tell you to.* I know it isn't easy to quit a game. I know how a little voice keeps urging that things will change. I know the temptation well. But I also know the old adage that a man will stand longer losing than winning. I have learned to quit before I am too badly losers.

Remember, if you do quit, be a man about it. Don't cry your woes to the world. (This is mental disciplining too.) You lost. No one asked you to play or made you belly up to the table. And don't, whatever you do, tell anyone, yourself in particular, that you're playing for fun and "don't mind" paying for it. There's no fun to be had walking down the street with your behinder bare to the world. The only real fun in gaming is when you're winning.

Lady Luck comes and goes. She tries to hit most of us. She does not favor us by religion, race, color or creed. She does, however, seem to admire the confident person who has brought himself to her table with a clear and win-conditioned mind. She conveys her wishes through the cards and dice just as though she didn't know they were only celluloid cubes and rectangles of paper.

The day you accept this and start preparing your mind for the game before you step up to the table, that day you will find yourself winning more than you lose. I swear it. It's a finding. I repeat: I have spent thirty years making these findings from a closer-than-ringside seat. If you were to heed them well you would carry home great chunks of my money.

17

♣ ♣ ♣ ♣

Luck, Hunches

And ESP

THERE IS SO very much of the occult involved in successful gambling let us consider it further. Games of chance being what they are, with built-in risks and odds against the player, there has to be something supernatural going for those who win. Indeed, what are hunches but mysterious messages coming out of the deeps of our minds through some sort of mental telepathy?

Men of scientific mind are examining this mystery today and already have concrete evidence that it does influence cards and dice. Extrasensory perception, as they call one channel of it, is a recognizable gift of some individuals among us. It intrigues me both as a gaming house operator who could be bankrupted by it and as a man turned loose on this mortal coil to make or break.

So does luck, tangibly intertwined with ESP. Bad luck, which runs in observable cycles through my daily life, has cost me many a dollar and many a heartache. Good luck helped make Harolds

255

Club the gigantic phenomenon it is. Good luck has made millions for the Smith family and, on several occasions, saved this life of mine.

Let me describe an incident. One night my son Junior and I were driving down from Lake Tahoe. The Mount Rose road is a steep and twisty mountain lane with breathtaking dropoffs into precipitous canyons, the conditions plain to any wary driver in frequent signs warning: NO MORE THAN 20 MPH.

It was 3 AM and very dark when we started down. I always drop into my low gear on that road to let the engine's compression hold me back and save the brakes. I was in low this night and creeping along when the greatest fool I've ever encountered careened out of the curve ahead, coming up. (I've watched foolish people at the gaming tables but this man was playing with mortal lives, including his own.) The man had to be going 50 when he came out of that curve. He hadn't seen my headlights because they were pointing out into space. I hadn't seen his for the same reason. He was driving one of those small hot cars with terrific acceleration and came up on the wrong side of the road. He was squarely in my lane. Considering that he was doing at least 50 and I about 27 or 28, the cars were closing on each other at 77 miles an hour at a distance of approximately 60 yards. There was less than a second to square away, I would guess. I knew it was happening so fast I didn't have time to get scared. My reflexes wanted to pull me to the right, which would have been over the cliff. His reflex was quicker. He saw me, cut in and passed, all so swiftly it can only be described as miraculous.

"That certainly was lucky," you say, and there's that word "lucky" for us to consider. We use it so often to sum up an incident we don't comprehend. To me, the interesting thing is that we don't comprehend because it's all so far past easy comprehension. It is supernatural.

Ah yes. There is also the matter of coincidence. Now it has always been my habit to be punctual. When I was working the concessions at Riverview Park, in Chicago, during the two seasons of 1929 and 1930, I made it a point to be at my stand each evening at ten minutes to six. Every night at 5:50 you could count on my being in front of that nail game setting up the nails. I wanted to open at six sharp and did. One night I was 10 minutes late.

Now here's the coincidence. At 5:50 that night they had an accident. A large wooden water truck pulled by a caterpillar tractor was going down the Midway. The pin came out of the coupling between cat and truck. The water tanker crashed into the nail game booth at precisely the place I stood every night at that moment. It tore out the entire front of the booth, knocking the stand back four to six feet. It would have crushed me. "Your lucky stars were shining on you that night, Harold," you might say. Yes, but why? That was the only time I was 10 minutes late in two full seasons, and a season comprises 110 nights. In 220 nights, then, I was late once and that one night avoided an accident that could have killed me. I can't even tell you why I was late that night. Luck?

I can't help but think of these things in connection with gaming, wherein an accumulation of incidents often contributes to a big win. Just the other evening, for example, a man here ran $10 up to $14,000. Right away, someone pegs him as lucky. Yes he was lucky. I think of the multiple situations in that card game in which something beyond our comprehension intervened to set aside the factual odds against his play. It has to be in the area of the occult or supernatural.

Bad luck also cancels normal odds, I have noticed, to defeat a player. This goes right back to those peculiar days when Lady Luck deliberately looks the other way and you couldn't win if you played solitaire and cold-decked yourself. I've seen days when I've played every kind of game we have in this city, all in one day, and lost at them all. I have lost as many as 13 and 14 consecutive bets. This is incredible. The percentage against your losing 15 bets in succession must be approximately 2,000,000-1, at least 1,000,000-1, and yet I have done it.

♠

As the years have passed, and I have looked one way and another for answers, I come to one conclusion. It isn't scientific, perhaps, but it's the only one I can comprehend. I believe that life turns in cycles for all people. There are good cycles and there are cycles when things for you individually won't go so good. I think this is meant to be.

And, while it may seem out of place in a gambler's book, I want to say I believe this whole sequence is set by the Big Gent upstairs. I don't mean to say He touches the dealer's hands as the cards come out or that He tumbles the dice to anyone's choice. I do mean that we're meant to live in good times and bad, in variations of the Bible's seven fat and seven lean years, all for our individual experience. Beyond that simple belief, I don't attempt to explain the tremendous Intellect behind all this. I merely look for the signs. Gambling is a fascinating activity in which to observe signs.

The cycles are very obvious. Speaking again as the professional gambler, I say that when the cycle is good, and if we possibly can, we should take advantage of it. When the cycle is not good, we should try to discipline and deny ourselves, specifically our emotions. It wouldn't be good, even if it did happen, for anyone to have things go to his satisfaction all the time. It just doesn't seem to help us as persons, or as characters, to have everything we touch, or do, or are associated with, come out a tremendous success. We wouldn't be trained for life's bigger battles. We really better ourselves when we get our lumps mixed in with the blessings. I apply this to gambling as surely as I do to earning a living, getting along with people or growing up.

I believe the Big Gent puts us to the test occasionally and with me it shows in my gambling. I have, as a matter of fact, recently been going through a very trying time in all my affairs, domestic to financial. I don't particularly like it, but I believe it will result in better times to come. Patience, as the Good Book reminds us, grows out of impatience, confidence out of lack of confidence, success out of failure. If you don't have confidence, hope and faith, at least in your own abilities and good fortune, you don't win in life or at our tables. If you're one to fall by the wayside, quit when the going gets rough and complain about it, something is lacking. We're not evangelists in the gaming casinos and we don't have the right words for it, perhaps, but we recognize the lack. There's no place on earth where a man's tenacity, patience and confidence show up as they do at the tables. If any man thinks every day is going to be rosy, that he isn't going to be disappointed and disillusioned, then he's not using that God-given intellect that makes him only a little less than the angels.

Gamblers and veteran players recognize a few other facts in this area of the not-quite-explainable. We know, all of us, that there are some dealers, for instance, who simply always "have the nuts on you." That's a gambling expression meaning that they'll dominate your play and beat you every time. Some towns have the nuts on people in the same way; they just don't get ahead in that particular environment. Some days are like that too. It's all part of the occult picture gambling draws so visibly for the one who will look.

Sometimes I wonder just how much any one of us does have to do with his own success. How much is the result of his own doing? How much falls in his way? Or how many times he comes around a mountain road and something, that vague something, gives the other driver the reflexes to swing around in time and prevent an accident. That luck business again.

Many, many people stop me in the club to make the obvious observation: "It must make you feel wonderful to have this big club . . . ." Oh, bless me, and pass the succotash, I was lucky, and you, the reader, now know how lucky. If I hadn't had help over and above my own efforts, as you have seen, I couldn't have done it. A whole series of events in my life, to which I might have objected at the time, prepared me peculiarly for this unique club. The work on my part was necessary, of course, but something else set aside the odds on the criterion hands.

Yes I have been lucky but one form of luck is that you make your own breaks. Nowhere else is this truer than it is in gambling. In no one else does it show so clearly as the man who gambles successfully. Take the dice-playing lumberman from Oregon who came in and beat us for a bundle right after his sawmill burned to the ground. He wasn't worried about his future. He was a self-made man with tremendous self-confidence. While his mill was being rebuilt, he came down to Reno and relaxed at the gaming tables. He came in his confidence and he beat us. He radiated success. I said it before and I say it again, his attitude influenced the dice. He had some of the supernatural going for him.

Certainly he had hunches and obeyed them. I'm still trying, incidentally, to define a hunch for you. Let's say it is a feeling that a given result is going to occur. A very good hunch forecasts the exact outcome. In gaming, you train yourself to recognize the hunch when it hits and to back it with your bankroll. I agree completely with my old friend Eddie Sahati that good hunches are better than money in the bank because with them you can make your money earn more than bank interest. (In gambling, that is, and I repeat here my admonition to my son: "If you're going to gamble, be sure you've got some business going for you to earn the money you must have to eat. Have some enterprise that is steady and stable, even if it's only a peanut stand.")

There's something of mental telepathy and extrasensory perception in hunches. I have no doubt about that. When that electric tingle hits you, as it has hit me so many times, you *know* specific things can happen. It may be an assurance that now, right now, you could get good cards. Or you know the dealer's hole card intuitively and therefore whether to hit or stand. And you'd better act on the hunch when you feel it.

A hunch, I have found, will not repeat itself. It doesn't stand and tap on your mind. It simply indicates a condition that may apply right now. As a matter of fact, if you think you're getting repeated hunches on a certain card or the way the dice will act, ignore them. This, undoubtedly, is wishful thinking. You're probably talking yourself into the mental image of what you want. Your wishes, hopes, wants or ego are talking. A hunch is sharp, electric, illuminating and quick-lived.

There are necessary conditions for hunches. This is why I urge every reader not to gamble if he's confronted with serious worries. I know as surely as I know the expression in my round blue eyes that if I have any problem, marital, financial or with business, if I'm emotionally upset by the illness or death of someone close, physically ill or unduly elated, I won't get a hunch I can trust. Even if I did, I would be slow to act upon it properly.

As I write this chapter, for instance, I wouldn't gamble 25¢ on winter coming again. I have too much on my mind. I don't want to gamble. I know I would be under a very serious handicap. I wouldn't be giving my money a chance to win. As soon as things are settled and I'm reasonably content again, the hunches will come. Then I'll play and I'll play for big money. I'll bet with that confidence that seems to flow into me, from wherever it comes.

There's another condition necessary for hunches. You cannot play too long or too steadily and expect to get them. Hunches are most accurate and sharply defined when you've laid off gambling a while. I, for example, know that if I haven't played dice for a few weeks and go up to a crap table a hunch will tell me the dice are going to be hot or cold. If I play that day and win some money, getting the hunches and backing them with my bankroll, I am almost literally "spending" something from that extra-sensory bankroll. It just won't be there if I call on it tomorrow. On my second day of gambling, invariably, I either have no hunches or am confused as to the sense of the ones I do have. Any man who plays every day is dulling his hunch-center. A good gambler must know himself thoroughly and decide how long a rest he needs between games. It may be a day or two, a week, even months.

I've had to stub my toe again and again before I understood this and I see people violate it daily in my club. Maybe they're way out in front and have more money stacked before them than they've ever had in their lives. They'd be thousands of dollars ahead if they'd quit now. Their hunches have stopped; long play has dulled their sensitivity. But they play on. Instead of driving a new Cadillac home, they will have to borrow money to take a bus. The only players I've ever known who could pursue games doggedly hour after hour through day and night and still hope to win were Eddie Sahati and Nick the Greek. Not many of us mortals are like them.

♥

I'll try once more to pinpoint for you what a hunch is. But how do you describe a sensation? How accurately can you put into words your enjoyment of a particular cup of coffee? A poignant moment? A sudden pleasant thought? Only you, with your accumulated experience, *feel* what it means to you. A hunch isn't obtained by reasoning. It must be felt.

I remember distinctly the one I had when Bobby Thomson came to bat in the ninth inning of that fantastic 1951 playoff game between Brooklyn and the Giants for the National League title. I was among the 45,000 fans looking on at the Polo Grounds. Bernie Einstoss, who had a bundle of money riding on Brooklyn, was sitting directly in front of me with his wife. The Giants trailed going into the last of the ninth. Then they got men on first and second. A single brought the man home from second, and Thomson came to bat. Suddenly it was just as though I saw a preview of the next play, which is now baseball history. I actually had a vision of Thomson hitting a home run.

Ralph Branca was now pitching for Brooklyn. "He can't pitch to Thomson," I declared to Bernie. I didn't mention my hunch glimpse. I talked like a fan. "He's been hitting the ball," I said. "He'll kill it."

Branca could, of course, have been ordered to walk Thomson, deliberately loading the bases but keeping him from hitting. Had I been the Brooklyn manager at that moment, knowing what I had visualized, that's what would have happened. Bernie said angrily: "You can't put the winning run on base."

"Be that as it may," I contended. "I wouldn't let him pitch to this man."

The first pitch was a ball, the next a strike, and the next the end of the Dodgers' pennant hopes. Thomson smacked that ball, exactly as I had visualized it, straight up and into the second tier of seats. There was, I remember, a crack like a .45 shot as the bat hit the ball and the crowd watched that white pellet soar. Forty-five thousand human beings sat stone silent trying to comprehend what was happening. There was utter stillness during the first moment of this tremendous experience. Then bedlam. It was worth the entire trip to New York City. A moment that made the ensuing Series with the Yankees almost anti-climactical. How often I've thought of Bobby Thomson since. He was the instrument in one of the most graphic hunches I ever had. I simply knew they couldn't pitch to him. As I have told you, though, I was receiving hunches clearly during that period. I won $1300 on that ball game alone.

I have another hunch as I write this. My daughter June is expecting a baby. I know it is going to be a boy. I can't tell you how I know it. I just do. I have $6000 bet against $3500 that it will be a boy. By the end of the book you'll know how good this hunch was.*

I see, though, that I've wandered a little afield. Down in the club a moment ago I heard a weekend player rattling the cubes over his head and shouting: "Come on, dice! Baby needs shoes!" I couldn't help but give him a wry smile, knowing that if he does have a baby and if it does need shoes from the money he's betting there won't be any shoes. His money will stay on the table. This age-old cry of the amateur dice player is, I believe, the best way to tell Lady Luck to go away. She just doesn't like to hear that needed money is being played. Those supernatural forces I've been talking about will turn those dice to craps.

Eddie Cantor tells in his book *The Way I See It* how he promised himself on a certain trip to Las Vegas that he wouldn't gamble. Lady Luck, if you please, has heard this promise many, many times. Mr. Cantor broke his. He gambled. In fifteen or twenty minutes he found himself signing a check for $15,000.

Later Mr. Cantor made another trip to Vegas with his son-in-law. They promised each other they wouldn't gamble. Eddie left his son-in-law for only a few moments and returned to find him at the dice table. He'd already lost several thousand dollars. He stopped when he saw Eddie and was most contrite. Mr. Cantor, being the loving person he is, didn't admonish or find fault. "Don't worry about it," he said. "I'll win it all back for you."

* I missed. June had a beautiful baby girl, Pamela Jean, born on Mother's Day, May 14, 1961.

He did, too, and my point in repeating the story is to show that Eddie Cantor went into this game, unlike his first one, thinking positively. He knew exactly why he was going to play. He wasn't using needed money. He was playing to do something nice for someone. He won back his son-in-law's money and quit a substantial winner. Here again is concrete proof of the supernatural aspects of the airy lady we call Lady Luck. Whether he had a hunch or not—or even recognizes that there are such things as hunches—Mr. Cantor played confidently and alertly. Expecting to win, as he said he would, he was prepared to double or re-double bets with the money he was winning. He was feeling neither greedy nor guilty. He did an excellent job of throwing the house money back in their own faces and making them pay more and more. In my mind there can be no doubt but that his positive thinking controlled the actual roll of the dice.

Weird? Eerie? Recondite? Yes, but also so necessary if you'd be a gambolier.

Some people unquestionably have greater talent than others for tapping into the supernatural. All who would gamble should develop the faculty. It is vital to gaming. It is vital to living. It is vital to success of any kind.

18

♦ ♦ ♦ ♦

For Winners Only

WE COME NOW to the point in this book where I must keep my promise to show you exactly how I play the various games we offer our customers in Reno. I shall call this my Primer On Gambling. If you were to study closely and put into practice everything I advocate here, I honestly believe you could come into Harolds Club on a given day and beat us for a substantial sum of money.

I don't guarantee that you will. As you now have seen, there are factors in gaming beyond the control of any of us, no matter how well we know the game. Above all, there's that vital factor of human nature and the hidden percentage it gives the house, the known fact you will stand longer at a table losing than you will winning.

Some of what I shall tell you is repetitious. You've now seen it demonstrated by experts and duffers in anecdotes scattered through my earlier narrative. Some of it you know from your own experience and observation. Some is simple logic. In stating my ABC's, though, repetition will help to emphasize the key points.

Let us preface our Primer with a review of some of the findings I've made in more than a quarter century as player and operator. There are, as we know, players who've waited many years for just one good hand. There are reasons why they've never known a lucky streak. There are reasons why other people win most of the time they play. Let's look again, very closely, at what gambling is and examine once more the makeup of the really good gambler.

◆

Gambling involves games of chance. No system of play can possibly eliminate all the risks involved. No system yet devised can change gambling into a sure thing. The slight edge which is in favor of the house must always remain in favor of the house.

All manner of systems have been concocted. Many players have advised me they have one which really will hurt Harolds Club, and ask permission to use it. I welcome them invariably with open arms; they're like money in the bank. In the entire history of my club, no system player ever has quit a winner. Some system players win a few times. Each of them invariably has returned to repay his "temporary loan" in full. I repeat: No system yet devised can change gambling to a sure thing.

The good gambler, the steady winner, knows that gaming must always remain games of chance. He is prepared to take his losses. For this reason he never plays with borrowed money or needed money. He doesn't "hock" anything to get gambling money. He does not, and need not, write checks. Generally he comes to the table with cash. Any loss which might occur will cause him no real suffering.

The expert gambler is a doer, not a crowd-follower. He is self-reliant, independent, thinks for himself and comes to his own conclusions. He has courage. He backs his judgment with his money. He is master of his own ego, controlling all emotions, and particularly greed. He *thinks* through problems rather than resolving them by *feeling*.

The good gambler decides beforehand what he can afford to lose and how much he will bet at the outset. This may be an amount as small as $5. He will bet the $5 of his own money to start, but when he begins to win he'll increase the bet unit from winnings. This type of person, you usually find, has established policies governing most areas of his life.

The expert gambler manages his money while playing. (Later I will describe my method of managing money in gambling games.) Since it takes such a very short time for the average player to lose his money, it should be obvious that it's more difficult to manage the money than it is to play the game. My own findings are that it's about five times more difficult to manage money properly and hold on to winnings than it is to win the money in the first place.

♠

Success is difficult to take. I've seen lucky streaks cause people to move to Reno on the assumption a few hours play each day will earn more for them than their present jobs. I recommend strongly against such rashness. I remember one player well who won continuously for two years, then dropped $100,000 in less than forty-eight hours. It broke him and he had to leave town to avoid the bad checks he'd written. Any businessman knows what it is to make a great deal of money in one year and be strapped the next. The principle is the same at the gaming table except that the action is faster.

The good gambler sets out to make big money and concentrates on his game. His mind does not wander. He thinks big money and winning at all times. He throws the house's money back in its face and doesn't "drag" a bet merely because the house has taken several from him. He knows that the chances of his making the next bet are exactly the same as was his chance of making his first bet. He has told himself this confidently and believes the cards or dice will get the message. He does *not* claim to anyone that his playing is only for fun and enjoyment and he "expects to pay" for that pleasure. The expert expects *to be paid*.

The good gambler plays methodically and with intent. The

losing gambler, on the contrary, trusts far too much on luck and blames *all* his losses on bad luck. Such bad luck, I hasten to assure you, will only continue so long as the player plays badly. Bad players can, and do, completely mess up hot hands and lose when everyone else is winning.

For example, I saw such a man make either eleven or twelve passes in a row with the dice once. This is a fantastically hot hand and he could have made more than the President of the United States. The man next to him did. He was betting $5 until the hot streak started; he increased his bets radically as the streak continued and was $20,000 ahead when the run ended. The shooter, because he bet badly, actually lost $50 on the run. Luck, as I say, can bring hot hands or a profitable evening but it takes more than luck to win more times than you lose.

The frequent winner at gaming is also a good businessman. It doesn't follow, however, that a good businessman is *per se* also a good gambler. So long as money is involved, a gambling game is a business transaction and should be treated and respected as such. Many a good businessman, very successful in his own line, has lost sight of this fact and dropped a bundle. The truly expert gambler never does. He analyzes the problem, invests or withdraws his money accordingly, and makes decisions as cautiously as if he were operating a store.

The good gambler is adept at applied psychology. In addition to understanding himself thoroughly, his own feelings of despair or happiness and the fact that things come in cycles, he is also aware of, and masters, his emotions. He makes certain his decisions aren't based on emotion. He refuses to let himself be carried away. He steels himself to think clearly and remain alert while he is thinking.

Expert gamblers are disciplined men. Self-disciplined men, I should say. When we gaming club operators get together for a game, for example, the contrast between our play and that of amateurs is marked. We're out to make a bundle of money for one thing and the stakes are high. There is almost no talk and absolutely no drinking. (A few men will have drinks, widely spaced, to aid them.) Most of us, as I now do always, drink black coffee or orange juice, which gives energy. We invariably play for only a short time, generally one or two hours, knowing how difficult it is to concentrate as deeply as we must for any longer period. Mental fatigue, we understand, muffles hunches. A fatigued mind and body brings only wrong decisions or slow decisions.

The expert gambler believes implicitly in the supernatural and develops his extrasensory perception to its ultimate keenness. With some, it would almost seem they can carry on conversations with other people simply by knowing how the others feel and without uttering a word. Hunches and ESP are closely intertwined, and good hunches are worth money in the bank. I have walked into a competitor's casino intending only to say hello and been hit at the doorway by a shock of knowingness that almost knocked me over. It has told me the dice will be hot for me and I have followed it to win as much as $25,000 in twenty-five minutes. By the same token, the expert gambler obeys the hunch which warns him not to gamble this day.

The truly skilled gambler is almost invariably a self-confident individual. Often he's a self-made man. He has plenty of money which he has acquired through his own efforts. Having won confidence through achievement, he radiates success and I find I generally like this man on first contact. He isn't a weak mortal. The confidence radiated by his personality carries over to the gaming table and wins for him.

I have given this considerable thought, incidentally, in view of our experience at Harolds Club during World War II and during the post-war period. Why, I have asked myself, were the big winners during the war only $10-$20,000 while the big winners of the post-war period took away sums of $40-$50,000? The reason, I now am convinced, lay in the confidence of the players of the two periods.

During the war, as I experienced myself, men carried the subconscious dread of going overseas. There was a constant fear of the unknown, a worry or tension that couldn't be suppressed. I never had a lucky streak during the time I was in the Army. I could only make the dice and cards perform, it seemed, after I returned to civilian life. In our club operations, of course, winners took away somewhat smaller amounts because our limits were lower. But there was more to it than that.

Immediately after hostilities ended, waves of ex-service men descended on us, jumped at the new high limits and clobbered the club. They were playing with surplus money, of course; discharge pay or accumulated pay. This is the luckiest money of all. But there was also a confident spirit about them. The serviceman who got home was thrilled to be alive. He'd made it! He had come through the great ordeal successfully while some of his buddies didn't. He was alive and he didn't have to suppress his fears any longer. This man made it big.

I remember one sailor who won more than $50,000 at a dice table in just a few hours. When I questioned the dealer about it, she said: "He couldn't do anything wrong and he was betting his luck. He took the 'proposition bets' (like betting 11, which pays 15-1, or 12, which pays 30-1) and they paid off for him." I was satisfied with her explanation. He was doing exactly what I advocate: take these high-odds bets when you're ahead and can use the house's money. The payoff always is tremendous because the odds in favor of the house are so much more than they are on the ordinary Line or Come bets. Fortunately this sailor decided he had enough when he won the $50,000 and telegraphed most of it home.

I say I like the strong, confident man. I do, even though he wins our money. The weak man with no particular success to his credit radiates discouragement. To my knowledge, no man of this stripe ever has been a large winner in Harolds Club.

The good gambler, I should add, understands perfectly how fear or anxiety cancels confidence. He works at his subconscious to remove or reduce fear tendencies (or else he avoids gambling). He tries to bring confidence into his conscious mind. He refuses to be like the steady loser who thinks only how wonderful it would be to win and what he would do with the money if he did win. He makes three or four passes with the dice, not concentrating on his betting, and wonders what is happening to his money.

The serious gambler, which again means the good gambler, knows that sex and dice (or cards) don't mix. I only have to glance at some players, note their inattentiveness, and know they won't be winners. I see them at a 21 table and notice they're more concerned with what's happening at the next table than they are with the play at their own. Or they're working at getting acquainted with the attractive woman playing next to them. Your mind can't serve two masters or two ladies. It's Lady Luck you're supposed to be wooing at the gaming table.

The really good gambler does not count on good luck alone, or supernatural coincidence, to win for him. Just as it takes more than a beautiful body to make a great actress, so does it take more than personal policy, confidence and luck to make a complete gambler. There must be some luck, certainly, but there also must be talent for the game and a wealth of experience. My model gambler sharpens his talents and builds consciously on his experience.

The expert gambler is, above all, a realist. He knows he can't expect to win all the time and that there will be days when he won't win at all. He prepares for such days, keeping his losses down so he can afford to try again when the tide turns. He knows the game will still be there tomorrow and that his cycle will make a swing. Then, when he's right again, he will plan to take fullest advantage of it. He will "get on that lucky train while it's going through town his way." Thus his winnings over a year should greatly exceed his losses. The player who thinks he can win all the time deludes himself badly and will pay for it.

Finally, the really good gambler knows how and when to quit. He is aware that all lucky streaks must end and that there's a time to get off the train before it turns around and returns him, broke, to his original starting point. No amount of confidence, skill or policy can halt that train once it turns around. The expert, then, is the man who, having won a great deal and seeing the dice now rolling against him, picks up his winnings and stops. It is this ability above all, I suspect, to walk away from a table winners that separates the good gambler from the bad. It is, incidentally, an ability I have acquired only recently and after many and many a spectacular failure to do so.

Now then, before we proceed to the games one by one, let me try to reduce all this to its essence. Let me give you my own Ten Commandments of Gaming.

1. Know and understand the game you play.
2. Prepare your mind to win.
3. Do not play needed money.
4. Do not borrow money, cash checks or pawn anything to play.
5. Manage your money to win.
6. Control your emotions, especially greed.
7. Listen carefully for hunches; avoid wishful thinking.
8. Concentrate on the game or leave the table.
9. When the tide turns, get out.
10. If you lose, don't cry.

The 11th commandment: Have patience.

Preparing to deal 21, I spread and check the deck.

I examine my hole card quickly and covertly

As a good dealer, I courteously answered player's questions.

I wait for players to study their hands.

Ace counts 1 or 11 and the man has taken two hits. Does he want another?

Good news for the players. I "break" and must pay all hands.

I instruct dealer Lavon Chambers in proper way to spin the little ball in roulette wheel.

Paying off a winner on Number 4 at 35-to-1

Paying off a split bet (on Numbers 4 and 7) at 17-to-1.

I pay off at 8-to-1 on a bet laid correctly to bracket four numbers, 4, 5, 7 and 8.

Another winner. Chip is laid to cover correctly Numbers 4, 5 and 6. Pays 11-to-1.

This Proposition Bet on Red is paid off at even money, chip-for-chip.

There's one right way to shoot craps. Bounce those dice. I'm going for the dough here.

This Line Bet pays the player. The shooter has "passed"—thrown seven on his first roll.

Bad news. Two Aces on the first roll. The house takes the Line Bet.

Here's a winning Proposition Bet in craps on Number 11. It pays off at 15-to-1.

Good bet on 4. I pay off the Line Bet at even money and the Odds Bet at 2-to-1.

This Don't Side Bet wins. The 12 (crap) came up on the first roll.

"Three winners, three losers," chants the Chuck-a-Luck dealer.

Happy? I have Ruggiero Ricci for my first Reno concert.

Junior, Kay Starr, Jan Peerce and I after another successful concert.

Ma petite femme, Lily Pons, captivated Reno, and me.

Lily Pons made those dice "sing" too.

Next came lovely
Elisabeth Schwarzkopf.

Mercedes Hoover, my confident
secretary, brews many a pot of
coffee to get me through
trying days.

Another dear face, my newest grandchild, joins my office gallery.

A happy grandpa, me, with Katherine, daughter Joan's second child.

A little older, a little wiser, but still in business at the same old stand.

19

♥ ♥ ♥ ♥

My Primer

Of Gambling

In GAMING, AS in too many areas of life, people simply don't plan their action. They depend on luck or happenstance. We may not notice the results immediately in most things. In gaming, which involves immediate and substantial risks, planning is the difference between winning and losing.

The great majority of players do not capitalize on their luck when it is running. Too many increase their bets while losing on the theory their luck "must turn some time." This is the wrong procedure.

You should increase bets only with the house's money, only after you see that luck is going with you. That can be only after you've had at least one winning bet.

My own experience proves to me that my luck doesn't begin to change until I've had that first winning bet. It's why I never increase after a losing bet. This might be the first of a series of losing bets and I don't want to go broke trying to buck a trend.

When the tide turns, however, I want my bankroll intact. I want to make up for my losing bets swiftly. Too many players consistently keep their bets small, even in a winning run, but double or triple them in a losing streak. For example, I have seen a man bet $2 and continue to bet only $2 in a good winning streak. He won five bets in a row and had $10. Then he lost a bet and began to double his wager in the hope of getting even. In no time he had lost $50 and was out of the game.

The only obvious solution to this is to plan your method of play before you sit down and *manage your money* so it will carry you through the lean cycles, being always prepared to hop on the bandwagon and increase your bets *with the house's money* when the tide turns. You soon can discern how the cards or dice are running. Your plan takes care of any eventuality except a straight day of bad luck, on which you'd better get out of the game anyway.

My plan of money management calls first for a betting unit. This you will decide in advance, depending on your bankroll, and you will also decide what your absolute losing maximum is to be. The betting unit may be one dollar, five dollars, ten dollars or a hundred.

This management method may be employed, incidentally, for most of our games: dice, 21, baccarat, chuck-a-luck or roulette if you're betting the red and black.

Assume that your betting unit is $1. This you will put up, and continue to play, after every losing bet. Thus, if you have three losing bets in a row, you have lost only $3. You will not change the amount of this bet until you have had a winning bet. Cards, after all, can run in favor of the dealer just as they sometimes do for the player. *Do not increase your bet even after losing three or four in a row.* The chances on each succeeding bet are exactly the same as they were on the first and it matters not, so far as the odds are concerned, that you may have up to fifteen losers in a row. The next one may start the winning cycle.

Let us say that I now get my first winning bet. To my betting unit of $1 the house pays me a unit. From my bankroll, I add a unit. This makes three units, or $3, I now am betting. If I win again, the house pays me $3. I drag that and put it with my bankroll.

I will now play the new betting unit of $3 until I lose (at which point I will revert to the original betting unit of $1 and build up again) or until I see that the cycle has come clear around for me and I am winning. If it is going real good, I increase my betting unit from $3 to $4 to $6 and on up. (In my own case, I may start with a betting unit of $20 and, depending on house limits, be up to $300 in a good streak.)

Remember, there's always a slight percentage in favor of the house and, because the odds against a player apply on *every* bet he makes, he doesn't have a 50-50 chance. If he is playing 21, for instance, he will make a bet every two or three minutes. Assume that, in one hour, he makes 30 bets, the percentage against him is 30 x 2.5% or 75%. This means simply that 75% of the time he must be money behind after 30 bets. The longer he plays, the higher the mathematical percentage working against him. The more likely it is he will be a loser.

With my system, you need to win two bets in a row to win any money but if you do start to win you will end up winners though you lose more bets than you win. You can still be winners though you average over-all only four winning bets to every five you lose. If you can average three winning bets in a row before you have to drop back to the original betting unit, you will win a great deal. Five to seven times your original bankroll is a reasonable amount to expect.

With my system, you drag only part of your winning bets as you go up, using the house's money against the house. You control yourself and your bankroll through losing cycles. You are in position, if you have a very lucky day, to pick up for some of the unlucky days you're bound to have.

Above all, you have a plan. You will not be stampeded by your own emotions. You can play hunches with the house's money and collect big bets. You can be conservative with your own.

Learning to manage your money is the only "system" I offer to those who would try to equalize the inherent odds against them in games of chance. It is just as important as knowing the rules and strategy of the games themselves.

21

In 21 you and the dealer each start with two cards. The object of the game is to make 21 points. You may call for as many more cards as you wish, to try to make 21. Face cards and tens count for 10, aces either 1 or 11. All other cards are at face value. The best of all hands, obviously, is a blackjack, any ace-ten (or face card) in the first two cards dealt. Otherwise, the hand nearest 21 (but not over 21) whether yours or the dealer's, wins the bet.

Twenty-one is a game of judgment as well as luck. The dealer turns her first card face up. You must attempt to guess what her hidden hole card may be and whether it gives her a hand you can beat, whether you should call for one or more cards and take the risk of going over 21, thereby breaking, or whether she will have to "hit" herself with a card and go broke.

The game as played in Reno's gaming houses offers certain optional gambles which may pay off if you take them. If, for instance, your first two cards add up to 11—a 6-5, 8-3, 7-4—you may turn them face up and double your initial bet. One card will be dealt face down to you. You are hoping, obviously, it will be a 10 or picture card to give you the perfect 21. But you also might get a 7, 8 or 9 which, with your 11, would constitute 18, 19 or 20, all good hands. Some players don't like to double-down, as we call it, if the dealer has a 10 or picture card showing, believing her hand too strong for the gamble. *I double down on every 11, regardless of what the dealer shows.*

In some casinos you may also double down on a 10. I usually do if possible, and especially if the dealer is showing a 3, 4, 5, 6 or 7. I am hoping I can add to my 10 the one card to beat her. (She may have anything from 13 to 17. She may also have a hidden card that gives her a good hitting hand.) *I certainly double down on 10* if the cards have been running favorably for me and even though the dealer has a 10 showing. An ace, being either 1 or 11, would make my hand 21.

In most gaming houses you are permitted to split pairs. You

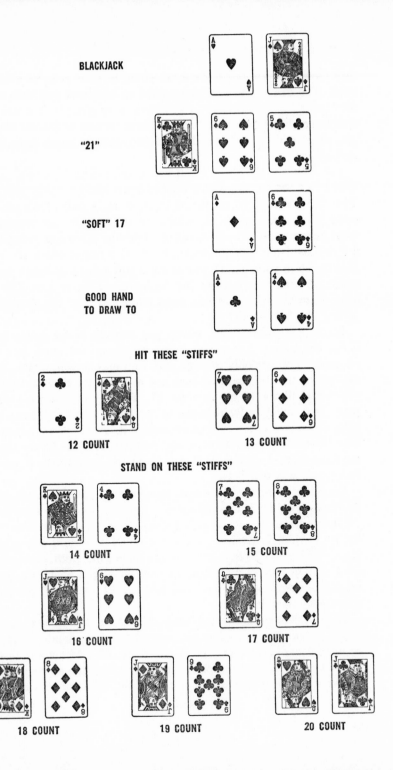

BLACKJACK

"21"

"SOFT" 17

GOOD HAND
TO DRAW TO

HIT THESE "STIFFS"

12 COUNT   13 COUNT

STAND ON THESE "STIFFS"

14 COUNT   15 COUNT

16 COUNT   17 COUNT

18 COUNT   19 COUNT   20 COUNT

turn them face up and place a bet equal to your original unit on each. The dealer will give you a card on each and you then may hit or stand as you choose. The object of splitting is to break up a weak combination in your original hand (a pair of 8's, for example, which add up to 16) and create two stronger hands (two 18's, perhaps).

I *do* split 3's, 2's, 6's or 7's. I *never* split paired 5's or 4's. Two fives is, of course, ten and a double-down hand, so why split it? Two fours, with a 10 or picture card, is 18, a pair of 6's on the other hand, adds up to 12, which we call a "stiff" or breakable hand because any 10 will break it. Splitting 6's might bring you a 5 or 4, which is a double-down hand. If it brings you a 10 (and thereby 16 in your hand) you've got a stiff again and aren't much better off than you were in the beginning. *I never split 10's or picture cards.* Why ruin one good hand and take the chance of getting two bad hands?

Splitting a pair of aces, which you may do in the Reno area, is another matter. When you split aces you get one card, face up, on each. You get only the one card and may not hit again. You are betting that one card on each ace will beat the dealer. Ideally, you would like a 10 on each for 21. Frankly this is not a good play. It is always advantageous to the house when you have two bets, which is why the casinos encourage it. As a player, however, I *do recommend* splitting aces, and particularly if the dealer shows anything from 7 under. You *can* catch two face cards, if you're lucky, and win two bets.

Speaking of house come-ons, incidentally, Harolds Club pays $5 bonuses on certain hands—a 6, 7 and 8 in the same suit, three 7's in one hand, or seven cards adding up to 21. Players like this, but it's obviously advantageous to the house because it encourages you to hit on two 7's or 7 and 8 in the same suit. Both, remember, are breaking hands. To offset all that, we give a $5 bonus for a blackjack composed of the Jack and ace of spades. There's no house advantage in that.

With certain exceptions, *I never draw to a stiff hand* (12, 13, 14, 15, 16). These, as you see, are all breaking hands. One 10 or picture card will break them. If, however, I feel I am casing the dealer's hole card correctly, and it will beat me anyway, or if I have a strong hunch that a non-breaking card will come, I *do* hit a stiff hand. Sometimes I win just because I do. I always watch the trend of the cards as other hands are hit. They may indicate, on this evening, that only 10's are coming on my 12's, but they may also indicate 4's and 5's are falling to my 16's. All things in gaming, remember, are relative. You can take chances one day that you couldn't on another. When luck really is with you, you can do nothing wrong.

Let's look now at the "soft" hand in which an ace serves either as 1 or 11. You always hit soft hands—ace-deuce, ace-trey, etc., up to ace-6. Some people don't hit "soft 17" (ace-6) but I always do. I do it for no other reason than that the Reno house dealers must and do. If the house does it, you know it's advantageous. A 10 or face card won't hurt the hand. A 2 or 3 will improve it. A 4 makes it 21.

What do you do when the dealer shows an ace but not a blackjack? (She would turn it immediately if it were blackjack). *I draw every time*, including to stiff hands, when the dealer shows an ace. If she hasn't a hidden hand already—a 7, 8 or 9 in the hole to give her 18, 19 or 20, she can draw enough cards to make at least 17.

Generally these are my do's and don'ts, my ABC's of 21. Sometimes they lose. Usually they win. In the final analysis, though, you play every hand as it lays.

CRAPS

There's only one logical reason in the world for shooting craps and that is to win money. The basic elements of the game, including percentages, I shall leave to authorities like Hoyle. Here I have time only to suggest what I think are your best chances for beating a crap game in a legal gaming casino and to recommend certain cautions.

Let me pass on some of the lore I learned from Eddie Sahati who, in his heyday, was one of the greatest dice players I ever watched. Eddie always played in the same way. He would make a Line bet; that is, *with* the player shooting the dice. This is a bet wherein, if the shooter, on his first roll, throws a 7 or 11, he and all Line players win. If a 2, 3 or 12 (craps) appears on the

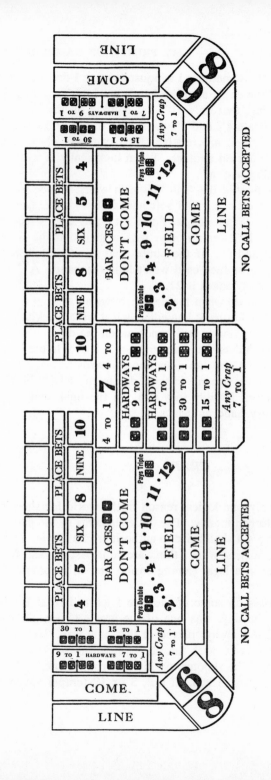

first roll, however, the shooter and all Line players lose. If he rolls a 4, 5, 6, 8, 9 or 10 on the first roll and repeats the number before a 7 appears, he and all Line players win their bets. If a 7 appears before the point is repeated, they lose.

Supposing the point to be made is 6. Eddie would make what we call a Come bet on the next roll. This is like a new Line bet, or making a Line bet for the "come-out" roll, thus betting on every roll of the dice. (I should explain right here the one expression that truly confuses the inexperienced player. It is "coming out." Let me make it very simple: *Any roll of the dice is "coming out."*)

If, on the first roll, the dice add up to a 4 or 10 (now to be made) the odds are 2-1 that he will shoot a 7 before he will shoot another combination of 4 or 10. If the first roll is 5 or 9, the odds are 3-2 a 7 will appear before either of them. Eddie always took the odds on 4, 10, 5 or 9, but was prejudiced against taking odds on 6 and 8, contending the odds on these two numbers (6-5) weren't big enough to warrant the risk. When I gamble, however, *I take every Come bet* including the odds on 6 and 8. I have seen these numbers repeat so often the odds to me appear reasonable; particularly if my timing of the cycle is correct. (The cycle when 8's and 6's are repeating.)

I always take at least simple odds. This means I now put an amount of money equal to what I wagered on the Line behind my first bet. (Just outside the Line and toward you). Double odds means I lay *double* my original bet in this position. *I strongly urge that you take odds or stay away from dice.* My reason? By taking odds, there is no percentage for you or against you. You now have a dead-even break for your money. The dice must seven-out for you to lose.

Assume that a new shooter gets the dice. On his first roll he throws a 4. He will continue to shoot the dice until he makes another 4 and wins. However, if he shoots a 7 before the 4, he loses, and then hands the dice to the next shooter in turn. While attempting to repeat the 4, he may roll a 5, 6, 8, 9 or 10. Taking all the Come bets, you may have all the numbers from 5 to 10 (except, of course, 7) covered. You win whenever one of these appears. Give me twenty minutes with few sevens and I'll have the entire board covered with bets. Every roll will be a winning one unless the shooter throws the 2, 3 or 12.

My finding from twenty-five years at the table is that the only way to beat a crap game is to take the Come bets with odds. I cannot emphasize this enough. I have seen Eddie Sahati win $25,000 in half an hour playing $400 plus $400 odds, or a total of $800 on each bet. Generally he would also play the propositions, which are the "Hard-way" numbers, if he was money ahead.

I contend, however, that a player should not take the proposition bets unless he feels very lucky or is using money already won. They pay longer odds for the house and against the player and therefore are not advantageous to you.

Let's look at these combinations. A Hard-way 4, for instance, is two deuces, a Hard-day 6 two treys, Hard-way 8 two fours, and Hard-way 10 two fives. Supposing an 8 is thrown and you wish to bet that it will repeat and will be made up of two 4's; in other words, the "hard way." You put your money out in the bracketed area marked for this in the center of the table. (The area is called fittingly "The Hazard.") For you to win, the shooter must throw an 8 made up of two 4's. Hard-way 8 and Hard-way 6 pay odds of 9-1, Hard-way 10 pays odds of 7-1. You will lose the bet if a 7 is thrown or if the shooter makes his 8 "the easy way," that is with a 5 and 3 or 6 and 2. This costs you your Hard-way 8 bet. (He didn't make the 8 with two 4's.) Money hasn't gotten that cheap to me yet. On proposition bets you may put your money down at will and sometimes I do play these bets—*if I have a hunch* or if the dice seem to be in a repeating cycle. I have cleaned up many a crap game this way. However, *I do not recommend this bet.* These are one-shot rolls.

Other proposition bets I don't recommend are on two 6's or two aces.

You win or lose on one roll of the dice regardless of the Line bet. This is true of all proposition bets. They have nothing to do with the other bets on the table. They pertain only to this roll of the dice. Your proposition bet wins or loses as it lays for the action.

I do not recommend the Big 6 or Big 8 bet in which you bet simply that a 6 or 8 will be thrown before a 7 appears. Here again you can pick up your bet or lay it down at will. I don't recommend the bet although I do play it when 6's or 8's seem to me to be coming in pairs.

One bet I absolutely do not play is the ace-deuce. My reason? I won't bet Do and Don't at the same time. It is simply illogical to have a Line bet supporting the shooter to make 7 or 11 on his first throw (or a point to be made later) and another bet on a 3, on which he would lose.

When I play the Do Come side, as I almost always do, I like to put my money on Number 11. That way, if the 11 comes, I will be paid both for the Line bet and for my 11. I may, for instance, have $200 on the Line and $25 on 11. Eleven comes and I get paid even money for my Line bet plus my 11-bet at 15-1 odds. Once in a long while I may even put $200 on the Field, which I don't advise at all. It's an idiotic way to play. I did it once and won $24,000 in 30 minutes. You can lose just as fast. *I certainly don't recommend this.*

Finally, I do not advise Place bets. Such a bet might be $5 on 10, which you can make at will or lift at will. You are betting that a 10 will appear before a seven. The bet has nothing to do with any other bets on the table. The percentage against you is greater than on a Line bet. Here's why. The moment you laid that $5 bet, one-half of the first dollar already was the house's. If your $5 wins, you will get $1 of it at even money (there went the house's percentage) and $4 at 2 to 1. (It wins $9 for you.)

Remember, please, in all gambling games that there is a difference between odds of 10 *for* 1 and odds of 10 *to* 1. In Las Vegas, for instance, the tables may be marked at odds of 15-*for*-1 on Number 11. That means that if you bet $1 and win you will receive your bet plus $14. At odds of 15-*to*-1 you would receive your bet back *plus* $15. Personally, I can always use another dollar.

A final word. Dice do "act crazy" at times. There's nothing you can do about it. Just hope you're not playing when they do and when they can't seem to repeat numbers thrown on the first roll. Over a long period of play—perhaps 10,000 rolls of the dice —the so-called law of averages will apply, but for a short duration of an hour or two anything can happen. I have seen seven 11's in a row, four or five craps in a row, and a player make as many as 35 passes in a row, all unusual. The good gambler knows that for the few hours he is going to play he'd better *watch carefully what is happening now,* and *don't count on any law of averages.*

CHUCK-A-LUCK

Chuck-a-luck, most simply, is a gambling game in which you have three large dice in an hourglass-shaped wire cage. When the cage is turned on its pivot the dice fall into various combinations. You bet the combinations into which you hope they will fall.

On the green felt layout are numbers from 1 to 6. Say you place a $1 bet on Number 1. If one ace shows, your $1 bet is paid at even money. If two aces fall, you are paid 2-to-1, and if three aces fall, 3-to-1. The same system applies to the other numbers up to 6.

In the "Hazard" area of the layout are certain combinations on which you may bet and which pay big odds. If, for instance, you bet Number 17 and the three dice fall into that combination (say two 6's and a 5) you will be paid off at 60-to-1.

You might also bet on the Jackpot ("Raffle," as it is called in some gaming houses). You then would be betting your $1 that the three dice will all fall with the same number up. Any three of a kind pays 30-to-1.

You might also bet High or Low. If you bet High, you are wagering that the combinations of numbers on the dice as they fall will add up to 11 or more. If you played Low, you would be betting that they added up only to 10 or less.

Now I will tell you some facts. The house odds against you on the simplest bet above $1 on an ace showing are 3.5%. After that simple bet, and as you get into the Hazard bets, the odds against the player soar. Chuck-a-luck is, therefore, not a popular game in Nevada. People by far prefer dice because the percentage of 1.41 against them is so much less. Always remember in choosing your game that whenever the house offers you bigger odds on your bets, such as the 35-to-1 in roulette or the 80-to-1 in Chuck-a-luck, it must have more percentage going against you. It would be awfully hard for you to beat Seabiscuit at the race track with a plug horse and you would deserve, and get, the 100-to-1 odds you would be offered.

I play almost no Chuck-a-luck myself. When I do, it is usually a courtesy bet and usually just a couple of dollars on the Raffle, or Jackpot. I can walk away from Chuck-a-luck as easily as I'd walk away from a seaweed salad.

SLOT MACHINES

There is no known system for playing and winning on the slot machines. They are strictly mechanical and the mechanical apparatus takes care of itself and you.

We have always been proud of the payoff on our machines at Harolds Club because *the player does have a chance to win.* My daddy cut the odds against the player on our machines very low early in the game. (This is possible, I repeat, only because of the gross volume of play our machines get.) I prefer not to tell you just how low the percentage against you is because I don't think you will want to believe it. However, I do say that Harolds Club was the first club in Nevada where people played the slot machines *for jackpots* rather than just for payoffs. That should speak for itself.

My only advice to you in playing slot machines is to manage your money. I will repeat, too, what I say of all gambling: Don't cash any checks. Don't hock anything to keep playing. Don't borrow money to play. If you follow this advice, you can't get hurt too badly by the slot machines.

If you win, consider yourself lucky. If you lose, don't be surprised. No gambler who is a real gambler even thinks of playing slot machines.

However, and I have told this to thousands of persons who have come into Harolds Club, you will be far better off to play the slot machines than the other games because the mechanical apparatus will take care of you. You will not have to gamble on your own thinking, alleged skills or judgment. Just insert your coin, pull the handle and see what happens.

Again, and I emphasize the statement Daddy has made so often: "If you gamble, gamble only with the change in your pockets." (I, unfortunately, have violated this advice many times.)

ROULETTE

Roulette, though the betting may appear complicated to a novice, actually is rather a simple game. You place your bet, or bets, on the number at which you hope the wheel will stop. The little ball is spun in the wheel and the number at which it stops is the one paid. There are, of course, many combinations of bets that may be made simultaneously on the layout in the hope the ball will favor one or more of them.

I would say that this game is comparable to the slot machines in that it is automatic and takes care of you. You cannot make a silly bet though you may make losing bets. Once the ball spins, there is nothing you can do by skill or judgment to alter the outcome.

In all the roulette layout, including the columns of numbers and the Hazard, or proposition bets, there is only one I cannot recommend. Let me explain it.

Up and down the Vegas Strip and in Reno we have roulette layouts with what are known as "house numbers"—the Single-O and Double-O. On this type of green you might make a bet in which you would lay your chips on 1, 2 and 3 plus the Double- and Single-O. This is the bet I do not recommend. Why, since it pays 6-to-1 if you win? I do not recommend it because, while the normal house percentage against you in roulette is 5-5/19%, on this bet it becomes 7-34/38% against you. That, obviously, is raising the odds too high against yourself and I would never play it.

Otherwise, roulette is a beautiful, a quiet game, a polite game. Over a quarter of a century as operator and player, I have noticed that this is the game professional men, doctors in particular, prefer.

One thing I do recommend strongly when playing roulette: Use chips instead of silver. Roulette chips are of several distinctive colors and you alone will be using the color you buy. When you win a bet, there will be no dispute over it. Silver on the table confuses both the players and the dealer. I have paid off bets of 35-to-1 many times simply because players had silver down and were confused as to who won. I knew who won but I wanted to

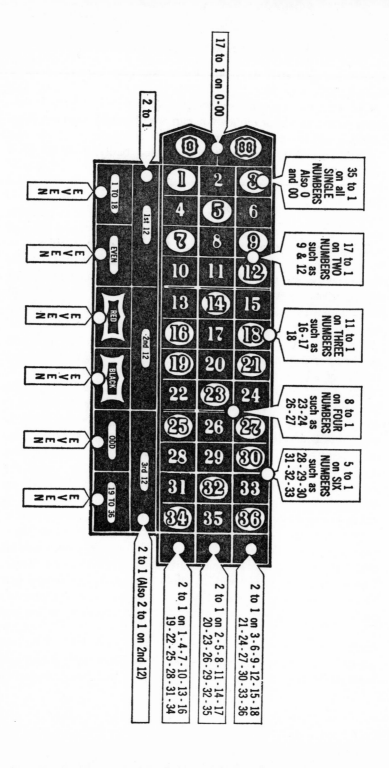

keep peace and so I paid off. *When you play with chips there need be no confusion.*

One final caution with roulette, as all gaming. Decide in advance what amount of money you can afford to play. Do not hock anything, do not borrow money or cash checks to play. If you heed this warning, you won't get hurt too badly, even on your unlucky day.

BRIDGE

Being a professional gambler, and therefore quite familiar with cards, I suppose I am more of a perfectionist at the bridge table than most people who play. I have played this game avidly for thirty-five years; ever since the early auction days. I love it and play it at least once a week now. Without going into technical details of the game and how it is played, I should like to make some strong suggestions for the person who attempts to play it for as much as a penny a point.

First of all, be a *partner* and not a soloist. Most partners in bridge, I find, do not seem to respect their partner's judgment. They do not seem to consider the potential value of his hand though obviously they must take it into consideration if they wish to win. Subconsciously at least, the average bridge player seems to think of himself or herself only as holding 13 cards, of which at least 7 may be high.

In the game of bridge, remember, you have an opportunity to see 26 cards, the 13 in your own hand and the 13 in the dummy, which is exactly half of the deck. Knowing them, you must and should attempt to seek out the value actually in your partner's hand. You have some idea from the declarant's bidding. You've seen half the deck. It shouldn't be too hard, if you have reasonable card sense, to decide where other cards may be. Remember, if you please, bridge is not solitaire but a co-operative endeavour.

You must study your partner and your opposition in bridge. We all have human nature to reveal us. A gambler is better than the average player of any game because he attempts to look to the marrow of his opponent's bones. Try it at bridge and see if your game doesn't improve.

Another cardinal rule for bridge was taught me by the very first bridge teacher I had. *Never double your opponents unless you can put down at least two tricks.* That may help check your enthusiasm. *Never go for a Little Slam or Big Slam unless you are almost positive you can make it.* Remember always you can jeopardize winning the rubber by being too enthusiastic about your cards or by your vanity getting the better of you and letting you try to make 6.

With almost all Big Slam bids, you will find, you will have to make at least one finesse to accomplish the slam. You have to take all the tricks, remember.

Equally true, though not quite as stringent, is the likelihood when you're going for a Little Slam you will have to make at least one finesse. You can lose only one trick to make your Little Slam.

There are many books on how-to-play-bridge and many reputable systems for playing the game. My advice is that if you are going to attempt to play by any of two or three systems be positive you understand all of them thoroughly. Otherwise, decide on one system and stick with it. You won't get into trouble that way and confuse one system with another.

Playing for money, I would remind you, is altogether different from tournament bridge. When you're in a tournament you're playing for masters' degrees or credits. When you go for the dough, you're going to win or lose your money. As with all forms of gambling then, you must be lucky as well as skillful *on the day you play.* Your own human nature will be an ingredient of the game you play for money.

I should like to point out that it is most discourteous when you are the dummy, and whether you're playing for money or credits, to look at the hand or hands of your opponents. For one thing, if you *do* look at their hands you cannot, according to the rules, call a renege should that be necessary.

Remember, too, I suggest, that playing bridge for money can sometimes make the worst of enemies out of the best of friends. So choose your partners, study your partners and play as though your partner's hand was a part of your own, as it is in bridge.

GIN RUMMY

This is a great game at which to gamble since you don't have to depend on a partner as you do in bridge. It is what we gamblers call a "head-and-head" game involving, as it does, two persons. Here, definitely, you notice how you have good days and bad.

I have several strong recommendations for the playing of gin. I hope you find them profitable to you.

First, in picking up a hand and starting your play, I strongly recommend that you play (or discard) a King. It is the top card of 13 in a suit. It can only fit with two other Kings or with the Queen-Jack of the same suit. Therefore its use to you would be limited. By discarding the King, you lighten your hand by 10 useless points.

The next card to discard would be the ace. This also is at the extreme end of 13 cards in a suit. It can only team with two Aces or at the low end of 2 and 3 in the same suit. It probably would not help you.

From my own findings, I would say the two most workable, or valuable cards in the deck for the gin rummy player are the 7 and the Jack. Retain them. If your opponent has two Jacks and you should discard yours, it would lessen his hand by 30 points to take your Jack and he would now have a three-card combination.

The 7 is obviously workable in a gin hand. It can pair with two other 7's. It can go with an 8 and 9 or with a 5 and 6.

I should add a word of warning for times you play gin rummy. Just as you would at poker, never let anyone who may be standing around see your hand. Remember that it is hard enough to control your own countenance so it won't convey whether you have a good or bad hand. When a kibitzer also is watching he may, by just his expression, reveal that information. It could be the tipoff and your opponent *might* take advantage.

One final thing. Before you ever entertain the idea of playing cards for big money, first play for pennies for a long time. Until you really know how to play cards. This applies just as surely to bridge as to gin rummy or 21.

BACCARAT

Baccarat is a classic variation of Chemin-de-Fer, once known as the game that "breaks the bank at Monte Carlo." The object of the game is to achieve a total of 9 with two cards or an additional third card. In the event 9 isn't made, the next highest hand wins.

The game is played between one individual and the Bank (or Banque) and all other participants bet on the hand being played. Picture cards and 10's have no value. All other cards count at face value, including the ace, which is one point. Any hand totaling ten points or more must subtract 10 points. Any hand totaling 20 points or more must subtract 20 points.

PLAYER		BANKER		
HAVING		HAVING	DRAWS when giving	DOES NOT DRAW when giving
1-2-3-4-5-10	Draw a Card	3	1-2-3-4-5-6-7-9-10	8
6-7	Stay	4	2-3-4-5-6-7	1-8-9-10
		5	4-5-6-7	1-2-3-8-9-10
8-9	Turn Cards Over	6	6-7	1-2-3-4-5-8-9-10

Baccarat is the only game in our club that is played solely with currency (although we may use $500 chips when the play gets very heavy). Baccarat is comparable to dice in that you play with or against the Bank. (Or, in dice, *with* the shooter or *against* him.) Being a positive thinker, I always advise Baccarat players to bet *with* the Bank.

There is a more concrete reason for this than philosophy of course. The percentage against the bank is 5%, which the house takes off the top when you win a bet. (It takes none when you lose.) When you bet on the player side (and against the Bank) the house has a positive 2½% against you in the game. (That is

$2.50 on $100, or 2½¢ on every dollar.) This 2½% is going *with you* when you bet with the Bank.

I urge Baccarat players to watch the Bank and see how the cards are running just as they would watch the shooter in a dice game and see how many passes he is making. Playing with the Bank is, of course, comparable to playing the Do side in a crap game.

In our club, the condition open to the public is $5 minimum bet up to $500 maximum bet or "any way you can get to it" (any combination from $5 to $500) as the gamblers say. If you really want to plunge, you may, by speaking to the management, get the limits increased in Harolds Club to a $20 minimum and $1500 maximum. As we say, you establish a new condition.

Baccarat is not for peanuts and you can win or lose as your luck runs. One night in Las Vegas I had lost $5000 at 21 and happened to stop at the Baccarat table in The Sands. I played *with* the Bank and won $7500. My last hand netted me $2600 and I went home singing.

So there, briefly, is my Primer on Gambling. I don't attempt the details of Hoyle or his illustrious successors. I simply hope to offer you some of the more valuable "do's" and "don't's" I have discovered in my years at the games. I don't discuss poker because I don't play poker any more. I don't care for horse-racing with that 15% percentage going against me the moment I bet. I have already told you what I think of Faro. My hope is that by not burdening your mind with a myriad of technicalities I can at least help you go home one day winners. Let's hope I have done that.

♠ ♠ ♠ ♠

Play It As It Lays

I CONSTANTLY AM asked the recipe for the success of Harolds Club. I state it as simply as I can: "Policy." And my questioners go off with a blank look. Herewith, then, I shall attempt to draw a picture, or series of pictures, of our policies and how we arrived at them.

Let me repeat, if you please. If there's any single key to the success of this gaming house, aside from luck, timing and the golden smile of Mother Providence, it has been our policy. We have been most fortunate in that since we came into this business without the necessary knowledge to create long-term policies.

What do you do, for instance, about loans to customers? You don't want a man to walk out broke after you've won all his money. What about liquor mixed with gambling? Fights, violence, disputes over the games? How do you hire employees who also can be firm diplomats? What about your own manner in the club where people are winning or losing? These are only a few of the general areas in which a gambling house operator must maneuver.

Remember, if you please, that I was practically a babe—only twenty-six years of age—when we opened our doors. My dad was a carnival and amusement park man, a pretty rough nugget though shrewd as a Vermonter can be. We'd operated as semi-gamblers in places where gaming was, for the most part, illegal. We had no idea that one day our cubbyhole would become the largest gaming club in the world. As you've seen, we just grew, like Topsy.

Early in the game, we had to determine how we would handle disputes. My brother Raymond says a quitter never wins a fight and my personal policy has always been never to walk away from one. But fights of any kind are no good in a club. Consider the facts. Say there's physical violence. There's always the obvious possibility some one, possibly an innocent bystander, will get hurt. Lawsuits will follow as surely as 10 follows 9. But there's a larger consideration, the over-all atmosphere of your club. Is it a happy place for fun and recreation or a place of contentiousness and violence where the customer never feels safe? The answer lies with the operator and his employees.

I have worked diligently to school my son and other employees in the facts. "If you walk around with a chip on your shoulder," I tell them, "you can fight five, six or seven times a day. There will be that many opportunities in a place like this where emotions are cooking. Now what the Hell kind of businessman would you be, fighting four or five times a day down in Harolds Club? To begin with, I couldn't stand up to it physically. I wouldn't have any teeth and I'd be all banged up. I'd have the reputation of a troublemaker and my club a name for trouble. So what's it going to be? You've got to have a policy."

Over twenty-five years, in which I have mediated countless arguments, I have hit only one man. He called me a name beyond all bounds of decent tolerance. Remember, if you will, that I'm frequently called a son-of-a-bitch, to my face, and with varying shades of conviction. I have developed an offhand answer for that. "I didn't know you knew my middle name," I reply, "the one I use to cash checks." However, the name this man called me was wanton, something I could not tolerate. Furthermore, he repeated it with embellishments and we had an audience. I tried to walk around him and get the bouncer, Red Bolster, but we had a curious situation here in those early days. Every time trouble started Red was out of the house. He was out eating.

The trouble had started at a table where Doris, who is still with us, was dealing roulette. The man had been drinking. I didn't want him annoying her, so I walked over politely and said: "Would you please cash in your chips? Tomorrow's another day. Come back then." He started the name-calling and I looked for Red, figuring he could clean it up without a mess. As I passed the table again, the man demanded: "Are you the one who asked me to quit?" He didn't know salt from pepper. I replied that I was. He called me that dirty name and I swung. I didn't even take time to remove my glasses. I clipped him on the jaw and knocked him against a 21 table nine feet away where Raymond was dealing cards. Then I yanked off my glasses and squared off for battle. At that moment a club employee grabbed the man's arm. I snatched his other arm and we ran him toward the door. It was a perfectly timed maneuver. Another employee was coming in and just happened to have the door open. We threw our man right through it and he slid on his nose across the sidewalk. Two city detectives collared him before he could resume hostilities.

That was my one fight and the genesis of our policy. An operator would be silly, I realized, to play bouncer. What does he think he's running? A gymnasium or a gaming club? Anyone who wants to fight is silly. (I ought to know because I heal so slowly.) When I encounter a damned fool like the man above I try to figure: *There's just a person who's more ignorant than I am.*

That's the way I have trained myself. Somehow I have to get it over to employees. "You are mediators," I instruct my floor bosses, "not arbitrators or referees. Therefore, approach a trouble-maker politely. Use a modulated tone of voice. Take it very easy. He's already excited and annoyed and probably the dealer is too. Someone must quiet this beef and that is your job. If you approach it with a suave demeanor, self-composure and control, you're going to be far more successful."

Ninety-nine times out of a hundred in a gambling club the dispute results from a player's mistake. Remember, if you please, dealers are trained carefully and work their game every day. Players are not schooled and don't play daily. They are, for the most part, amateurs participating in a highly professional activity. Now we add other considerations, including alcohol. We sell more whiskey at seven bars than is sold under any other roof in

304 • I WANT TO QUIT WINNERS

the world. All right, now you sold a man some liquor. He is not at his best. A floor man must consider that point. He is coming up to pacify a situation.

Point two. When an argument starts, and especially if it gets loud or leads to a fist fight, action on all other tables slows or comes to a stop while the players watch. Two or three or four tables may stop. As an operator, you must bear one cold fact in mind—at least 98% of the people from the outside will be sympathetic to the outsider embroiled in a quarrel. That is human nature. They are biased in his favor. They're gambling. Maybe they're stuck, heavy losers, either to your club or a neighboring one. Gambling house operators don't have the noblest reputation in the world. So you, the floor man, had better not stride up there like a cop in a new uniform as if to announce you're going to assert yourself.

I have developed pat answers over the years for situations such as this. Perhaps the player has gone beyond the loudly irate and is now so high-handed about you and your club you're up against a stone wall. You try to appease him with gentle courtesy but it only makes him angrier. "There's no use trying to argue with me, sir," I say at this point. "I'm too ignorant." Almost invariably a new expression comes over the disputant's face. Perhaps he was getting embarrassed with his own loud bawling and you've let him off the hook. It always eases the tension; that I know.

Let me describe another rather common situation. It has to do with the laying of bets. A dealer must at all times be clear on one thing: *Is it a bet or is it no bet?* In a gambling house we simply can't have "call" bets—a player shouting he wants "$5 on number 13" or saying "Count me in, I'm digging for my dough." We want to see his money on the line. Otherwise there's too much chance for leakage and arguments. So we have another expression which is cardinal law in the gambling business: *"It goes as it lays for the action."* If that needs to be made simpler, it means that the action is started and your bet will be considered for exactly what it is and where it is.

We come now to the situation rather common at roulette. A player is betting several numbers. Now the ball's about to stop. He calls out: "$2 on Number 2." The money isn't on Number 2 but the ball stops and it hits Number 2. The player demands that he be paid $70. I am thinking of one of these incidents when the dealer was a woman. She wasn't quick enough to shout: "It is no bet" or "Too late this roll." Perhaps his call came only a fraction of a second before the ball hit the number. But the ball *is* in Number 2 and you know, and I know and everyone knows, if it had stopped in Number 6 this player wouldn't insist upon paying the $2 called. (There are a few honest souls who would, but only a few.) So here we are. It was a call bet, made verbally, and I've been called to the wheel where the dealer is just as hot over the situation as the player.

Here, potentially, is a nice, excitable, angry argument. If I approach it with any but a serene attitude I'm going to make it worse. The more you stir fire the more it burns. This man, being halfway gambling wise, has loudly informed the dealer: "You should have said 'No bet.' " That gave me an opening. "We don't accept call bets in Harolds Club," I explained. "Have you any idea of the confusion they create?" He should have had since he was in the middle of some he'd created. "She should have called it 'No bet,' " he insisted. I agreed, but pointed out: "When you're back of these tables eight hours a day you're sometimes not as alert as you should be." He brushed that aside with: "Are you going to pay me?" "No," I said. "I'm sorry but the dealer is correct and I must back her play. If I were to pay you we might have another incident in thirty minutes. The next call might be for $15 or $20. I'd be running around here all night and never knowing where we stood. We have to stand on our policy of no call bets."

There is another common situation which has prompted signs over our crap tables: NO DICE ON 4 SILVER DOLLARS OR 4 CHIPS IN A STACK. This means simply that if either or both of the cubes should come to rest on a stack of four or more chips or four or more silver dollars, it is no play. The dice must be thrown over. I innovated this policy many years ago and you've no idea how much trouble it prevents. Dice bounce pretty good, as we know. The majority of the money wagered in a dice game is usually bet along the front line or "Do" side. But there's also heavy wagering against the shooter on the "Don't" side. We'll say someone has 20 silver dollars stacked on the Line and the shooter's point is 8. One of those damnable dice bounces up and comes to rest on the dollars. If permitted, it contributes to a seven-out craps, and the Don't side people clamor for their money. The Do players, waiting for their 8, clamor just as loud. In gambling it's pretty hard to satisfy everyone. People's money is involved and so, naturally, is their opinion and temperament. What do you do?

I remember such an incident during the war when a Navy commander threw the dice and one went on top of 25 silver dollars. This time, however, it favored the Do side winners. They wanted to be paid. The Don't siders shrieked in protest. We couldn't take their money—they wouldn't let us. Yet we had to pay off the Line betters. Clearly, if I didn't come up with a stated policy, I was in a position where I couldn't win but I could lose. That's when I set four silver dollars or four chips as the limit and posted my signs.

Another incident. A lady film writer from Hollywood was playing roulette. She was a little, mousey-gray person, the pity-me type, in slacks, and she was betting $30 a hand. It was the way she laid her bet down, on the line between the second and third 12 sections, that caused the trouble. We have that line for the convenience of players who can't reach the Single- and Double-0 sections at the end of the table. They place their chip on the line but edging it over to right or left to indicate they want Single-0 or Double-0. It is understood they don't mean it as a bet on either of the 12s into whose territory it encroaches. Our lady, however, had intent. She dropped her chip over the line carelessly so that if the 0 hit she could claim a 17-1 payoff; if the 12 hit, she wanted 2-1 for her money. I had alerted the dealers to watch for this and always ascertain which bet she meant and line up her chips accordingly. This they had done five different times that day, informing her politely she was crossing the line. Well, you can guess what happened. The lady looked all day until she found one dealer momentarily looking the other way and the Single-0 hit. She wanted her 17-1 payoff. The dealer, vanity stung because she'd been taken advantage of, pointed out that the bet was at least 85% into Section 12 territory. She was excited now too, you see and wanted to argue, which never gets the job done. I was summoned to the table.

Some fifty people, hearing the dispute start, gathered to see what would happen. The lady film writer waited serenely, a look on her face that said plainly: *They're robbing me, a poor, tired little woman.* The spectators said nothing, waiting to see what I would do. Among them was a man named Waldorf Red, who has dealt roulette around this country for twenty-five years. It wasn't good. I knew and she knew she'd been corrected five times already. "I am going to pay this bet," I announced, "but I should like to explain this table to you again." I handed her $510, which was her winning bet at 17-1 odds, and explained clearly that the money must go as it lays for the action. Everyone was happy. I stepped away from the wheel. Waldorf Red was at my elbow. "That's the first time I ever saw a 2-1 bet paid off at 17-1," he declared, "especially when the house really won the bet."

"Red," I replied, "I will bet you a $100 bill that this same lady, within a year's time, will come back with that $510 and I will get it back from her." He declined the bet. Nine months later she was back, having now worked out a system to beat the dice game. I don't recall how many trips she made to the powder room to get more money from her purse but I do know she lost at least $2000 on the dice. The moral? You may pay many a bet you've really won in order to keep peace in the club but patience and time will rectify all errors.

Let's look at another kind of incident. A gentleman, obviously a working man not used to big money, had run $20 up to $6000 on the 21 table while drinking and was getting boisterous. This was just after the war, when our men employees hadn't returned yet, and we had a lady floor boss on duty. Anticipating trouble, I went in to deal to the man. He won another $1000 and I left, thinking everything was all right. Soon after that, apparently, his luck changed. He had only $350 left when he cashed in. The lady floor boss got the cash and handed it to him. Without a word of warning, he hit her in the mouth and knocked her cold. It took four of us to overpower him. Ironically, as the police were taking him out, he shoved the $350 to me. "Hold it for me, Harold," he said. I did, returning it to him on the day of trial. He now was angry because he'd been incarcerated overnight. There is this type of person, I have found, who crows when he wins and cries when he loses. "I won't go to Harolds Club no more," he tells everyone. Frankly I don't want his business, but I told the judge: "I'm here to testify in the hope this man will take it easy in the future when he's drinking. I don't think he's the kind of man who wants to do this sort of thing. Actually he was angry at himself for having had all that money and losing it back." It softened the blow for him. While I obviously can't have customers clobbering the help, my personal policy must include some understanding of the human passions involved. Today, if a customer appears potentially menacing, the dealer can step on a button and have a floor man at her side instantly.

I have tried to exercise perception in hiring personnel and here again I have idiosyncrasies. When I'm interviewing an applicant, as sometimes happens, and he makes a production of his honesty and what a hard worker he is, I don't hire him. My finding is that the more a person protests his honesty the more you'll have to watch him. If he emphasizes how hard he likes to work you're liable to have a cry baby on your hands because no one can appreciate how much he does work. I try never to hire a weak prospect because later, if you have to discharge him, you've created another enemy. The gambling business, as any other, wants as few enemies as possible.

The same principles apply to cashing checks in a gaming house. If a man announces to the Credit Office: "This check is as good as gold," don't cash it. If he says: "I'll take an oath on my mother's grave," look out. He probably has practiced that phrase with reason. It would amaze you to know how valuable little clues like these can be in the operation of a club.

Then there's the matter of lending money. I remember an incident that occurred when operators could still play at their own tables. I was shilling—encouraging the play—at a dice table and playing the Line, or Do side. The gentleman in question was playing the Don't side. I shot a hot hand and wiped him out. He dropped probably $80 and it was obviously a lot of money to him. He came around to me after I finished playing and asked for a loan. By then I had learned the facts of life. I turned him down. You as a gaming club operator simply can't loan money. People will pay the laundry bill, phone bill, room rent, restaurant tab, hospital and even the doctor before they'll pay money back to a gambler. You lose the money and the customer.

Time was I made loans of $50 or $100. Later the person would come up to me and say: "Harold, where in Hell were you the last two-three hours? I had that $50 to pay you but you know how it is, I got to horsing around the dice table—" "Well," I would suggest, "why didn't you put it in an envelope and leave it at the Credit Office with my name on it?" The invariable answer: "Oh, I wanted to give it to you personally." Rather than loan money, I found, it's better to use the refund book and *give them the money.* They'll continue as customers. Eventually you'll get that money to the vault.

There's another truism in this area—you always buy the last marker. A marker, as I have explained, is a man's IOU for a gambling credit. It's a courtesy extended to big players who are good customers or are recommended by someone who is. It creates very difficult situations for the operator. His customer may be a respected business or professional man and perfectly good—solid, as we say in the gaming houses—for $2000, $3000 or more. Over the years he gets stuck and takes a marker, gets even, then stuck again and even again, wins your money and hurrahs you for quite some time. Then he gets into a very, very unlucky streak, tries to gamble his way out and overextends himself. Now he needs $10,000. You have misapprehensions—you're aware of his unlucky streak—but he has always been good on markers before. You've no tangible license to turn him down. You grant the $10,000. This marker you will buy. He simply can't, or won't, bring himself to redeem it. Knowing this, you must be philosophical. You don't want to ruin the man—or shouldn't want to—so you tote up his losses to the club over the years and mentally write it off. (But keep a copy in the files.) This isn't a five-minute finding of mine, I hasten to assure you. I contend you always end up buying the last marker with no exceptions. I have one in my desk right now for $40,000. It is Eddie Sahati's. That story you know.

Serving liquor in a gaming club was to take us through a number of interesting experiences. Daddy, as I have said, was against it until he reckoned the economic loss from players going elsewhere. As our first bar grew into seven bars on three floors, we had to establish a whole code of policies. One was we would not encourage drinking with gambling. We would not send hostesses —"rum runners," I believe they call them—to offer free drinks at the tables. Many other clubs do this, and with intent! We don't, though on rare occasions when I've made a big kill at the tables myself I may order free drinks around. Instead, we have certain times when we announce that "Mr. House" will buy during the next hour for everyone who cares to go up to the Seventh Floor. It's surprising how many players decline the invitation. "Tomorrow night maybe," they seem to say, "but not now. I'm stuck or I'm winning. I've got a lucky streak going and I'm not going to leave this table and this dealer now." He knows the free drinks are available and he's welcome to them but that isn't what he came to Reno for. The rum runner will bring drinks to him at the table, but only if he calls for his and pays. It's also surprising how little real drunkenness we encounter.

There are times, to be sure, when we notice a man has too much and must stop his play until he sobers up. I shall skip all talk about integrity or honesty or love for our fellow man. That's a consideration, to be sure, but there's a far more cogent reason for our concern. It is bad business for us to gamble with a man who doesn't know what he's doing and it is good business for us to stop him. How can we determine when he "doesn't know what he's doing?" It isn't hard. When we see a man at the 21 table, for instance, with a face card and an eight (18) in his hand ask the dealer for another card and go broke, as he almost inevitably must, we know this man doesn't know salt from pepper. He's not losing his money; he's throwing it away. He hasn't a chance to win. And we probably sold him the liquor on which he got intoxicated. We'll suggest to him he quit playing for a while.

It isn't easy to control a man's drinking. Ask any wife. The gentleman is over 21; he remembers that distinctly when he forgets everything else. He is intent on drinking and to interfere with him is a good way to get yourself punched in the nose. If a man shows he has taken on too much at the bar, we can and do refuse to sell him any more. But we can't go around giving sobriety tests. We have to use our judgment, attempting to ascertain his condition by the manner in which he conducts himself. This isn't easy either. Some people can absorb a lot of booze without showing it immediately. Some take a lot aboard and go on to gambling and it hits them as suddenly as if the roof fell in. All we can do is remember that our customers are our friends. We treat them as you would a friend who has been invited to your home, partakes of your hospitality and finds himself suddenly drunk.

Just the other night I observed a man at a 21 table near our Silver Dollar Bar. He was playing five hands at $500 a hand and had run it up to $80,000. I knew he'd been drinking and heavily. He was a big man physically who apparently could handle it. He played his cards a little slowly and with some fumbling; it sometimes took a moment for the pictures to get through to him but he knew what he was doing. He was quiet and courteous, a type I guarantee would punch you in the nose if you invaded his privacy. If I or a floor boss went to him with a lot of wisdom about the dangers of drink we'd be inviting trouble. The fact is this man cashed in $45,000 winnings.

The amount of money involved is not the criterion with us. Eighty dollars can be a Hell of a lot of money to some people. I remember the summer of 1924 when I worked like a dog all season for Daddy, saved my money and returned to Cleveland with $200. It was a fortune. I also remember one night when I first was in Reno and went over to the Bank Club to try my luck. I had a few bottles of beer and maybe some whiskey and lost $40. Those 40 silver dollars seemed as big to me as the typewriter here on my desk. I was so sick when I got home I had to throw up. It wasn't all from the beer and whiskey either.

More than one player has blessed us for saving his bankroll when he's been drinking. I remember distinctly a man who came up to me one morning to borrow money. "But you've got $800 in the vault," I protested. He looked blank. I learned then he had been drinking the night before and one of our men had persuaded him to sock a little aside. He'd forgotten all about it by the morning after. Believe me, you never saw a happier man. To him it was like finding $800.

Saving people from themselves, let me assure you, is probably harder to accomplish in a gaming house than anywhere else in the world. I remember an instance involving Chuck Webster, manager of our day shift. It was shortly after the war when we had many ex-servicemen playing at the club. Some of them had been in war zones where their salary accumulated and added to their discharge pay. They were the most reckless and lucky gamblers I've ever seen. This chap was playing 21 and had built up

$18,500. Chuck, who's a big, good-natured chap, asked the soldier if he didn't want to put some away for safekeeping. He said he did not. He continued to play another 24 hours and lost it all. Then he asked for enough money to buy a bus ticket home. Chuck arranged it for him. Instead of buying the ticket, though, the soldier took the $50 to the 21 table. Soon he was $17,500 ahead.

"How about putting $15,000 in the vault for safekeeping?" Chuck asked. "You'd still have $2500 to play with."

"Listen, Dad," the serviceman said, "why in Hell don't you mind your own business?"

He was in the office the next morning broke. This time Chuck bought the bus ticket personally and escorted the soldier to the depot.

Incidents, policies, customers, passions, employees—the club is a world apart. A man must be understanding, he must be philosophical, and he must be sober. That's one reason we're positively insistent no employee drink on shift.

And the boss? Well, he has to remember that all these factors are involved in his livelihood. He knows, for instance, that the biggest hours of business in a gaming club are from 8 PM to 1 AM and that's when he'd better be available. Troubles or worries he may have but he'd better not let them show. He wants to make friends and keep friends under conditions that often are trying. You can go about your rounds observantly, I constantly tell the floormen, and still be smiling. If there's heavy play at a table I don't want a caucus of floor men eagle-eying every play, as some clubs do, making the player feel self-conscious. Naturally we're interested in what's going on. There's no reason why we can't stand there with a pleasant look on our kissers and still observe the play. Do we *have* to look severe? Who the Hell are we impressing? The bus boy or the janitor? The player isn't impressed if his luck's running good. If it's running badly I'd just as soon not impress him with my presence. The basic question is: Are we down there to impress people or are we down there to make money?

Make no mistake about it, dear reader. We may make it appear very sad for us to take your money when you lose, we may shake our heads and buy you a drink on the Seventh Floor, paternally protect you from yourself and extend a few dollars from the refund book to get you home. All these things we do with studied and smiling countenance. They are policies and successful ones. But our basic reason for operating a gambling casino is never out of mind. We're here to make money. Yours, if you care to wager it.

21

♣ ♣ ♣ ♣

My Shift's Almost In

MANY PAGES AGO, when we started this chronical of a gambler and his games, I promised to give you an honest accounting. This I have tried to do and now, if you please, the job is about done. Gaming itself, as we know, will end only when human nature has changed completely and there are no more bets to win. That will be never. But for every human narrative, and I said this would be one, there must be a conclusion.

We all know the condition of life's game. The Big Dealer sets a time limit for each of us. There is little we can do to change it. None of us wants to quit, yet all of us hope to quit winners. I am no different in this than the next player. At the age of 51, I look ahead as intently as any man; as intently, in fact, as I have been looking backward in the writing of my story. For all my hunches and extrasensory perception, however, I cannot case the future as I might a dealer's hole card. Life, while loaded with chances, isn't a gambling game.

The day must come sooner or later, I know, when it will be time to rack and count my chips. In the probate of my estate, the bottom line will show what material things I've won or lost. I will not be able to cash in the $100 chips, stuff my wallets with green and take it with me. When that last big hand has been played, I won't be catching the Bonanza Air Lines plane back from Vegas or walking on air across familiar old Virginia Street. Where I go—wherever it may be—the accounting will not be in chips of red or gold. It will be with me as it is with every other player in life's game. What have I done with my life or failed to do with it?

You, by now, may have your own ideas. You have seen far more of that 15-inch ruler that symbolizes my life than anyone ever has been privileged to see before. You've now seen a fair sampling of my failings and my failures. You've watched me stray from the straight and narrow and you comprehend enough of my nature to understand why, perhaps, in the time left to me, I mean to play it a little closer to my chest. I have some things not connected with gaming that I wish to do. Things, if you please, I must do.

I feel a certain recurrence of the boyhood vibrato in my inner voice as I speak of them. Of course, being now a consummate, poker-faced professional gambler, I control it. None of us wears quite the face that peers out shyly from deep inside. Life's vicissitudes help to wrap us all in sheaths of sophistication and personality. I'm not made of marble, as I've said so often, but I have learned to discipline my emotions. I have learned to look to the marrow of the bones of people who gamble for money in my club. I also have gazed to my own marrow and I am only a little surprised at what I find. Basically, I still am the sensitive boy in Cleveland who wanted more than anything to be a concert violinist and see a World Series ball game. At rare moments I am even, almost, the uncomplicated six-year-old who took his First Communion in Buffalo, N. Y.

Ah, you say, the gambler's had his fun and made his millions and now he's getting religion. Like the Prodigal Son of scripture, he wants, after his riotous living, to return to the pale again. Well, that is a consideration. I *would* like to be a better person than I have been. And that, I believe, is the purpose of religion. As I look into me with my round blue eyes, though, I believe I am only returning to what I basically have always been. The herring has been marinating there a long, long time.

As for the millions made, they wouldn't buy many stars for a crown. Sure I've made it big but I've always kept my money in circulation. I don't have the millions today that people expect me to have. I've gambled away a lot. A lot more has dribbled away through divorce, cowboying about and family foibles. No, I'm not the bloated millionaire trying to insure my bets for the hereafter. Definitely not, though I don't expect to cash out in the poorhouse.

Before you turn completely cynical in all this discussion, if you please, I'll ask you to recall that period of months I spent on the frontier of insanity. You'll remember how, in my desperation, I turned submissively to the Big Gent upstairs. Many a tough man before me has done the same thing, in the wilderness, on life rafts, in fox holes. They've made fervent contracts with God as I did. There's one thing you learn as a gambler. You keep the contract you make or lose everything. Remember Eddie Sahati?

I remember well what I said in that psycho ward. *This is my lot*, I acknowledged. *I accept it. So be it. Thy will be done.* Show me the conditions of the game as I must play it now, I asked, and I'll play it Your way. But, please, give me back my sanity. I still wasn't quite oriented when I came out of the hospital. It took more time, more help; it took the keeping of my word. I had bound it all with an oath not to drink for four years and I kept that oath. When my term of oath ended, in January, 1960, I drank again, with intent, for 13 days. Then I voluntarily took another oath not to drink for six years. It will terminate at the time my daughter Diane comes of age.

What then? I will play it as it lays. I am seeking guidance every day of my life. In that connection, I plan to take a walking trip, alone, through the Holy Land, in the hope of coming even closer to the source of inspiration. Perhaps after that I will have my first drink in a sidewalk cafe in Paris. Perhaps I'll come back to Reno and really empty a few bottles. Perhaps I will never drink again. Whatever I do, I assure you, it will be no accident. It will be with intent.

Changing me has never been an easy job. I'm afraid it never will be. Take the matter of gambling. Gambling, as I have admitted, is a passion with me comparable to the supreme love act.

Gambling has also been my means of livelihood, my institution of higher learning, my golden goose and the cross I have borne at times. Lately I have toyed with the idea of taking an oath not to gamble any more. It is, after all, not merely a pastime or recreation with me. It's always a binge or a spree as violent as any with booze. But I must see how I am directed in this. In my first outing after considering such an oath, I won $18,000 at the 21 table and woke up contrite with my pockets full of dough.

It isn't unnatural, I feel, that the play of my life should turn this way. We all make our own monsters and I surely have helped to shape mine. I have always carried a load of guilt when I was romancing highest. Maybe this is what the padres call conscience. Whatever it is, I know that I drank longer and harder than most men can and there was always a part of me soberly condemning the action. I gambled big, yet the mere sight or thought of Daddy could ruin my play. My cowboying through the treed-up lands appalled even me while I was doing it. At my worst, as I have noted, and though I wasn't eligible for the sacraments of my church, I found myself wandering in again and again like a hungry beggar to watch and listen. I never stopped praying. Looking back, it seems almost symbolical that the little prostitute I met in the days after my divorce from Dorothy did not interest me carnally. I gave her a bath. In my drunken stupor I was trying somehow to clean things up.

Let's not be silly though. Passion hasn't died in me, nor has the flesh grown completely weak. I haven't traded my silk suits and Western clothes for sackcloth and I don't turn my eye from a pretty ankle. Excuse me, but that's anti-human nature. There are times when I almost ache for a replay of the old days. The fun ones, of course; not the miserable ones. Well then, if the flesh is still so strong what's the answer? It's just, perhaps, after a monstrous experience with insanity and feeling the odds of life grinding away on me, that the spirit has grown a little stronger. Among other things, I don't want another nervous breakdown. I doubt that I could survive one.

The tides that swirled and churned through my life to make me a professional gambler are now, I feel, swirling in new directions. I feel their pull. I see new conditions to the game. Daddy's getting older, for one thing, and while he's far from senile, I realize he won't always be here as the steady rock of reality in Harolds Club. Mama has lain in St. Mary's Hospital for weeks now, no longer goaded by a lifelong need to flit about. My daughters, babies such a short time ago, are themselves mothers now. Junior, the perennial gay boy bachelor and caballero, was married in a big church wedding only the other day. At the reception, I danced a wild rhumba with a French girl from our *Can Can* show and was roundly criticized in Reno town. I'm not the Harold of old even in other people's eyes. Perhaps it was the way the lights hit my bald spot as I pirouetted.

Of course it hurts. It hurts in a very special way to know that I mustn't go down in the club, order a bottle and start flirting with the green eyes, brown eyes and blue eyes that still turn my way. Thinking back to those fun days, I'm sick with nostalgia. I'm sick, too, whenever it hits me poignantly, that I can't call Eddie Sahati and start off gaily to romance a crap game now that I know how. I had a passion for fun despite those voices inside me and it isn't dead. But the good Lord does set a time on our game and at 51 I realize I don't have time to waste climbing treed-up places in Never-Never Land. I don't want to quit losers.

I now know that I was blessed, as I have been in so many, many, many ways, with a good mind. Circumstances of family, environment and temperament prevented it from being trained through formal schooling. Instead, I learned the gaming profession from Daddy, a great teacher, and in the process learned much of human nature, including my own. For some years now I have been trying to catch up on the book knowledge I missed. I find I love words and their meanings. I constantly am buying new dictionaries and studying them. When I hear or read a word that intrigues me, I look it up in several of my dictionaries and type out the definitions. Then I practice the word until I can use it correctly in conversation. And I do use it. In fact, people meeting Harold S. Smith, Sr., today are inclined to think he's some sort of fascinating freak full of affectations. Let them think it! I'm learning. My reading is improving constantly. I've long known the difference between salt and pepper. Now I know something more than the odds on roulette or the nicest way to distract a 21 dealer. I know something of this brain of mine and what makes it tick. I'm acquiring friends outside the gambling fraternity,

learned men who teach me things with every sentence. To be
sure, I'm the knowing gambler to them and must still talk gambler
talk to sing for my supper of erudition, but every game has its
conditions. I listen to my good music in my office and hideaway
while I meditate, or to Shakespeare on records, and I buy the old
Bard's admonitions to "Know thyself" and "To thine own self be
true." It's that "own self" deep inside I'm trying to reach. I find
such wonderful things to mull over. Like the word "serendipities,"
which describes special aptitudes for making fortunate discoveries
accidentally. My life has been filled with serendipities.

It was my need to be an expert gambler, for instance, that sent
me into a detailed study of hunches, extrasensory perception, the
supernatural. This has led full circle to the realm of the subconscious mind, rooting ground for many of life's mysteries, a place
of marvelous wonder.

In one of his critical moods, Daddy once said to me: "Harold,
you will never become a big man. You are too sensitive." A big
man? In what way? I had already made a million dollars when
he said it. Hadn't I made that million through my own efforts? I
was offended. Today I look at it differently. A million can make
a man a pretty big shot in this treed-up land but now I've seen big
shots and been one. It doesn't wear well. This sensitivity is what
I was born with and I've tried to control it all my life. Now I see
that only because I was sensitive could I feel and understand what
is in the human heart, the thoughts a man has when he wins, the
pain when he loses. Now I'm proud of that sensitivity though I
realize that, like every other emotion, it must be kept under
control or it can consume and destroy. I needed sensitivity. I
couldn't, otherwise, have attempted to set down my story in this
book. Growing older, I can look back on a full and interesting
life and believe that now the interesting part begins for me. Up
to now it was preparation. Now, perhaps, I can be a big man in
the truest sense of the word.

I'm not ashamed of my life. Let's make no mistake about that.
Nor am I ashamed of Harolds Club in any way. I have been a
professional gambler, true, a whole-hog one but a good one, and
above all an honest one. The reputation of Harolds Club speaks
for that. You will recall how we took our club name from the
fact Chinese boys in San Francisco's Chinatown mistook me for

Harold Lloyd. The great movie comedian had just made *Grandma's Boy*, a wonderful, wholesome, fun picture. That was the attitude with which we wanted to operate; it is the way we have. We have a tremendous name in the gaming industry; no one can touch it. Yet I don't want to be remembered only as a man who developed one of the world's finer skills for taking your money. We never meant to have the world's largest gambling house, you'll recall. We were only trying to make a living with our penny roulette wheel.

I should like to be remembered as a man who contributed a little, too. I don't mean the club's well-known charities, either, or the scholarships we have given to University of Nevada students, or the many thousands of dollars that have dribbled out of our pockets into needy hands. No, that isn't what I mean. I am thinking in intangible areas now. Like this book. I really believe it should make a contribution to a life somewhere or I would not have gone to the trouble of writing it. I don't need best seller money or fame or notoriety. In many ways, in fact, the book may prove to be a headache, coming back again and again to haunt the club or me.

It's harder to explain intangibles than odds on a dice game. Much harder. For instance, I return often to the psycho ward where I was incarcerated for months. I always bring candy, cigarettes, magazines, a word of hope. I am always given the run of the place and there aren't many outsiders with that latitude. It is interesting that neither the attendants nor patients have any fear of me. That is an intangible. I was *there* once. I hope to show other patients that they, too, can recover. I must constantly remind myself I can't go back there. I would quit losers if I did.

But that isn't enough. I'm a vital, restless man in the prime of life. I have been gifted with imagination and trained in certain specialties. Carrying candy and cigarettes to psycho ward patients isn't going to get the job done for me. I still have those dreams of the small boy back in Cleveland. They all center on music.

I've never actually been far from good music. When I worked for Daddy in San Francisco, I went to concerts every chance I got. Always, when I visit New York, I attend the concerts at Carnegie Hall or the operas at the Met. I am always amazed, incidentally, by the attitude of New Yorkers who look upon us faraway Nevadans disdainfully because we don't have the great advantages of culture out here in the sagebrush. Bless me and pass the succotash! Of course they have advantages, such as the Met and Carnegie, but what are New Yorkers boastful about? With nine million of them in the Big Town, I always find I can get seats. Those boastful people aren't taking full advantage of the very advantages they're so proud of. Yes, I sometimes get into big gambling games among the skyscrapers but I always treat myself to the good music too. In that, if not the World Series, I *have* been again the little boy enjoying a treat.

This is good. It is great. It is wonderful. I admit that great music hasn't thrived on the Nevada deserts. Oh, we've had concerts of sorts but they weren't the greatest and they weren't always done with the quality of the big time. There are, after all, certain limiting conditions to culture in a city of only 60,000. For a long while it occurred to me: why couldn't some of us with great funds to tap bring some of this fine music West? Why couldn't Harolds Club do it?

I decided to try, and this was a part of the new Harold Smith, Sr., who came out of the psycho ward. In 1958 I announced my first concert, featuring the great violinist, Ruggiero Ricci. Immediately there were those who said it was only a club promotion. It was, in a sense. But it was *quid pro quo*, something for something, and in this case something very fine. Some said it was simply a case of a professional gambler trying to wrap himself in a cloak of culture. True. It was that, too. But it was also the little boy who loved, and could never fulfill his love for, good music. I had thought so often of that small boy who desired to be a concert violinist and learned at painful last that he simply didn't have the talent. Maybe, I thought, out there beyond the bare brown hills of Nevada, there is another boy or girl who has talent and needs only to have it awakened. Let our auditors reckon the cost and charge it to promotion. I would know the true value of our concerts if they helped just one small spirit to soar.

There were, to be sure, arched eyebrows when I announced we were going to bring other great artists to Reno. Would the great ones I promised even come? What would be the advantage, aside from money, of making their great music in a one-night stand in the divorce mill? What would we use for a concert hall? How could our artists perform over the deafening din of the slot machines? I fixed that. I took my concerts to the auditorium of Bishop Manogue High School, far from the gaming halls and their atmosphere. Harolds Club gladly paid all expenses and the proceeds went to the parochial school's building program. Our townspeople all turned out, too, though I must confess that many came just to watch Harold as an impresario and laugh if he had a flop. I didn't. I summoned up a dignity and *savoir-faire* people here didn't realize I had (perhaps because it isn't necessary in dealing a 21 game) and we had one tremendous success after another.

It wasn't, if you please, the fabulous funds of Harolds Club that got the job done either. Let me cite my experience with Lily Pons as a case in point. I wanted this great woman to appear as the star of my second concert in 1959 and approached her through an agent. That gentleman, without even consulting her, booked her into Reno. The next thing I heard was that Madame Pons (which is how the agent told me to address her) absolutely would not keep the Reno date. For one thing, her schedule was almost solidly booked and she would have had to come here two nights after a recital in Texas with all the annoyance and weariness of plane routing. More important, and any lady can understand this, she resented being booked into Reno without so much as a telephone call to ask her wishes. Under those circumstances, I should have said the same thing: "Deal me out."

But I was determined to have Lily Pons sing in Reno and I meant to correct any errors. I called her and made an appointment to see her at her home in Palm Springs. She was still adamant, I noted: *She was not coming to Reno.* I laid my plans accordingly. I arrived in Southern California a day ahead of the appointment, bursting with confidence, and stopped in to see my daughter Joan. "Don't get too excited, Daddy," she warned. "Madame Pons may not come into Reno."

"Joan!" I said positively, "she's coming in." (To myself I said: *You, too, Joan—et tu—would try, at least subconsciously, to deter your father when he's trying to do something good.* I since have gotten that attitude out of Joan's talk).

My appointment was for 2 PM in Palm Springs. Knowing that

any big artist is a perfectionist—being one myself—I knew that meant 2 PM sharp. I rented a car and drove out to the Springs the night before, eliminating any chance of a breakdown or accident on the road that might delay me. The next morning I hired a taxicab to pilot me do Madame Pons' home, which was high in a hillside canyon behind a fence with a sign which said the grounds were patrolled by officers. I followed the cab in my rented car so I would remember each turn and street. I cased the job thoroughly. Then, at 1:30 PM, I parked my car 70 yards from her gate and read a magazine article about Johnny Longden, the jockey, until 1:55.

I had set my watch by radio time and checked it twice. At five minutes of two precisely I rang the doorbell. There was no answer. *Fine,* I thought, *she is truly a perfectionist. We will get along wonderfully.* I sat on the veranda and waited until one minute of two and rang the bell again. Lily Pons opened it herself. She then was the gracious lady showing an invited guest the lovely, tranquil home she had designed herself and chattering about a bird that had adopted her. Every pillow, every painting, every piece of furniture was perfection. I knew instantly the type of person with whom I was dealing.

"This agent," she stormed, "is a jerk! Not even telling me I am to be booked into Reno."

I could understand her anger. The true artist is not to be snared lightly in the net of commercialism. Reno is not noted as a cultural center. I had a little selling job to do. That was why I had come alone, counting on my own earnestness and understanding to accomplish my mission.

"Lily," I said, "I cannot call you 'Madame.' I've never seen the woman who wants to be called madame. It should be 'la petite femme.' "

"Yes," she exclaimed. "Little one. Not big one!"

Now don't muff it, I warned myself. *You're not giving away Beacon blankets in a bingo game.* I paused in front of her and laid out a file of photographs I'd made up from Ruggiero Ricci's Reno appearance. A lady likes to look at photos. She can see much in them that words do not convey. I had selected pictures which showed Ricci *after the concert* quite obviously very happy. Still berating her agent, Miss Pons studied them.

"Lily," I said, "please listen. Every songbird has its favorite song. Every comic has his favorite story. Every great teacher has his slogan that tells it all." I knew her to be most religious, a wonderful Catholic. "What did our dear Christ say, Lily? 'Forgive them,' He said. 'They know not what they do.'"

She glanced at me, gauging my sincerity. I was completely sincere. "You have license to be angry with the agent," I assured her. "But forgive him."

She tossed her head.

"I know it is hard to do," I said. "I have to do it all the time in my club. Now you, too, must forgive. Come to Reno. You will be happy, I promise you. Ruggiero Ricci was happy. The pictures tell it all."

She pondered for perhaps another second. "I'll come," she said. "I will get my calendar."

I breathed a deep sigh of relief. With a person such as this, if she said she would come it was better than seven contracts. I was so happy I kissed her hands as I left and I guess I squeezed too hard. She grimaced. But I had treated her as a man should treat a lady. Lily Pons is, above all things, a beautiful, majestic lady.

Reno outdid itself for her. There were cocktail parties at the Mapes and Riverside for I wanted my competitors in on the festivities. This great occasion, I was determined, was to be for all my neighbors. And Lily outdid herself for them. On the night of the concert, which of course produced a packed house, I was full of penicillin against a bout with flu and had another of my iritis attacks. But the show went on. And the moment that bell-like voice trilled in the hall I got well. Later we had another party and Lily went through Harolds Club playing the games. The next day she and I took a wonderful drive up through the Sierra to Tahoe and everything was beautiful. She said so and Lily Pons recognizes beauty. She also recognized my sincerity. Today we are good friends.

Not the great artist and the big gambler, remember, but Lily Pons and the grownup boy from Cleveland.

So now I see a course of action by which, in my own way, I can indeed bring benefits to this Never-Never Land that has been good to me. Now I see clearly how I can bring the really big things— not the biggest jackpots or no-limit games—to my town. I can't change the spirits of people, I know. But I can exalt them for an hour or so. After Lily Pons, I brought in Jan Peerce, the great tenor and man of wisdom. Then Elisabeth Schwarzkopf and we televised her recital to every ranch within range of our channel. Jan Peerce came back by popular request. My concerts finally had made a place for themselves in Reno town. I hope now to bring in Dorothy Kirsten backed by the San Francisco Symphony Orchestra. Then, one day, I will present opera out here by the banks of the Truckee. Do you hear the din of slot machines slowly fading? Well they won't fade completely because those busy contraptions which give some people pleasure are going to help pay for the music that will bring others real rapture.

That isn't all of it by any means. I want not one penny from the operas. All proceeds will go to help pay the $2,000,000 bill for a new wing the Dominican Sisters are building on their hospital. The gambler has got religion? Why not? But gamblers may come and go; the sick are always with us. I know what it is to be sick and I know the gentle care of the good sisters. Give them the facilities and they'll be getting a job done long after my chips are racked, counted and spent again by someone else. If I can do that, I figure I'll quit winners for sure.

The only difference between the winner and loser often enough is just a turn of a card. By that little, Dr. Roy Parkinson once almost gave up the study of medicine and I can't guess what would have happened to me if he hadn't been the one man available with relief for the agonies of iritis. I can't begin to say what might have happened to me as a person without his wise counsel. I still have to watch every card as it is played in my life and I still have to control my impetuous self. In recent years I have, in fact, developed a habit of biting hard on my forefinger to remind me not to say the wrong thing under trying conditions. For you see my peanut stand is still my gaming house. Hate it though I must, I still must live with chicanery in all its forms.

My daddy, as you have gathered, is often a thorn in my side. In 1960 he bought out Dorothy's one-third interest in Harolds Club and became an equal partner with Raymond and me. He makes so many speeches about gaming, in fact, many people think *he* is the Harold of Harolds Club. He dominates the scene and me, his 51-year-old son, and he's still a pretty rough old nugget. When Ricci played his recital here, I recall, it was Daddy who ambled up to the stage and asked me: "Could you have your fiddler play *Melody of Love?*" He has a million ways of exasperating me. Yet I still say he's the only man in the world I would want for a father. I don't forget that he *did* buy me my violin, he did bring me to San Francisco when Cleveland palled and he did teach me the business that has made us rich.

I see Dorothy, my ex-wife, often, and I always suffer a little pang of regret when I remember those wonderful first years of our marriage. Sentiment is a hard burden to carry. Forgiving isn't quite as easy as I made it sound to Lily Pons. But here, too, I have learned to live with reality. Nothing remains as it was in the beginning. You must learn to play them as they lay for the action. Dorothy helped present the Christmas party for our employees this year and I made a point of telling her how pretty the decorations were and how well she looked. Old bitterness is more easily forgotten when I remember her as the mother of three of my wonderful children.

When Daddy irks me I try to recall that King Herod had his John the Baptist in whom he saw strength and to whom he would go and talk frequently. Maybe he envied the spiritual strength in John the Baptist and I would like to believe that Daddy, in a small way at least, finally sees strength in me. Certainly the success of my concerts amazed him—"all those people trooping out to Manogue to see a show Harold presented!" With no gimmicks, no carnie attractions, no Beacon blankets! Daddy was impressed and maybe he was pleased. I have tried so long and hard to please him.

Yet, and it rankles me, there still is a basic difference between us. I wasn't completely daffy on the night of my breakdown when he wouldn't let me talk of God. My Daddy is so self-sufficient I sometimes wonder if he realizes there *is* a God and that he, Raymond I. Smith, had better re-examine his hand before he goes to his rest. I want to see him look up just once and pray—just once, as sincerely as my drug addict friend, Eddie Sahati, did. I want to see a look of real compassion on that stony Vermont face when he's not wooing the elusive buck. I want to see him attend just one funeral or appear at one Christmas dinner without discussing business. I want all this so I can really, fully admire him as I did when I was a six-year-old at my First Communion in Buffalo, New York. Maybe the little boy will be back in me then. I have carried too much resentment for my parents far too long.

So how does all this affect you? You, who only wanted to know how to make those slot machines talk or beat the cards and dice once in a while? It needn't change your game at all. We're still in business at the same old stand and I'm still very much the professional gambler wanting to see you win. Just because I have all my big chips in the center doesn't mean you have to quit. Your game may go on for a long time after I check out.

However, I said at the beginning of this I would give you a look inside this gambler's heart. I promised in my Openers I would let you see the real me, Harold S. Smith, Sr., professional gambler, impetuous sentimentalist, dreamer, doting father, grandfather, businessman and human being. I told you there have been heartaches and I've shown you a lot of them. I've given you facts and findings about games of chance that I had to learn the hard way over twenty-five years on both sides of the table. I've studied myself carefully, as you can see. I know that when those pearly gates swing wide I won't be able to grease any headwaiters or captains to get a preferred throne. I won't be able to bluff it as I might in a Lo-Ball game. I have no illusions at all. I simply will have to play it as it lays and maybe the best I can say is I tried.

Now perhaps you can see why a psychiatrist should spend his first year of practice in Harolds Club. Why clergymen, too, may find sermon material here. There's sin and human nature here but we aren't utterly crazy people. We're just human nature rubbed a little thin at times. We're far too logical to waste time on bosh or hypocrisy. Neither of those make the dice bounce differently or pay for the lights.

Do I urge you to try our games? Never. I have never urged anyone to gamble. I do say there's fun and recreation in gaming when you are mindfull of the pitfalls, too. None of us can win all the time, as our Harolds Club signs plainly state. All of us like to win some of the time. Plenty of people still want to try. So I shall be running my gaming house when you come by. I'm not taking vows of chastity, poverty and obedience. This is the only trade I know. It and you have been the great education of my life. Play confidently, I say. Play to win. And have fun.

May the Big Gent always be guiding your hand, and as our PA announcements urge: ALWAYS GOOD LUCK!

INDEX